Susman & Chambers, American History

Selected Reading Lists and Course
Outlines from American Colleges
and Universities

American History
Vol. I: Survey and Chronological Courses

edited by Warren Susman and John Chambers
Rutgers University

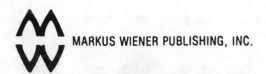

MARKUS WIENER PUBLISHING, INC.

R
016.973
S 964
v. 1

Second Printing 1985
© 1984 by Markus Wiener Publishing, Inc.

ISBN 0-910129-04-5
Library of Congress Card No. 83-061362
Printed in America

TABLE OF CONTENTS

VOLUME I

INTRODUCTION

SEE PAGE 207 FOR TABLE OF CONTENTS
OF VOLUME II, VOLUME III AND WOMEN'S HISTORY

PREFACE

Looking through books of syllabi and reading lists about American history may seem as exciting and useful as leafing through compilations of old business receipts, but such is not the case here. Rather, these volumes can prove both intellectually stimulating and educationally valuable. Because most historians are teachers as well as scholars and because the quality of teaching is one of the more serious concerns faced by the profession, we present the following course outlines and reading lists not only to help faculty members to prepare or revise courses but more importantly to encourage further examination and dialogue within the profession about the teaching of U.S. history.*

These materials were selected for publication to illustrate a variety of approaches, intellectual and pedagogical, to the teaching of various aspects of American history, primarily at the undergraduate level, at universities in the

* This series includes a separate volume on women's history edited by Annette K. Baxter

United States. (#1, footnotes at end of preface) The approximately one-hundred syllabi and reading lists contained in these three volumes were chosen to demonstrate the innovation and diversity existent in the teaching of American history to undergraduates. (#2) We put them forward not as models for emulation, although many are certainly worthy of it, but rather as suggestive examples for critical appraisal and stimulation of discussion of what, how, and why historians teach American history as they do.

This compilation indicates that the majority of courses continues to be organized by particular chronological period, subject, or field. Few syllabi for thematic courses were received, and we suspect that few are taught. The reading lists and syllabi that are included have considerable value as documents of basic organization and choice of reading materials. As such, they demonstrate the broadening of the profession's instruction to include the sources, methods, and findings of the "new" social, cultural, economic, and political history. It is also clear from the documents we received that many historians have sought, with varying degrees of success, to integrate the new data and interpretations of these fields into traditional chronological or subject-oriented courses. The course materials included in these volumes will, we hope, contribute to the forum of discussion about the advantages and disadvantages of the manner in which American history is divided for instructional purposes as well as the methods by which particular courses are themselves organized and taught.

Careful examination of these syllabi and reading lists confirms that there are many different ways to achieve the educational aims of professional historians; it also demonstrates the importance of clear definitions of those pedagogical goals. As numerous symposia and publications on the teaching of history have indicated, there is general agreement within the profession over the goal of teaching history as inquiry, that is of helping students to develop particular intellectual skills. (#3) Use of the historical method can teach students how to analyze critically evidence that is sometimes conflicting, to recognize and distinguish between statements of fact and opinion, and inferences and assumptions, and to be able to assess the merits of differing interpretations. The study of the past, particularly in a classroom setting in which the student is encouraged to be an active participant in the process of analysis and synthesis, can also equip students with the ability to construct explanatory generalizations based on logical arrangement of evidence from a variety of sources and to be able to communicate those conclusions in a coherent and concise manner. These, of course, are basic skills for an educated person--the ability to perceive, think, write, and speak critically and effectively.

But of course, history is more than method; it is also experience. Undoubtedly the acquisition of factual knowledge of other times and peoples and comprehension of the process of change over time can help students to understand how the present derived from the past and to be aware of forces shaping the contemporary world. In the past, one of the functions of the teaching of history was to provide an understanding of a common heritage and system of values, but such a dominant consensus has eroded if not disappeared in the wake of the rediscovery and legitimation of the racial, ethnic, and sectional dimensions of American society. Given the lack of a common history or a common historical cultural awareness in contemporary society, what is the pedagogical role of the historian as he or she transmits the knowledge of the specific area of the past which is his or her area of professional expertise? What is the knowledge to be imparted?

An examination of the syllabi and reading lists included in these volumes confirms the importance of the role of the individual teacher/scholar in his or her own particular field of specialization. Based upon reasonable and public criteria within the discipline, the arrangement of a course and the materials within it is a personal creative act, influenced by the teacher's conceptual framework and analytical point of view which is his or her own. Even when materials and organization are quite similar for different instructors, in self-expression, classroom innovation, and class expression, two courses, very much like two books on the same subject by different authors, cannot be exactly alike. We draw upon others, certainly, but within the particular classroom environment provided by a particular instructor and students, the result must of necessity differ in some measure, if not in factual knowledge and understanding, then certainly in the experience of learning.

It is our belief that giving a course should very much resemble the writing of a book, not only in the attention paid to preparation and presentation but in the role of each in the stimulation of thought and learning. In a course as in a book, there will be a thesis, perhaps several, and it can be beneficial to a student to learn this and to become aware of the manner in which the issues and material are selected on the basis of established criteria of explanation and interpretation. The clearer and more logical are the formal order of a course, its conclusions, and its meaning, the more effectively can students participate in the process of examining the evidence, testing the thesis, debating the issues and explanations and arriving at their own conclusions. The course and the classroom thus can become not merely a place where a body of factual data is transmitted but a place of learning that encourages independent judgment as well as comprehension of the nature of social change in the past.

We put forward these syllabi and reading lists with the hope that they will stimulate further discussion within the profession of the goals and methods of historians as teachers as well as writers of history.

Warren Susman

John W. Chambers

New Brunswick, N.J.

November 1, 1983

Acknowledgments

The authors wish to thank all of those people who so generously contributed to this project: the scholar-teachers who responded to requests for course outlines and reading lists and Markus Wiener, our publisher, whose active participation and unflagging enthusiasm turned an idea into these volumes.

1. This compilation includes materials for some graduate courses (which are so identified), but for the purposes of this project it was decided that on the whole, it would be more appropriate to focus on material for undergraduate courses. Those interested in the extensive reading lists characteristic of graduate courses are referred to bibliographies in recent historiographical articles, pamphlets (such as those in the American Historical Association series or the Golden Tree series published by Appleton Century, Crofts) or books such as Michael Kammen, ed., The Past Before Us: Contemporary Historical Writing in the United States (Ithaca, N.Y.: Cornell Univ. Press, 1980).

2. Within the limitation of space which prohibited exceptionally long reading lists, the materials for approximately one-hundred courses included in these three volumes were selected from the nearly three-hundred received according to criteria of innovation, variety of approach, and the need to include materials from many different fields and chronological periods within U.S. history. Because of these considerations, many excellent syllabi and reading lists which we received could not be included. We wish to thank all of the teachers who responded to our requests.

3. For a more extended discussion of goals and methods, see Warren Susman, "Annapolis Conference on the Introductory Course," AHA Newsletter (Nov., 1982), 18-23. See also Paul L. Ward, Elements of Historical Thinking (Washington, D.C.: American Historical Assn. pamphlet, 1971).

UNIVERSITY OF CALIFORNIA, LOS ANGELES

History 7A
Winter. 1983

Professor Joyce Appleby
with Teaching Assistants
Paul Frisch, Susan Neel,
Bruce Tyler, Joan Waugh, and
Intensive Writing Instructor
David Hawkes
Office: Bunche 6254
Hours: Monday, 12-2 p.m.;
Wednesday, 9-10 a.m.

Texts: American History to the Civil War

Edmund Morgan, The Birth of the Republic, 1956.
James Thomas Flexner Washington: The Indispensable Man, 1969.
John Mayfield, The New Nation, 1800-1845, 1982.
Stephen B. Oates, With Malice Towards None: The Life of Abraham Lincoln, 1977.
The United States Constitution, 1787.
Scott Waugh, ed., Writing Historical Essays, 1982.

This introductory course in American history will present an interpretation
of how Americans, first as British colonies and then as citizens of a new nation,
created a distinctive society and a unique political culture. Our focus will
not be on the events so much as the values and beliefs of the men and women who
made the events. We will explore the assumptions and goals of the different
groups who settled English North America as a way of looking at the developments
which gave shape to their communities. During the revolutionary era which began
in the 1760s and ended with the election of Thomas Jefferson in 1800, the Americans
formed a particular national ideology which guided them in the early nineteenth
century as they worked out their basic political and economic systems. The same
ideas that influenced American nation building also fueled the sectional conflicts
that led to the American Civil War. It will be part of our task to understand
this paradox of a political ideology that laid the basis for the American nation
at the same time that it caused fundamental cleavages. Since we are still living
with the institutions and ideas that took shape at the end of the eighteenth
century, you will discover in this period of American history something about
yourself and the country you are a part of today.

Your grade will be calculated on the basis of the following distribution:
final examination (40%), three papers and a rewrite (10% each), and sectional
participation (20%). It goes without saying that attendance at all lectures and
section meetings is required. No one missing more than three section meetings
will be entitled to the 20% section grade.

No late papers will be accepted; no incompletes will be given except by
permission of Professor Appleby in cases of documented illness or hardship.

Week 1: The Colonies in 1750

         Writing Historical Essays.

Week 2: The Forces of Change

         Washington, pp. 1-54.

1

Week 3: Resistance Becomes Revolution

The Birth of the Republic, pp. 1-111.

Washington, pp. 55-184.

FIRST PAPER DUE IN SECTION MEETING THIS WEEK

Week 4: A Society Transformed by Revolution

Washington, pp. 185-314.

Week 5: A Nationalist Consensus

The Birth of the Republic, pp. 112-155, 160-183.

SECOND PAPER DUE IN SECTION MEETING THIS WEEK

Week 6: The Politics of Opposition

Washington, pp. 315-433.

Week 7. Taking up the National Domain

The New Nation, pp. 3-83.

THIRD PAPER DUE IN SECTION MEETING THIS WEEK

Week 8: Liberalism, Democracy, and Nationalism

With Malice Towards None, pp. 3-106.

The New Nation pp. 87-105.

Week 9: Slavery and Its Enemies

The New Nation, pp. 151-229.

With Malice Towards None, pp. 111-191.

Week 10: The Collapse of Compromise

With Malice Towards None, pp. 195-436.

REWRITTEN ESSAY DUE IN SECTION MEETING THIS WEEK

FINAL EXAMINATION is on Wednesday, March 23, 3:00-6:00 p.m.

UNIVERSITY OF VIRGINIA

HIUS 251   American History, 1607-1865   Fall 1979

Mr. Michael F. Holt
Office: 203 Randall Hall
Phone: 924-7146
Office Hours: Wednesday, 2-4, Friday, 9-12

The following paperback books are to be purchased at the Newcomb Hall Bookstore.

     John Blum, et. al., The National Experience, 4th edition, Vol. I (textbook)
     Edmund S. Morgan, The Puritan Dilemma
     Peter Wood, Black Majority: Negroes in Colonial South Carolina
     Richard Jellison (ed.), Society, Freedom, and Conscience: The Coming of
          The Revolution in Virginia, Massachusetts, and New York
     James Sterling Young, The Washington Community, 1800-1828
     Robert Remini, Andrew Jackson and the Bank War
     Paul Johnson, A Shopkeeper's Millenium: Society and Revivals in Rochester,
          New York, 1815-1837
     Michael F. Holt, The Political Crisis of the 1850s
     David Donald (ed.), Why the North Won the Civil War

Course Requirements:

     There will be a midterm examination on Wednesday, October 17, that will
count 20% of the final grade. The final examination, which will cover the
entire semester's work, will count 40% of the final grade. Students will also
write three (3) three-page critical book reviews on the assigned reading during
the course of the semester, which will count 20% of the final grade. The
specific topics for those papers will be assigned by section leaders. Finally,
students are expected to make informed and intelligent contributions to the
weekly discussions of the reading, and the overall grade for students' performance in section will count for the last 20% of the term grade.

Schedule of Lectures and Readings

Week 1   Sept. 3   The European Background to Colonization
         Sept. 5   Contrasting Patterns of Settlement

              Reading: Text, pp. 3-49

Week 2   Sept. 10   The Puritan Experiment
         Sept. 12   The Transformation of New England Society: 1650-1720

              Reading: Morgan, The Puritan Dilemma; Text, pp. 50-73

Week 3   Sept. 17   The Shaping of Southern Society in the 17th Century
         Sept. 19   A Factious People: Colonial Life in the 18th Century

              Reading: Wood, Black Majority

Week 4   Sept. 24   The Great Awakening
         Sept. 26   The Changing Pattern of Empire

              Reading: Jellison, Society, Freedom, and Conscience; Text, pp. 76-101

3

Week 5   Oct. 1   The Logic of Revolution
         Oct. 3   The Impact of Revolution

            Reading: Text, pp. 103-153

Week 6   Oct. 8   The Debate over the Constitution
         Oct. 10   The Federalist Ascendancy

            Reading: Young, The Washington Community; Text, pp. 155-177

Week 7   Oct. 15   The Federalist Demise
         Oct. 17   Midterm Examination

            No additional assignments this week; sections can meet to review
         material.

Week 8   Oct. 22   The New Nationalism, 1816-1824
         Oct. 24   The Origins of the Jackson Movement: Politics in the 1820s

            Reading: Remini, Andrew Jackson and the Bank War; Text, pp. 178-231

Week 9   Oct. 29   Andrew Jackson and Jacksonian Democracy
         Oct. 31   The Nature of the Jacksonian Party System

            Reading: Johnson, A Shopkeeper's Millenium; Text, pp. 232-253

Week 10 Nov. 5   Abolitionism and the Antislavery Movement
         Nov. 7   American Women, 1815-1860

            Reading: Holt, The Political Crisis of the 1850s, pp. 1-138; Text,
               pp. 254-299

Week 11 Nov. 12   American Negro Slavery in the 19th Century
         Nov. 14   The Old South and the Development of Southern Sectionalism

            Reading: Holt, Political Crisis, pp. 139-259; Text, pp. 300-321

Week 12 Nov. 19   Manifest Destiny and the Slavery Extension Issue
         Nov. 21   Politics and the Sectional Conflict

            No assignment; no section meetings; Thanksgiving holiday

Week 13 Nov. 26   Know Nothingism and the Party System
         Nov. 28   Why Did the Republican Party Succeed?

            Reading: Donald, Why the North Won the Civil War; Text, pp. 322-355

Week 14 Dec. 3   The Civil War and the American Negro
         Dec. 5   The Civil War and the American Political System

            No section meetings.

University of Connecticut

History 231   Survey of American History from   Richard D. Brown
Spring 1983   the Colonial Period to 1877

1. Introduction: Why Study History?

I. Colonial America

2. European Imperialism
3. Virginia Settlement
4. New England Settlement
5. Pennsylvania
6. New England Begins/Library Video Theater
7. Englishmen and Indians
8. Colonial Politics and the Imperial Government

II. The Emergence of the United States of America

9. The French and Indian Wars
10. Reform and Resistance
11. Revolutionary Idology
12. Coercive Acts and Independence
13. Discussion (Knox, Paine, and the Declaration of Independence)
14. The Revolutionary War
15. Revolutionary Ideals and Slavery
16. Confederation and Constitution
17. George Washington
18. Discussion (Federalist No. 10, the Constitution)
19. Hour Exam
20. World of Franklin and Jefferson

III. The Trials of Nationhood

21. National Government and Politics
22. American Nationalism
23. American Culture (slide lecture)
24. The Population of the United States, 1760-1880
25. Territorial Expansion
26. Industrialization and Urban Growth
27. Slavery: Perceptions and Realities
28. Riot and Violence
29. Popular Politics
30. Discussion (Douglass)
31. Destruction of the Party System
32. Election of 1860 and the Secession Movement
33. Discussion (the first Lincoln-Douglas debate)
34. Fighting and Dying
35. Union Victory
36. Abraham Lincoln
37. Reconstruction or Reunion?
38. Modern America
39. Discussion (the past, the present, the future)
40-42. Review Sessions.

Readings. All books should be purchased, however copies have been placed on Library Reserve, with the exception of J.M. Blum, et al., The National Experience.

I. Colonial America

Bernard Bailyn, et.al., The Great Republic: A History of the American People, Second ed., vol. I (Lexington, Mass: D.C. Heath, 1981), Ch. 1-4, pp. 2-119.

Richard D. Brown, MODERNIZATION: THE TRANSFORMATION OF AMERICAN LIFE (New York: Hill and Wang, 1976), chs. 1-3, pp. 3-73.

II. The Emergence of the United States of America

Bailyn, et. a., Great Republic, vol. I, chs. 5-10, pp. 122-272.

Brown, MODERNIZATION, chs. 4,5, pp. 74-121.

Robert A. Gross, THE MINUTEMEN AND THEIR WORLD (New York: Hill and Wang, 1976), entire, 220 p.

Old South Leaflet, No. 210. "William Knox on American Taxation, 1769," 24p.

Thomas Paine, COMMON SENSE (Philadelphia, 1776), 50p.

Declaration of Independence, Bailyn, et al., Great Republic, appendix, pp. v-vi.

Constitution of the U.S.A., Bailyn, et al., Great Republic, appendix. pp. xii-xx (through the 15th amendment)

Hamilton, A., et al., THE FEDERALIST, No. 10 (James Madison)

III. The Trials of Nationahood

Bailyn, et al, Great Republic, vol. I, chs. 11-20, pp. 275-555.

Brown, MODERNIZATION, chs. 6-8, pp. 122-201.

Frederick Douglass, NARRATIVE OF THE LIFE OF FREDERICK DOUGLASS (Boston, 1845) entire, 160 p.

Lois W. Banner, ELIZABETH CADY STANTON: A RADICAL FOR WOMEN'S RIGHTS (Boston: Little, Brown, 1980), entire, 173 p.
OLD SOUTH LEAFLET, no. 85, "The First Lincoln and Douglass Debate," 32 p.

<u>EXAMS</u>: There will be a one-hour essay exam at the end of Part II (Emergence of the U.S.A.). The date to be announced. It will count for approximately 20 percent of your grade. A two-hour essay exam covering the <u>entire</u> course will be given during the final exam week, and it will count for approximately 50 percent of your grade. Your continuous involvement in the readings, lectures and discussions is an important part of the course. Before exams students are required to hand in suggestions for questions.

<u>DISCUSSIONS</u>: From time to time we will discuss readings in relation to course material. On the day of the discussion you should hand in a brief (one or two paragraph) comment on the scheduled readings. No grade will be assigned, but credit will be given for handing in your comment.

<u>PAPERS</u>: Every student is required to write a 5-8 page essay that treats a single topic. Normally these are to be selected from the attached list, but if there is another subject that interests you deeply, please let me know. All students must come in to discuss their topics and sign up for them immediately; the deadline is February 7. <u>Your paper will be due April 18</u>. It will count for approximately 30 percent of your grade.

Suggestions for Paper Writers

1. Papers should be double-spaced, with liberal margins. Allow space for reader's comments.

2. Don't use a faded typewriter ribbon.

3. Put page numbers on each page in case they become scrambled.

4. Staple pages together in upper left-hand corner.

5. <u>QUOTATIONS</u>

   a. All direct quotes should be placed within quotation marks and precisely footnoted.

   b. Quotations should be used sparingly, for emphasis, when the particular words carry a special punch. Otherwise <u>paraphrase</u>. Avoid the scissors-and-paste approach.

   c. When you do quote, integrate the quotation into the prose. Do not simply drop quotes in without identification or connection. Phrases like "he said," "she argued," "they asserted," are often sufficient. Note that punctuation goes <u>inside</u> the quotation marks.

6. Proof-read your final copy carefully. If your essay was worth spending hours to create, it is worth a few minutes more to proof-read.

*Indicates book exists in paperback.

Christopher Columbus (1451-1506), Samuel E. Morison, ADMIRAL OF THE OCEAN SEA
    (1942), 2 Vols. Genoese explorer.

John Smith (1579-1681), Philip Barbour, The Three Worlds of Captain John Smith.
    A remarkable adventurer.

John Winthrop (1588-1649), Edmund S. Morgan, THE PURITAN DILEMMA: THE STORY OF
    JOHN WINTHROP (Boston: Little, Brown, 1958).* Key leader of Massachusetts
    Bay colony.

Roger Williams (1603-1683), Ola Winslow, MASTER ROGER WILLIAMS (1957). Puritan
    dissident and founder of Rhode Island.

Benjamin Franklin (1706-1790), Verner W. Crane, BENJAMIN FRANKLIN AND A RISING
    PEOPLE (Boston: Little, Brown, 19).* Boston boy who made good in
    Philadelphia, London, and Paris.

Thomas Hutchinson (1711-1790), Bernard Bailyn, THE ORDEAL OF THOMAS HUTCHINSON
    (Cambridge, Mass.: Harvard University Press, 1974).* Staunch defender
    of the British cause caught in the Revolutionary crisis. Bailyn's biography
    is superb.

Roger Sherman (1721-1793), Christopher Collier, ROGER SHERMAN'S CONNECTION:
    YANKEE POLITICS AND THE AMERICAN REVOLUTION (Middletown, Conn.: Wesleyan
    University Press, 1971). Connecticut's leading Revolutionary politician.

Ezra Stiles (1727-1795), Edmund S. Morgan, THE GENTLE PURITAN: A LIFE OF EZRA
    STILES, 1727-1795 (New Haven: Yale University Press, 1962). Liberal Con-
    necticut and Rhode Island clergyman who served as president of Yale. Morgan's
    biography is splendid.

George Washington (1732-1799), James Thomas Flexner, WASHINGTON, THE INDISPENSABLE
    MAN (Boston: Little, Brown, 1969).* A politician who "could not tell a lie."

John Adams (1735-1826), Peter Shaw, THE CHARACTER OF JOHN ADAMS (Chapel Hill, N.C.:
    University of North Carolina Press, 1976).* A Massachusetts leader in the
    Revolutionary era.

Thomas Paine (1737-1803), Eric Foner, TOM PAINE AND REVOLUTIONARY AMERICA (New
    York: Oxford University Press, 1976).* English immigrant and revolutionary.

Abigail Adams (1744-1818), Charles W. Akers, ABIGAIL ADAMS: AN AMERICAN WOMAN
    (Boston: Little, Brown, 1980).* and Lynne Withey, Dearest Friend:
    A Life of Abigail Adams (New York: Free Press, 1981). A brilliant wife.

Eli Whitney (1766-1825), Constance M. Green, ELI WHITNEY AND THE BIRTH OF
    AMERICAN TECHNOLOGY (Boston: Little, Brown, 1956).* Connecticut industrial
    innovator.

Andrew Jackson (1767-1845), Robert V. Remini, ANDREW JACKSON AND THE BANK WAR (New York: Norton, 1967).* Powerful President.

Henry Clay (1777-1852), Clement Eaton, HENRY CLAY AND THE ART OF AMERICAN POLITICS (Boston: Little, Brown, 1957).* Major western politician of the first half of the nineteenth century.

Thomas Hart Benton (1782-1858), William N. Chambers, OLD BULLION BENTON: SENATOR FROM THE NEW WEST (Boston: Little, Brown, 1956).* One of the western stars in the ante-bellum Senate.

John C. Calhoun (1782-1850), Margaret L. Coit, JOHN C. CALHOUN: AMERICAN PORTRAIT (Boston: Houghton Mifflin, 1950). The slavocracy's star in the ante-bellum Senate.

Martin Van Buran (1782-1862). Robert V. Remini, MARTIN VAN BUREN AND THE MAKING OF THE DEMOCRATIC PARTY (New York: Norton, 1970).* Masterful politician.

Daniel Webster (1782-1852), Richard N. Current, DANIEL WEBSTER AND THE RISE OF NATIONAL CONSERVATISM (Boston: Little, Brown, 1955),* or Irving H. Bartlett, DANIEL WEBSTER (New York: Norton, 1978). Nationalist senator from Massachusetts.

Lewis Tappan (1788-1873), Bertram Wyatt-Brown, LEWIS TAPPAN AND THE EVANGELICAL WAR AGAINST SLAVERY (New York: Asheneum, 1971).* Major organizer of political abolitionism.

Catharine Beecher (1800-1878), Kathryn K. Sklar, CATHARINE BEECHER: A STUDY IN AMERICAN DOMESTICITY (New Haven: Yale University Press, 1978).* Career woman and reformer of the mid-nineteenth century.

John Brown (1800-1850), Stephen B. Oates, TO PURGE THIS LAND WITH BLOOD: A BIOGRAPHY OF JOHN BROWN (New York: Harper & Row, 1970). Connecticut abolitionist firebrand.

Dorothea Dix (1802-1887), Helen E. Marshall, DOROTHEA DIX: FORGOTTEN SAMARITAN (1937); or Dorothy Clarke Wilson, STRANGER AND TRAVELLER: THE STORY OF DOROTHEA DIX, AMERICAN-REFORMER (Boston: Little, Brown, 1975).

Robert E. Lee (1807-1870), Earl Schenck Miers, ROBERT E. LEE (New York: Knopf, 1956). Confederate general.

Jefferson Davis (1808-1889). Clement Eaton, Jefferson Davis (New York: Free Press, 1977). Confederate President.

Abraham Lincoln (1809-1865). Read either: Stephen B. Oates, WITH MALICE TOWARD NONE; THE LIFE OF ABRAHAM LINCOLN (New York: New American Library, 1977) or Benjamin P. Thomas, ABRAHAM LINCOLN: A BIOGRAPHY (New York: Modern Library, 1968).

Theodore Parker (1810-1860), Henry Steele Commager, THEODORE PARKER: YANKEE
CRUSADER (Boston: Beacon Press, 1947). Reforming clergyman and backer of
John Brown's raid on Harper's Ferry.

Stephen A. Douglas (1812-1861), Gerald M. Capers, STEPHEN A. DOUGLAS: DEFENDER
OF THE UNION (Boston: Little, Brown, 1959).* Major Democratic politician
of the pre-Civil War decade.

Frederick Douglass (1818-1895), Nathan I. Huggins, SLAVE AND CITIZEN: THE
LIFE OF FREDERICK DOUGLASS (Boston: Little, Brown, 1980).* An outstanding reformer.

Ulysses S. Grant (1822-1885), Bruce Catton, U.S. GRANT AND THE AMERICAN
MILITARY TRADITION (Boston: Little, Brown, 1954).* William S. McFeely,
GRANT: A BIOGRAPHY (New York: Norton, 1981).

Thomas Wentworth Higginson (1823-1911), Tilden G. Edelstein, STRANGE ENTHUSIASM:
A LIFE OF THOMAS WENTWORTH HIGGINSON (New York: Atheneum, 1980).* Reformer,
soldier, and poet of the nineteenth century.

Carol R. Berkin BARUCH COLLEGE
CITY UNIVERSITY OF NEW YORK

History 151   U.S. History,
Miss Berkin   to the Civil War

The text book provides the background information and framework necessary for
both our class discussion and for the other, more interesting, readings. Please
keep your testbook reading up with the topics covered each week in class. Reading
a whole textbook, crammed with facts, maps, names and dates, the night before an
exam is a self-inflicted "cruel and unusual punishment." It creates ulcers, hostil-
ities, and bad exam papers.

There are three other history books that you will want to own for this course.
Readings in them are essential and frequent. They are all in paperback editions.

(1) Boorstin, Daniel. The Americans: The Colonial Experience (Vintage Books),
$2.45

(2) Fine, Sidney & Brown, Gerald. The American Past, Vol. 1 (MacMillan)

(3) Hofstadter, Richard. The American Political Tradition and the Men Who
Made It (Vintage Books)

You will be required also to read one American Novel on Pre-Civil War American,
and to write a critique for me of this book. You may choose from the following:

(1) Hawthorne, Nathaniel. The Scarlet Letter* (*paperback)

(2) Hawthorne, Nathaniel. Hawthorne's Short Stories, ed. by Newton Arvin
(Vintage Book V-15 only)*

(3) Melville, Herman. Redburn (Doubleday Anchor Book)*

(4) Stowe, Harriet B. Uncle Tom's Cabin.*

(5) Thoreau, Henry D. Walden Pond (Signet)*

(6) Twain, Mark. The Adventures of Huckleberry Finn (Signet)*

I Discovery: A New World.

II Building Societies: A Study in the Social Organization of Four Colonial
Ventures.

A. Virginia

Readings: Boorstin, The Americans, pp. 97-139.

B. French Canada

C. Georgia

Readings: Boorstin, pp. 71-96

D. Massachusetts

Readings: (a) Boorstin, pp. 3-32.
OR (b) Morison, S.E., Builders of the Bay Colony,* Ch. 3
"John Winthrop, Esquire," pp. 51-105.

11

III   Man and the Devil in America

   A. Satan Comes to Salem Village

          Readings: (a) Erikson, Fai, Wayward Puritans: A Study in the
                     Sociology of Deviance, pp. 137-160
          OR   (b) Hansen, Chadwick. Witchcraft in Salem, Chs. 6
                     and 9
          OR   (c) Starkey, Marion. The Devil in Massachusetts*
          OR   (d) Mather, Cotton. "Memorable Providences," or
                     "Wonders of the Invisible World," in G. L. Burr,
                     ed., Narratives of the Witchcraft Cases 1648-1708;
                     or in Samuel Drake, ed., The Witchcraft Delusion in
                     New England

   A. The Image of the Black Man
          Readings: Jordan, Winthrop. White over Black,* pp. 3-259

IV   A Maturing Society: Some Problems in 18th Century America

   A. Attitudes toward the New Frontiers
          Readings: (a) Bridenbaugh, Carl. Myths and Realities*,
                     pp. 155-167
          OR   (b) Douglass, Elisha. Rebels and Democrats*
                     (Chapel Hill, 1955), pp. 71-100; or in
                     Colburn, ed., The Colonial Experience*, pp. 186-
                     197.

   B. Political Organization
          Readings: Greene, Jack. "The Role of the Lower Houses of
                 Assembly in 18th Century Politics," in Fine & Brown*
                 pp. 66-84; OR IN Journal of Southern History, XXVII
                 (NOV 1961), pp 451-474; OR IN Goodman, Paul, ed.,
                 Essays in American Colonial History*, pp 425-444; OR
                 IN Bobbs-Merrill Reprint Series.

   C. The Question of "Democracy"
          Readings: (a) Brown, Robert. "Democracy in Colonial Massa-
                     chusetts," New England Quarterly, Vol. XXV,
                     No. 3 (Sept 1952); OR IN Fine & Brown, pp. 31-38;
                     OR IN Bobbs-Merrill Reprints #H-31.

          OR   (b) Sydnor, Charles. Genlemen Freeholders,* Ch. 9,
                     pp. 120-134; or under new title in paperback,
                     American Revolution in the Making,* Ch 9, pp. 107-
                     118

V   Challenge to Authority: The American Revolution
   A. The Reorganization of the Empire
          Readings: Gipson, L. H. "The American Revolution as an After-
                 math of the Great War for Empire," in Colburn,*
                 pp. 281-291; OR IN Einsenstadt, A., ed., American
                 History,* Book I, pp 157-172; OR IN the Political
                 Science Quarterly, LXV (March 1950), pp. 86-104;
                 OR IN Bobbs-Merrill Reprints #H-268

    B. On Authority and Legitimacy: The Revolutionary Ideology

    C. Dealing With Dissent: The Fate of the Tories

VI A New Experimentation

    A. The Articles of Confederation

    B. The American Revolution: Culmination or Counter-revolution?

VII "The People"

    A. "The People" -- A Problem in Definition

    B. Jefferson and the Birth of the "democrats"
               Readings: Hofstadter, Richard. American Political Tradition,*
                       pp. 18-44

    C. The Era of the Common Man
               Readings: (a) Hofstadter,* pp. 45-67

               OR   (b) Ward, William. Andrew Jackson, Symbol for an
                              Age,* (Galaxy Books, 1962), pp. 166-180

    D. In Defense of the Common Man
               Readings: (a) Schlesinger, Jr., Arthur. The Age of Jackson*
                              Ch 10, pp 67-74; OR IN Fine & Brown,* pp 383-
                              398
               OR   (b) Hammond, Bray. Banks and Politics in America*
                              Ch 12, pp 326-368; OR IN Brown & Fine,* pp 398-
                              422

    E. Query: Can the Common Man Manage His Government

VIII Westward Expansion: Upsetting the Balance, Triggering the Conflict

    A. Manifest Destiny and the Winning of the West

    B. Expansion: The Threat to Both Cultures

           Readings: Hofstadter*, pp. 68-92 AND pp. 93-136

    C. The Question of Compromise

IX The War Between the States

13

UNIVERSITY OF WISCONSIN
Department of History

Paul S. Boyer

History 102-001   THE UNITED STATES SINCE 1865   Professor Boyer
Fall 1930

Assigned Books: Available in University Bookstore and on library reserve

Horatio Alger, RAGGED DICK
John D. Haeger & Michael P. Weber, Eds., THE BOSSES
Richard Hofstadter, Ed., THE PROGRESSIVE MOVEMENT
George E. Mowry, ed., THE TWENTIES: FORDS, FLAPPERS AND FANATICS
Nathaniel West, A COOL MILLION
Max Boas and Steve Chain, BIG MAC
Paul Boyer and Mario DePillis, eds., YOUR FAMILY IN AMERICAN HISTORY
Allan J. Lichtman, YOUR FAMILY HISTORY
(Optional) Charles Sellers, et. al., A SYNOPSIS OF AMERICAN HISTORY   Vol. II

Office Hours: To be announced

Grading:

Discussion participation: 20%   Midterm Exam: 20%
Family History Research Paper: 30%   Final Exam: 30%

Family History Research Paper:

This written report will give you an opportunity to relate some aspect of your own
family experience to the "History" we will be studying in this course. In addition
to the written paper to be done by everyone, a few students will have the
opportunity to give an oral report in discussion section, for extra credit, on
their findings. Further information on the family history project will be provided
in the second lecture, and in discussion section. Note the deadlines in the
course outline below relating to this project.

Lecture/Discussion Schedule and Assigned Reading:

W   9/3   Course Introduction

F   9/5   Family History: Some Background and Practical Information (No discussion
                            section this week).

The Late 19th Century: A New American Society Takes Shape

M · 9/8   The United States in Your Great-Grandparents' Day· An Overview

W   9/10   The Impact of Industrialization

F   9/12   The Shock of Immigration: For the Immigrants

           Discussion #1: Get Acquainted; Overview of Semester's Work

M   9/15   The Shock of Immigration: For the Native-Born

W   9/17   Growing Pains of the Cities

F   9/19   The Varieties of Urban Reform

           Discussion #2: Haeger & Weber, The BOSSES.*

           *Note: The discussion assignments listed in this outline are general and
                   tentative only. Specific assignments will be made on a week-by-
                   week basis by the discussion leader.

14

M 9/22 The Black Experience 1865-1920

W 9/24 Working People I: Factories and Mills

F 9/26 Who Ran the Country? Politics and Power in the Gilded Age

Discussion #3: Alger, RAGGED DICK Brief written statement on proposed
family-history topic due today.

M 9/29 Working People II: Farmers

W 10/1 Agrarian Protest

F 10/3 Popular Culture in the Gilded Age: Nostalgia in the Music Halls

Discussion #4: Individual conferences on Family History Proposals

THE EARLY 20TH CENTURY: THE MIDDLE CLASS ORGANIZES ITSELF

M 10/6 Roots of the "Progressive Movement"

W 10/8 Teddy Roosevelt: The Politics of Morality

F 10/10 Woodrow Wilson: The Politics of Nostagia

Discussion #5: Hofstadter. ed., THE PROGRESSIVE MOVEMENT

M 10/13 The Woman's Movement, 1865-1920

W 10/15 The Social Impact of World War I

F 10/17 MIDTERM EXAMINATION

Discussion #6: Review Session

THE 1920s: THE STRESSES AND STRAINS OF "NORMALCY"

M 10/20 Politics in the 1920s I: Republicans Galore

W 10/22 Social Strains in American Society in the 1920s

F 10/24 Politics in the 1920s II: Rumblings Beneath the Surface

Discussion #7: Leuchtenberg, THE TWENTIES

M 10/27 Crash and Depression; Hoover's Response

THE 1930s: FDR AND THE NEW DEAL

W 10/29 Beginnings of the New Deal

F 10/31 The Later New Deal

Discussion #8: Family History oral report #1: The Depression Experience

M 11/3 The New Deal: A Balance Sheet

W 11/5 Popular Culture in the 1930s

F 11/7 The Homefront in World War II

Discussion #9: West, A COOL MILLION Written progress report on
family history paper due today.

THE UNEASY FIFTIES: WHEN YOUR PARENTS WERE STARTING OUT

M 11/10 American Society in the 1950s: Affluence and Its Price

W 11/12 "Modern Republicanism": They Liked Ike

F 11/14 Roots of the Cold War

Discussion #10: Boyer & DePillis, YOUR FAMILY IN AMERICAN HISTORY

M 11/17 The Cold War Gets Hotter: Korea

W 11/19 McCarthyism: The Politics of Fear

F 11/21 The Civil Rights Movement

Discussion #11: Individual conferences on family research paper,
as needed.

TURBULENT SIXTIES, TROUBLED SEVENTIES

M 11/24 The Ghettoes Explode

W 11/26 No class

F 11/28 Thanksgiving vacation

No discussion section this week   Work on family history paper.

M 12/1 Vietnam: Origins of a Quagmire

W 12/3 Vietnam II: Crisis

F 12/5 "Campus Unrest": Higher Education in the 1960s

Discussion #12: Family History Oral Reports #2: Postwar America

THE SEVENTIES: ROOTS OF CONTEMPORARY ISSUES

M 12/8 Over 30 Billion Served: The Standardization of Consumption

W 12/10 The Long Road to ERA: The Women's Movement 1920-1980

F 12/12 Environment and Energy

Discussion: Boas & Chain, BIG MAC

M 12/15 Reagan Rides Again: The Conservative Resurgence (Family History
Papers due today)

UNIVERSITY OF TEXAS, AUSTIN

History 315L, Fall 1983   Office: **Garrison 407**
Professor Michael B. Stoff   Off. Hrs.: **MWF, 2-3 & by Appt.**

The United States Since 1865

Note:

1. There will be two hour examinations, each worth 25 percent of your semester
   grade, and one final examination, worth 50 percent of your semester grade.
   The final examination will be comprehensive and may be given added weight in
   determining your final grade should you show steady improvement.

2. NO MAKE-UP EXAMINATIONS WILL BE GIVEN. You may be excused from one of the
   hour examinations only if you have a certified written explanation of a
   medical problem or an official university obligation.

3. NO TAPE RECORDERS are permitted in class.

4. Each student will be assigned a teaching assistant who will be responsible
   for grading your examinations and for helping you with any problems related
   to course work.

Required Reading (available at the Co-op and on reserve at UGL):

     John M. Blum, et al, The National Experience, Part II
     James W. Davidson and Mark H. Lytle, After the Fact
     William L. Riordon, Plunkitt of Tammany Hall
     Melvin Urofsky, Louis Brandeis and the Progressive Tradition
     Doris Kearns, Lyndon Johnson and the American Dream
     Michael B. Stoff, ed., The Manhattan Project: A Case Study (xeroxed documents
                                                                   available)

Lectures and Reading Assignments:
                    I. The Age of Transformation, 1865-1900

Aug.   30: Introduction
Sept.   1: Executive Reconstruction
Sept.   3: Congressional Reconstruction
Reading : Blum, National Experience, chaps. 15-16, Davidson and Lytle, After the
            Fact, Prologue, chap. 7

Sept.   8: The Consolidation of Industry
Sept. 10: The Rise of Cities
Reading : Blum, National Experience, chaps. 18-19; Davidson and Lytle, After the
            Fact, chap. 8, Riordon, Plunkitt, pp. 1-32

Sept. 13: The "New" Immigrants
Sept. 15: The Growth of the "Ghetto"
Sept. 17: The Urban Boss and His Machine
Reading : Blum, National Experience, chap. 20; Riordon, Plunkitt, pp. 33-98

Sept. 20: The Travail of Labor
Sept. 22: The Revolt of the Farmers
Sept. 24: The Quest for Empire
Reading : Blum, National Experience, chap. 21; Urofsky, Brandeis, chaps. 1-3

17

II. The Emergence of the Regulatory State, 1900-1932

Sept. 27: HOUR EXAMINATION
Sept. 29: The Seedtime of Progressivism
Oct.   1: Theodore Roosevelt and the Square Deal
Reading : Blum, National Experience, chap. 22; Davidson and Lytle, After the
           Fact, chap. 9

Oct.   4: Woodrow Wilson and Progressive Reform
Oct.   6: The Homefront at War, I
Oct.   8: The Symbolic Crusade: Prohibition and its Aftermath
Reading : Blum, National Experience, chaps. 23-24; Urofsky, Brandeis, chaps. 4-6

Oct. 11: The New Era
Oct. 13: The Politics of Provincialism
Oct. 15: The Great Crash
Reading : Blum, National Experience, chap. 25; Davidson and Lytle, After the Fact,
           chap. 10, Urofsky, Brandeis, chaps. 7-8

III. The Emergence of the Welfare State, 1932-45

Oct. 18: The Tragedy of Herbert Hoover
Oct. 20: Franklin D. Roosevelt and the Early New Deal
Oct. 22: Franklin D. Roosevelt and the Waning of the New Deal
Reading : Blum, National Experience, chaps. 26-27, Davidson and Lytle, After the
           Fact, chap. 11

Oct. 25: The Homefront at War, II
Oct. 27: Harry S. Truman and the Fair Deal
Oct. 29: The Black Pursuit of Civil Rights
Reading : Blum, National Experience, chap. 29

IV. The Emergence of the National Security State, 1945-73

Nov.   1: HOUR EXAMINATION
Nov.   3: The Diplomacy of the Second World War
Nov.   5: The New Atomic Age
Reading : Manhattan Project, Preface, Introduction, Parts 1-2

Nov. 15: "Point of Order" (Part II)
Nov. 17: The Bland Decade
Nov. 19: Dwight Eisenhower and the Corporate Commonwealth
Reading : Manhattan Project, Parts 5-7; Davidson and Lytle, After the Fact,
           chap. 12

Nov. 22: John Kennedy and the New Frontier
Nov. 24: John Kennedy and the Cold War
Reading : Blum, National Experience, chap. 30-31; Kearns, LBJ, chap. 1

Nov. 29: Lyndon Johnson and the Great Society
Dec.   1: The War in Vietnam and at Home
Dec.   3: The Rise of Richard Nixon
Reading : Blum, National Experience, chap. 32; Kearns, LBJ, chaps. 2, 6-8

Dec.   6: The Fall of Richard Nixon
Dec.   8: Public Policy and Inequality
Dec. 10: Finis
Reading : Blum, National Experience, chap. 33; Davidson and Lytle, After the
           Fact, chap. 13.

                    FINAL EXAMINATION: Tuesday, December 14, 9-12

History 22 (4)   Prof. John Kasson
American History Since 1865   Ms. Ruth Doan
Fall 1981   Ms. Julia Hesson

PATTERNS OF AMERICAN THOUGHT AND EXPERIENCE

This course will explore patterns of American thought and experience during
the nation's history since the Civil War. Emphasis will be placed upon various
problems of social and cultural division in American life and the search for
unity. While we will use a textbook to provide necessary background, our reading
will frequently center upon primary texts. By using primary and secondary
accounts in tandem, we want both to introduce you to some key problems in American
history and also to teach you something about the process of historical interpretation. Together we will learn history not only by reading what various
historians have said, but also by practicing history ourselves. Our aim will be
to become more self-conscious about the historical assumptions and interpretations
we currently hold, to test them in fresh studies of past events, and to learn how
to formulate strategies of analysis that are both critical and creative.

Class meetings in this course are divided into lectures and discussion
groups (the latter meeting roughly every two weeks). We intend the two formats
to complement one another, and we regard both as integral parts of the course.
The lectures will provide contexts for the topics under study and will also offer
interpretations for you to consider. Students should attend lectures faithfully,
listen critically, and raise questions. Attached as the instructor may be to his
own discoveries and formulations, he does not wish students simply to record his
words and commit them to memory. Rather, the aim is that students learn from his
efforts how to develop their own interpretations and, equally important, how to
communicate their discoveries (in papers and examinations, for example) clearly
in a way that can withstand critical scrutiny.

The role of the discussion groups is to assist in this process of learning.
Discussion groups should serve, in effect, as the course workshops, where people
come to exchange ideas about the various topics under study, to sharpen their
critical tools and to work toward new understandings and hypotheses, more satisfying
and penetrating than those they might have had before. Discussions, then, are
collective enterprises which, to function successfully, demand every member's
preparation, attendance, and participation. The job of teaching assistants is to
lead discussion, not to mount an additional lecture. They can help the class
define problems and formulate questions, but the success of discussions depends
upon each member accepting responsibility and demonstrating initiative in the
group.

In addition, please feel free to talk to us individually about any matters
relating to the course that interest or concern you. We will be holding regular
office hours and can also arrange for specific appointments at other times when
necessary.

Schedule of Class Topics and Readings:
    (Books marked with an asterisk should be purchased at Student Stores.)
1. Charting Our Course (Aug. 25)

2. Problems of Reconstruction (Aug. 27-Sept. 1)
   Discussion meetings (Sept. 2-4)
   Reading: Bernard Bailyn et al., The Great Republic, *2nd edition, vol. 2
            (1981), chapter 20.
            Materials on the Murder of John Walter Stephens:
            (a) Andrew J. Stedman, Murder and Mystery . . . (1870).
            (b) Albion Tourgée, A Fool's Errand (1879), chapters 30-31.

3. Social Divisions and the Search for Unity in the Late 19th Century (Sept.8-15)
   Discussion meetings (Sept. 16-18)
   Reading: The Great Republic, chapters 21-23.
            Edward Bellamy, Looking Backward* (1888).

4. The New South and the Black Predicament (Sept. 22)
   Discussion meetings (Sept. 23-25)
   Reading: Booker T. Washington, Up from Slavery (1901).
            W. E. B. Du Bois, The Souls of Black Folk (1903), chapters 1,3, 5-6.
            [Both books are included in Three Negro Classics.*]

   Essay Due Oct. 1
5. Progressive Reform (Sept. 29-Oct. 6)
   Discussion meetings (Oct. 7-9)
   Reading: The Great Republic, chapters 24-27.
            Jane Addams, "The Subjective Necessity for Social Settlements" (1892).
            Theodore Roosevelt and the Progressive Party (excerpts from articles
               and speeches, 1910, 1912).
            Woodrow Wilson, "Freemen Need No Guardians" (from The New Freedom,
               (1913).

6. Cultural Fragmentation in the Twenties (Oct. 13-15, Oct. 27)
   Discussion meetings (Oct. 21-23)
   Reading: The Great Republic, chapter 28.
            John Dos Passos, The Big Money* (1936; vol. 3 of USA).

   Midterm Examination Oct. 29
7. Encountering the Depression: America in the Thirties (Nov. 3-10)
   Discussion meetings (Nov. 11-13)
   Reading: The Great Republic, chapters 29-30.
            Daniel Aaron and Robert Bendiner, eds., The Strenuous Decade,
               documents 2, 5, 8, 10, 11, 14, 16, 21, 23, 30, 34, 56, 58.

8. Dreams and Disturbances of Post-War America (Nov. 17-24)
   Discussion meetings (Dec. 2-4)
   Reading: The Great Republic, chapters 31-33.
            Short selection from various writings including Garry Wills on
               Nixon's "Checkers" speech; the Army/McCarthy Hearings (1953);
               integration in Chapel Hill (1963-64); the My Lai massacre (1968);
               the riot at the 1968 Democratic convention; John Hersey, "The
               Year of the Trip-Hammer" [on 1968]; Joan Didion, "The White Album."
   Films: Nixon's "Checkers" Speech (1952).
            Peter Davis, Hearts and Minds (1974).

9. Course Wrap-Up. (Dec. 1).

FINAL EXAMINATION

RUTGERS UNIVERSITY

Department of History

Reading Lists for three courses on American Indians

Calvin Martin

(A) Indian Civilizations of the Americas (i.e. New World Prehistory and Ethnology) (Fall Semester, Rutgers University)

Peter Farb, Man's Rise to Civilization: The Cultural Ascent of the Indians of North America (2nd ed., rev.). Despite the unfortunate subtitle, a worthwhile book, and always successful with students. In my experience, this is the only prehistory text students will read cover to cover and enjoy.

Gary Witherspoon, Language and Art in the Navajo Universe. Extremely worthwhile book. I have not yet used it in a course, but intend to next year (1983-84).

Ruth Murray Underhill, Singing for Power: The Song Magic of the Papago Indians of Southern Arizona. Excellent book. Students enjoy it.

Ruth Murray Underhill, Red Man's Religion: Beliefs and Practices of the Indians North of Mexico. Good, but not as good as Hultkrantz (below). A trifle unsophisticated.

Boyce Richardson, Strangers Devour the Land: A Chronicle of the Assault upon the Last Coherent Hunting Culture in North America, the Cree Indians of Northern Quebec, and Their Vast Primeval Homelands. Deeply moving narrative. Invariably the most popular book in the course.

Dennis and Barbara Tedlock, eds., Teachings from the American Earth: Indian Religion and Philosophy. Short readings, well chosen. Students enjoy.

Ake Hultkrantz, The Religions of the American Indians. Very good. Philosophical.

***I do not use all of these book when I teach the course. I vary my reading list year to year. These are the books I have found to be the most successful over the years.

(B) The Indian in American History (i.e., the History of Indian and White Relations) (Spring Semester, Rutgers University)

Peter Nabokov, ed., Native American Testimony: An Anthology of Indian and White Relations, First Encounter to Dispossession. Students enjoy.

Robert M. Utley, The Last Days of the Sioux Nation. Marvelous book. The best, most judicious account of the Plains Indian Wars. Its real strength is its discussion of the Battle at Wounded Knee Creek (1890).

Theodora Kroeber, Ishi: A Biography of the Last Wild Indian in North America. Students love this classic -- and justifiably so.

Neal Salisbury, Manitou and Providence. Indians, Europeans, and the Making of New England, 1500-1643. I will probably use this for the first time in 1983-84. Strong on both Indians and whites.

George T. Hunt, The Wars of the Iroquois: A Study in Intertribal Trade Relations. Hunt's ethnohistory stands in need of correcting. Still, a useful book, and readable.

Nancy Oestreich Lurie, Mountain Wolf Woman, Sister of Crashing Thunder: The Autobiography of a Winnebago Indian. Subtle book. Good.

N. Scott Momaday, House Made of Dawn. Profound fiction, written by a Kiowa.

Robert Berkhofer, Jr., The White Man's Indian: Images of the American Indian from Columbus to the Present. Very good. Students enjoy.

Calvin Martin, Keepers of the Game: Indian-Animal Relationships and the Fur Trade.

William Faulkner, "The Bear," in Three Famous Short Novels. Very important statement about the American Indian. Ethnologically accurate. Students find it a joy to read.

***Again, I do not use all of these books when I teach the course. I vary my reading list year to year. These are the books I have found to be the most successful over the years.

(C) The Image of the Indian in Classic American Literature (Rutgers University)

Roy Harvey Pearce, Savagism and Civilization. Still a marvelous book.

James Fenimore Cooper, The Last of the Mohicans.

Francis Parkman, The Oregon Trail. (Obviously not fiction.)

Francis Parkman, selections from The Jesuits in North America and The Conspiracy of Pontiac. (Again, not fiction.)

D.H. Lawrence, Studies in Classic American Literature. Here we read "Hector

St. John de Crevecoeur" (chap. 3), "Fenimore Cooper's White Novels" (chap. 4), and "Fenimore Cooper's Leatherstocking Novels" (chap. 5).

Herman Melville, The Confidence Man. Here we read "Containing the Metaphysics of Indian-Hating" (chap. 26), and "Some Account of a Man of Questionable Morality" (chap. 27).

Ernest Hemingway, Nick Adams Stories. Here we read "Indian Camp," "Ten Indians," "The Indians Moved Away," and "Fathers and Sons."

William Faulkner, Three Famous Short Novels. Here we read "The Bear."

Willa Cather, Death Comes for the Archbishop.

Conrad Richter, Light in the Forest.

N. Scott Momaday, House Made of Dawn.

James Welch, Winter in the Blood.

***Books I may use in future include Ken Kesey's One Flew over the Cuckoo's Nest and Leslie Marmon Silko, Ceremony.

History 157C
UCLA Winter 1984
Professor Walter Williams

NORTH AMERICAN INDIAN HISTORY SINCE 1860

Required Reading:

Walter Williams, Southeastern Indians Since the Removal Era (University of Georgia Press).

John Neihardt, Black Elk Speaks (Washington Square Press).

Nancy Lurie, Mountain Wolf Woman (University of Michigan Press).

Edgar Cohn, Our Brother's Keeper (New American Library).

Vine Deloria, Custer Died For Your Sins (Avon).

Course Outline:

TOPIC 1: Eastern Indians and the Indian Territory to 1890: Civil War and Treaty-Breaking.
read Williams, Southeastern Indians.

TOPIC 2: Indians of California, the Great Basin, and the Northwest to 1890: Genocide and Overlooking.
read Neihardt, Black Elk Speaks.

TOPIC 3: Indians of the Southwest to 1890: Cultural Survival.

TOPIC 4: Indians of the Plains to 1890: Military Resistance and Defeat.
read Lurie, Mountain Wolf Woman.

TOPIC 5: U.S. Indian Policy and Native Reactions to Colonial Control.

TOPIC 6: Indian Demoralization and Forced Acculturation, 1890-1920.
read Cohn, Our Brother's Keeper.

TOPIC 7: Indian Reform, 1920-1950.
read Deloria, Custer Died for Your Sins.

TOPIC 8: Termination and Urbanization, 1950-1970.

TOPIC 9: Pan-Indianism, Red Power Protests, and Cultural Revival, 1960-present.

Course Requirements:

The books are listed in the Outline to be read before we discuss the topic in class, so do not let yourself get behind in your readings. To do well in this course, you must do all the readings and have a complete set of lecture notes.

Course Requirements (cont.)

Since much of the final exam is based on the lectures, those students who miss more than a few classes always find that they cannot answer the test questions -- and receive a very low grade. If you miss, you will be expected to consult the professor about dropping the course. The final exam counts 40% of your grade.

The other 60% can be earned by doing essays on the readings. Each paper should be doublespaced typed, clearly written, analytical, well-organized, and demonstrating your own critical thought about the subject. It helps to do an outline before writing. Students are encouraged to turn in papers before the deadline, so if you think you will not be able to get the paper in on its due date you should turn it in early. Papers turned in after the due date will be lowered in grade. Plagiarism of a paper is grounds for failure.

January 20 is the final date to turn in the first essay, on this topic: "From reading Southeastern Indians Since the Removal Era, briefly state (about 1 page) what you consider to be the two most important themes in Southeastern Indian history, 1840-1975, and then concentrate on your ideas of what themes were not covered in Chapter 11, which you saw in reading Chapters 2-10. Be original, creative, and don't be afraid to criticize." This essay should be about 3 or 4 doublespaced typed pages, and will count 15% of your grade.

February 17 will be the last date to turn in a mid-term essay on the two autobiographies of Black Elk Speaks and Mountain Wolf Woman: "Compare and contrast the attitudes of Black Elk and Mountain Wolf Woman toward their own cultures and toward white society. What viewpoints do they share which indicate continuity in Indian thought, and how do their differences show how Indian people have changed in the last century?" This essay should be about 7 or 8 doublespaced typed pages, and will count 25% of your grade.

March 14 will be the last date to turn in an essay on the two books Our Brother's Keeper and Custer Died for Your Sins (topic will be announced at mid-term). This essay should be about 5 or 6 doublespaced typed pages, and will count 20% of your grade.

If you have any questions, on either the lecture notes or the readings, feel free to ask at anytime, in class or out. Class reactions will be encouraged.

UNIVERSITY OF CALIFORNIA, LOS ANGELES

History 197/201
UCLA Winter 1984
Professor Walter Williams

AMERICAN INDIAN POLITICAL STATUS IN THE TWENTIETH CENTURY

This class is a seminar for students with some background in Indian studies
and/or exposure to Indian reservations. It is not designed for those who wish
an introductory survey about Native Americans, but focuses on the political
situation of Indian people since they have been under the domination of the
United States (from the nineteenth century to the present).

COURSE OUTLINE

Topic 1:   Introduction and U.S. Indian treaties (lecture by instructor)
            (students choose a research topic)

Topic 2:   The legal status of Indians to 1900: laws and court precedents
            (lecture by instructor) (Bibliographies die)

Topic 3:   Assimilationist policies and allotment, 1900-1934: the Bureau of
            Indian Affairs (lecture by instructor).
            and The Indian Reorganization act (oral report).

(ORAL REPORTS):

Topic 4:   The Supreme Court and the Question of Indian Sovereignty since 1900.
            Indian Claims Commission and Claims settlement.

Topic 5:   Termination, and terminated tribes.
            Public Law 280 and affected tribes.

Topic 6:   Federal policies since 1960.
            State policies since 1960.

Topic 7:   National Indian organizations, 1900-1960
            National Indian organizations since 1960

Topic 8:   Tribal governments and leadership since 1934: The Plains.
            Tribal governments and leadership since 1934: Oklahoma.

Topic 9:   Tribal governments and leadership since 1934: The Southwest.
            Tribal governments and leadership since 1934: The Far West and
            Alaska.

Topic 10:   Non-reservation Indian political status (unrecognized, state reser-
            vations, or off-reservation).
            Urban Indian political status and leadership

Alternate topic: Indian Treaties and the Question f Sovereignty.

Grading:

Each student will choose a research topic, and present an oral report and
discussion at the appropriate time during the class. When each student presents the oral report, she or he will pass out to each class member a short
general outline and bibliography (this oral report will count 40% of the
grade). By the last class meeting, each student will turn in a 12-18 page

(doublespaced typed) paper on this same topic, which will count 50% of the grade. Graduate students will be expected to base their research on primary sources, show a wide bibliographical use, and present a paper 20-27 pages in length. All papers should be well written, without mistakes, and demonstrating analytical thought. Notes should be at the end, in correct citation form (refer to Turabin, Manual for Writers or the University of Chicago, Manual of Style). Plagarism in a paper is ground for failure.

The other 10% of the grade will be based on class participation and discussion of the topics. This means students should be at all classes, in order to be able to participate. Those who miss two classes should immediately consult with the professor about dropping the class.

INTRODUCTORY BIBLIOGRAPHY

(consult with the Librarian, Ms. Salabiye, at the American Indian Studies Center)

Reference materials:

Francis Paul Prucha, A Bibliographical Guide to the History of Indian-White Relations in the United States (1977) also, Indian-White Relations...A Bibliography (1982).

Wilcomb Washbuen, ed. The American Indian and the United States: A Documentary History (4 vols., Commissioner of Indian Affairs Reports, laws, treaties, court decisions).
F. P. Prucha, ed. Documents of United States Indian Policy.
Vine Deloria, ed. Of Utmost Good Faith.
Jack Forbes, ed. The Indian in America's Past.
Virgil Vogel, ed. This Country was Ours.
Imre Sutton, Indian Land Tenure: Bibliography

GENERAL STUDIES

Richard Ellis, ed. The Western American Indian.
David Getches et.al. Cases and Materials on Federal Indian Law.
Monroe Price, Law and the American Indian.
D'Arcy McNickle, Native American Tribalism.
Edward Spicer, A Short History of the Indians of the U.S.
S. Lyman Tyler, A History of Indian Policy.
Wilcomb Washburn, Red Man's Land/White Man's Law.
Jennings Wise, The Red Man in the New World Drama (1971 revised edition by Vine Deloria).
Howard Bahr et.al. Native Americans Today.
Indian Voices: The Native American Today (2nd Convocation of American Indian Scholars, 1974, on water rights, education, land use, health, museums, and Indian Claims Commission).
Stuart Levine and Nancy Lurie, eds. The American Indian Today.
Deward Walker, ed. The Emergent Native Americans.
Lawrence Barsh and James Henderson, The Road: Indian Tribes and Political Liberty.

University of Chicago

History 737   Department of History   E. Cook

Seminar: Basic Problems in Early American Social History

* = U. of C. Bookstore

I.   Background and Organizational Session

      Henretta, James K., "Social History as Lived and Written," AHR 84 (1979),
          1293-1333.

      Schneider, David M., American Kinship: A Cultural Account. 2nd Ed.
          (Chicago, 1980), 1-54, 118-136.

      Stone, Lawrence, "The Revival of Narrative: Reflections on a New Old
          History," Past and Present #85 (1980), 3-24.

II.   The Town: Formal Structures and Resources

      *David Grayson Allen, In English Ways: The Movement of Societies and the
          Transferal of English Local Law and Custom to Massachusetts Bay in
          the Seventeenth Century (Chapel Hill, 1981).

      *Edward M. Cook, Jr., The Fathers of the Towns: Leadership and Community
          Structure in Eighteenth Century New England (Baltimore, 1976).

      Lecture Materials:

      Sumner C. Powell, Puritan Village: The Formation of a New England Town
          (Middletown, Conn., 1963)
      *Charles S. Grant, Democracy in the Connecticut Frontier Town of Kent
          (New York, 1961)
      Bruce Daniels, The Connecticut Town: Growth and Development, 1635-1790
          (Middletown, Conn., 1979), Chap. 1, 3, 5.
      Richard Holmes, Communities in Transition: Bedford and Lincoln, Massachusetts,
          1729-1850 (Ann Arbor, 1978), Chap. 1, 2, 3, 4.

III. Religion in Community Process

      *Richard L. Bushman, From Puritan to Yankee: Character and the Social Order
          in Connecticut, 1690-1765 (Cambridge, Mass., 1967)

      Rhys Isaac, "Religion and Authority: Problems of the Anglican Establishment
          in Virginia in the Era of the Great Awakening and the Parsons' Cause,"
          WMQ, 3rd Series XXX (1973) 3-36.

      Daniels, The Connecticut Town, Chap. 4

      J. M. Bumsted, "Religion, Finance, and Democracy in Massachusetts: The Town
          of Norton as a Case Study," Journal of American History 57 (1971) 817-831.

      Lecture Materials:

      Paul R. Lucas, Valley of Discord: Church and Society along the Connecticut
          River, 1636-1725 (Hanover, N.H., 1976) Chaps. 1-4, 6.
      Robert G. Pope, The Half-Way Covenant: Church Membership in Puritan New
          England (Princeton, 1969), Chap. 2, 5, 8, 9, 10.
      James P. Walsh, "The Great Awakening in the First Congregational Church
          at Woodburg, Connecticut," WMQ 28 (1971), 817-831.
      J. M. Bumsted, "A Caution to Erring Christians: Ecclesistical Disorder
          on Cape Cod, 1717-1738," WMQ, 3rd Series XXVIII (1971), 413-438.

Week III, Lecture Materials (Contd.)

William F. Willingham, "Religious Conversion in the Second Society
of Windham, Connecticut, 1723-43: A Case Study," Societas VI
(1974), 109-120.

Gerald F. Moran, "Religious Renewal, Puritan Tribalism, and the Family in
Seventeenth Century Milford, Connecticut," WMQ 3rd Series, XXXVI (1979)
236-254.

IV.   Community Culture

*Kenneth Lockridge, A New England Town: The First One Hundred Years (New
York, 1970).

*Paul Boyer and Stephen Nissenbaum, Salem Possessed (Cambridge, 1974).

*Michael Zuckerman, Peaceable Kingdoms: The New England Towns in the
Eighteenth Century (New York, 1970), Chap. 1, 2, 4, 6.

Lecture Materials:

Darrett Rutman, Winthrop's Boston: Portrait of a Puritan Town (Chapel
Hill, 1965)

David Konig, Law and Society in Puritan Massachusetts: Essex County,
1629-1692 (Chapel Hill, 1979)

William Nelson, Dispute and Conflict Resolution in Plymouth County,
Massachusetts, 1725-1825 (Chapel Hill, 1981)

John Demos, "John Godfrey and His Neighbors: Witchcraft and the Social
Web in Colonial Massachusetts," WMQ 3rd Series XXXIII (1976), 242-265.

V.   Demography, The Life Cycle, and Society

*Philip Greven, Four Generations: Land, Population, and Family in Colonial
Andover (Ithaca, 1970)

Lutz Berkner, "The Stem Family and the Developmental Cycle of the Peasant
Household: An 18th Century Austrian Example," AHR 77 (1972), 398-418.

Daniel Scott Smith, "The Demographic History of Colonial New England,"
Journal of Economic History, XXXII (1972), 165-183, or in The American
Family in Social-Historical Perspective, Michael Gordon, ed. (New York,
1973), 397-415.

Daniel Scott Smith and Michael S. Hindus, "Premarital Pregnancy in America,
1640-1971, An Overview and Interpretation," Journal of Interdisciplinary
History, V (1975), 537-570.

Walter J. Dickie, "The Representation of the Family," from "Family and
Polity in Atlantic England" (Ph.D. diss., University of Chicago, 1978),
15-47.

Lecture Materials:

John Demos, "Families in Colonial Bristol, Rhode Island: An Exercise in
Historical Demography," WMQ 25 (1968), 40-57.

Kenneth Lockridge, "The Population of Dedham, Massachusetts, 1636-1736,"
Econ. Hist. Rev. 14 (1966), 318-344.

Susan L. Norton, "Population Growth in America: A Study of Ippswich,
Massachusetts," Population Studies 25 (1971), 73-82.

Week V., Lecture Materials (Contd.)

    Robert V. Wells, "Family Size and Fertility Control in America: A Study of Quaker Families," Population Studies 25 (1971), 73-82.

    Robert V. Wells, "Quaker Marriage Patterns in a Colonial Perspective," WMQ 29 (1972), 415-442.

    Lois Green Carr and Lorena S. Walsh,"The Planter's Wife: The Experience of White Women in Seventeenth Century Maryland, WMQ 3rd Ser., XXXIV (1977), 542-571.

    Darrett and Anita Rutman, "Of Agues and Fevers: Malaria in the Early Chesapeake, WMQ 3rd Ser., XXXIII (1976), 31-60.

    Russell R. Menard, "Immigrants and Their Increase: The Process of Population Growth in Early Colonial Maryland," in Law, Society and Politics in Early Maryland, Land, Carr, and Papenfuse, eds., 88-110.

VI.   The Family - Standards of Living; Lineage and Power

    Sarah F. McMahon, "Provisions Laid Up for the Family: Toward a History of Diet in New England, 1650-1850," Historical Methods, 14 (1981), 4-21.

    Lois Green Carr and Lorena S. Walsh, "Inventories and the Analysis of Wealth and Consumption Patterns in St. Mary's County, Maryland, 1658-1777," Historical Methods, 13 (1980), 81-104.

    James T. Lemon, "Household Consumption in Eighteenth Century America and Its Relation to Production and Trade: The Situation among the Farmers in Southeastern Pennsylvania," Agricultural History XLI (1967), 59-70.

    John Demos, A Little Commonwealth: Family Life in Plymouth Colony (New York, 1970), 19-58.

    Jack Michel, "Economic Behavior and Social Structure in Early Pennsylvania: An Introductory Essay," (Unpublished paper, University of Chicago, 1980), 1-125.

    Lecture Materials:

    *John J. Waters, The Otis Family in Provincial and Revolutionary Massachusetts (Chapel Hill, 1968)

    Richard S. Dunn, Puritans and Yankees: The Winthrop Dynasty of New England, 1630-1717 (Princeton, 1962)

    Andrew Raymond, "A New England Colonial Family: Four Generations of the Porters of Hadley, Mass.," New England Historic and Geneological Register CXXIX (1975), 198-220.

VII.   Social Structure and Social Mobility

    *Robert Gross, The Minutemen and Their World (New York, 1976) (on reserve in Harper Library under History 155)

    *Jackson Turner Main, The Social Structure of Revolutionary America (Princeton, 1965), chaps. 1, 4, 5, 6, 9.

    Kenneth A. Lockridge, "Land, Population and the Evolution of New England Society, 1630-1790," Past and Present #39 (1968), or in Stanley N. Katz, ed., Colonial America: Essays in Politics and Social Development, 1st Edition, 466-491.

Week VII, Lecture Materials:

    P. M. G. Harris, "The Social Origins of American Leaders: Their Demo-
        graphic Foundations," Perspectives in American History III (1969), 159-346.

    Allan Kulikoff, "The Progress of Inequality in Revolutionary Boston," WMQ
        28 (1971), 375-412.

    Bissell, Linda A., "From One Generation to Another: Mobility in Seven-
        teenth Century Windsor, Conn.," WMQ XXXI (1974), 79-110.

    Dennis P. Ryan, "Landholding, Opportunity and Mobility in Revolutionary
        New Jersey, WMQ, 3rd Ser. XXXVI (1979), 571-592.

    Douglas Lamar Jones, "Poverty and Vagabondage: The Process of Survival in
        Eighteenth Century Massachusetts," New England Historic and Geneological
        Register 133 (1979), 243-256.

VIII. Historical Geography

    *James T. Lemon, The Best Poor Man's Country": A Geographical Study of Early
        Southeastern Pennsylvania (Baltimore, 1972)

    Robert D. Mitchell, Commercialism and Frontier: Perspectives on the Early
        Shenandoah Valley (Charlottesville, 1977).

Lecture Materials:

    *Carville U. Earle, The Evolution of a Tidewater Settlement: All Hallow's
        Parish, Maryland, 1650-1783 (Chicago, 1975)

    Douglas McManis, Colonial New England: A Historical Geography (New York, 1975)

    Daniels, The Connecticut Town, Chap. 6.

    Carville Earle and Ronald Hoffman, "Urban Development in the Eighteenth
        Century South," Perspectives in American History, X (1976), 7-80.

IX. The Rural Economy

    Winifred B. Rothenberg, "The Market and Massachusetts Farmers, 1750-1855,"
        Journal of Economic History, XLI (1981), 283-314.

    James A. Henretta, Families and Farms: Mentalite in Pre-Industrial America,
        WMQ 3rd Ser., XXXV (1978), 3-32.

    James T. Lemon, Early Americans and their Social Environment, Journal of
        Historical Geography VI (1980), 115-131.

    Michael Merrill, "Cash is Good to Eat: Self-Sufficiency and Exchange in the
        Rural Economy of the United States," Radical History Review III (1977)
        42-71.

Lecture Materials:

    Max George Schumacher, The Northern Farmer and His Markets During the Late
        Colonial Period (New York, 1975)

    Carl Bridenbaugh, Fat Mutton and Liberty of Conscience (Providence, 1974).

    Darrett Rutman, Husbandmen of Plymouth: Farms and Villages of the Old
        Colony, 1620-1692 (Boston, 1967).

    Margaret E. Martin, Merchants and Trade of the Connecticut River Valley,
        1750-1820: Smith College Studies in History #24 (Northampton, 1938-39)

*Starred materials in the lecture sections are books that other members of
the seminar ought to read if they can find time.

UNIVERSITY OF CHICAGO

History 234

Contrasting Communities: English and American Society 1550-1750

Course List   Mr. Cook
Fall 1981   Mr. Kishlansky

Class Schedule

I.   Introduction
          Oct. 1   Lecture - England: An Overview
          Oct. 6   Lecture - America: An Overview
          Oct. 8   Discussion

II.   Demography
          Oct. 13   Lecture - English Demography
          Oct. 15   Lecture - American Demography
          Oct. 20   Discussion

III. Social Structure
          Oct. 22   Lecture - English Social Structure
          Oct. 27   Lecture - American Social Structure
          Oct. 29   Discussion

IV.   Family Life
          Nov. 3   Lecture - The English Family
          Nov. 5   Lecture - The American Family
          Nov. 10   Discussion

V.   Agriculture
          Nov. 12   Lecture - Agriculture and Society in England
          Nov. 17   Lecture - Agriculture and Society in America
          Nov. 19   Discussion

VI.   Localities
          Nov. 24   Lecture - English Localities
          Dec. 1   Lecture - American Localities
          Dec. 3   Discussion

Readings

Books marked (*) have been ordered at the U. of C. Bookstore. All books and
articles have been placed on reserve in Regenstein.

I.   Introduction
          Peter Laslett, The World We Have Lost, 1-127
          Kenneth Lockridge, A New England Town: The First One Hundred Years, 3-118

II.   Demography
          Philip J. Greven, Jr., Four Generations: Population, Land, and the
              Family in Colonial Andover, Massachusetts, 21-40, 103-124, 175-221
          Lawrence Stone, The Family, Sex and Marriage in England, 1550-1800, 33-66
          Wrightson and Levine, Poverty and Piety in An English Village: Terling,
              1500-1700, 43-72
          Darrett and Anita Rutman, "'Now-Wives and Sons-in-Law': Parental Death
              in a Seventeenth Century Virginia County," in Thad Tate and David
              Ammerman, eds., The Chesapeake in the Seventeenth Century, 153-182
          E.A. Wrigley, "Family Limitation in Pre-Industrial England," Economic
              History Review, 19 (1966), 82-109.

III. Social Structure
    *Margaret Spufford, Contrasting Communities: English Villagers in the Sixteenth and Seventeenth Centuries, 3-92
    *Robert Gross, The Minutemen and their World, 68-108
    *Greven, Four Generations, 41-71
    Lawrence Stone, "Social Mobility in England, 1500-1700," Past and Present #30 (1966), or in Rowrey and Graham, Quantitative History, 238-271
    James A. Henretta, "Economic Development and Social Structure in Colonial Boston," William & Mary Quarterly XXII (1965), 75-92, or in Stanley N. Katz, ed., Colonial America: Essays in Politics and Social Development

IV. Family Life
    *John Demos, A Little Commonwealth: Family Life in Plymouth Colony, 59-125
    *Stone, The Family, Sex and Marriage, 69-180
    Lorena S. Walsh, "'Till Death Us Do Part': Marriage and Family in Seventeenth Century Maryland," in Tate and Ammerman, The Chesapeake in the Seventeenth Century, 126-152

V. Agriculture
    W. G. Hoskins, The Midland Peasant: The Economic and Social History of a Leicestershire Village, 90-179
    *David G. Allen, In English Ways: The Movement of Societies and the Transferal of English Local Law and Custom to Massachusetts Bay in the Seventeenth Century, 3-116
    *Wrightson and Levine, Poverty and Piety, 19-42

VI. Localities
    *Victor Skipp, Crisis and Development: An Ecological Case Study of the Forest of Arden, 1570-1674, 3-99
    *Paul Boyer and Stephen Nissenbaum, Salem Possessed: The Social Origins of Witchcraft, 1-109, 179-216
    *Wrightson and Levine, Poverty and Piety, 73-109

Course Requirements

1) Informed participation in class discussion.

2) A paper of 12 to 15 pages drawn from one of the 5 topics. All papers must be comparative in focus and will involve supplementary readings selected in consultation with the instructors.

3) A final examination.

ESCAPE FROM EUROPE
    E. E. Rich, "The Population of Elizabethan England," Economic
        History Review, 2nd ser., 2 (1949), 247-65
    Michael Walzer, "Puritanism as a Revolutionary Ideology," History
        and Theory 3 (1961), 59-90
    Edmund Morgan, The Puritan Dilemma, ch. 2
    Michael Zuckerman, "The Fabrication of Identity in Early America,"
        William and Mary Quarterly 34 (1977), 183-214
    *Sir Walter Raleigh, The Discovery of Guiana
    *William Bradford, Of Plymouth Plantation, ch. 1-4
    *Gottlieb Mittelberger, Journey to Pennsylvania

THE NEW FRONTIER
    Frederick Jackson Turner, "The Significance of the Frontier in
        American History," in The Frontier in American History, ch. 1
    Sigmund Diamond, "From Organization to Society: Virginia in the
        17th Century," American Journal of Sociology 63 (1958), 457-75
    Edmund Morgan, "The First American Boom: Virginia 1618 to 1630,"
        William and Mary Quarterly 28 (1971), 169-98
    Richard Dunn, Sugar and Slaves, ch. 8
    *Joseph Conrad, Heart of Darkness
    *John Barth, The Sot-Weed Factor, part II, ch. 6

RACE
    Winthrop Jordan, The White Man's Burden, pp. 3-25, 46-86, 99-122
    James Axtell, "The White Indians of Colonial America," William
        and Mary Quarterly 32 (1975), 55-88
    *John Rolfe, "Letter," in Lyon Tyler, ed., Narratives of Early
        Virginia, pp. 239-44
    *The Narrative of the Captivity and Restoration of Mrs. Mary
        Rowlandson, in Richard Van Der Beets, ed., Held Captive by Indians,
        pp. 42-90

RELIGION
    Tom Wolfe, The Electric Kool-Aid Acid Test, ch. 4, 11
    Edmund Morgan, The Puritan Dilemma, ch. 10
    Jon Butler, "Magic, Astrology, and the Early American Religious
        Heritage, 1600-1760," American Historical Review 84 (1979), 317-46
    *"The Diary of Michael Wigglesworth," Colonial Society of Massachu-
        setts, Publications 35 (1951), 311-444
    *William Perry, ed., Historical Collections Relating to the American
        Colonial Church, I, pp. 261-318, 434-501

THE FAMILY
    J. Hajnal, "European Marriage Patterns in Historical Perspective,"
        in D. V. Glass and D. E. C. Eversley, eds., Population in History,
        pp. 101-43
    Philip Greven, "Family Structure in 17th-Century Andover, Massachu-
        setts," William and Mary Quarterly 23 (1966), 234-56
    Edmund Morgan, The Puritan Family, ch. 2, 3, 6, 7
    Stephanie Wolf, Urban Village, ch. 7, 8
    Daniel B. Smith, "Mortality and Family in the Colonial Chesapeake,"
        Journal of Interdisciplinary History 8 (1978), 403-27

Robert Weir, "Rebelliousness: Personality Development and the
American Revolution in the Southern Colonies," in Jeffrey Crow
and Larry Tise, eds., The Southern Experience in the American
Revolution, pp. 25-54
*Annie Jester and Martha Hiden, eds., Adventurers of Purse and
Person: Virginia, 1607-1625, pp. 5-69

THE ECONOMY

Max Weber, from The Protestant Ethic and the Spirit of Capitalism,
in Talcott Parsons, et al., eds., Theories of Society, pp. 1253-65
Edmund Morgan, "The Labor Problem at Jamestown, 1607-1618," American
Historical Review 76 (1971), 595-611
Emery Battis, Saints and Sectaries, ch. 17
Frederick Tolles, Meeting House and Counting House, ch. 3, 4
James Henretta, "Families and Farms: Mentalite in Pre-Industrial
America," William and Mary Quarterly 35 (1978), 3-32
Aubrey Land, "Economic Base ₂nd Social Structure: The Northern
Chesapeake in the 18th Century," Journal of Economic History 25
(1965), 639-54
Richard Dunn, Sugar and Slaves, ch. 1
*John Cotton, "Christian Calling," in Perry Miller and Thomas
Johnson, eds., The Puritans, pp. 319-27
*Benjamin Franklin, Autobiography

CRISIS AND RESTABILIZATION

Edmund Morgan, "Slavery and Freedom: The American Paradox,"
Journal of American History 59 (1972), 5-29

COMMUNITY

Michael Zuckerman, "The Social Context of Democracy in Massachu-
setts," William and Mary Quarterly 25 (1968), 523-44
Sidney James, A People Among Peoples, ch. 1-8, 11
Richard Shryock, "British vs. German Traditions in Colonial Agri-
culture," Mississippi Valley Historical Review 26 (1939), 39-54
*Richard Hooker, ed., The Carolina Backcountry on the Eve of the
Revolution, part 1 or 2
*William Byrd, Prose Works, ed. by Louis Wright, pp. 41-153
*Charles Paullin, Atlas of the Historical Geography of the United
States, plates 40, 41d, 43b, 44d, 53a-d

POLITICS

Bernard Bailyn, The Origins of American Politics, ch. 2
Charles Sydnor, American Revolutionaries in the Making
Rhys Isaac, "Evangelical Revolt: The Nature of the Baptists' Chal-
lenge to the Traditional Order in Virginia, 1765 to 1775," William
and Mary Quarterly 31 (1974), 345-68
Patricia Bonomi, "The Middle Colonies: Embryo of the New Political
Order," in Alden Vaughan and Charles Biliias, eds., Perspectives
on Early American History, pp. 63-92
Robert Zemsky, "Power, Influence, and Status: Leadership Patterns
in the Massachusetts Assembly, 1740-1755," William and Mary
Quarterly 26 (1969), 502-20
Pauline Maier, "Popular Uprisings and Civil Authority in 18th-Century
America," William and Mary Quarterly 27 (1970), 3-35
*Richard Hooker, ed., The Carolina Backcountry, part 3

DECENTRALIZED TOTALITARIANISM

Leonard Levy, Legacy of Suppression, ch. 1, 2, 4

THE JOHNS HOPKINS UNIVERSITY

History 357   Sociology of Early Modern British
                                     Colonization: The Seventeenth Century

Professor Jack P. Greene   **Fall Term 1981**

   This is a discussion and writing course. Each student will be
expected to read from 100 to 300 pages each week and to write a short
two-page paper on a sharply focused topic on the basis of that reading.
These papers will serve as a starting point for class discussions. There
will be no examinations.

   All items on the reading list will be on reserve in the MSE Library.
Those marked by an asterisk are in paperback and should be available at the
JHU Book Center.

                        READING ASSIGNMENTS

PART ONE: THE NATURE OF COLONIAL SOCIETIES

September

   10   Orientation

               Herbert Lüthy, "Colonization and the Making of Mankind,"
                  Journal of Economic History, XXI (1961), 483-95.

   17   Theories of Colonization

               Adam Smith, "Colonies," Parts 1-3, in An Inquiry into the
                  Nature and Causes of the Wealth of Nations, any edition.

               Herman Merivale, Lectures on Colonization and Colonies,
                  73-98, 253-76, 300-10, 613-35.

               O. Mannoni, Prospero and Caliban: The Psychology of
                  Colonization, 97-109.

             * Richard D. Brown, Modernization: The Transformation of
                  American Life, 1-48.

PART TWO: TWO MODELS OF EARLY ANGLO-AMERICAN COLONIZATION

   24   The Chesapeake

               Sigmund Diamond, "From Organization to Society: Virginia
                  in the Seventeenth Century," American Journal of Sociology
                  LXIII (1958), 457-75.

             * Edmund S. Morgan, American Slavery, American Freedom: The
                  Ordeal of Colonial Virginia, 44-211.

                               37

PART TWO: Two Models of Early Anglo-American Colonization   (cont'd.)

September

24   The Chesapeake

* Thad W. Tate, ed., The Chesapeake in the Seventeenth Century, 51-125.

Wesley Frank Craven, White, Red, and Black: The Seventeenth Century Virginian, 39-72.

October

1   New England

Richard S. Dunn, "Experiments Holy and Unholy 1630-31," in K. R. Andrews, N. P. Canny, and P.E.H. Hair, eds., The Westward Enterprise, 271-89.

T. H. Breen and Stephen Foster, "Moving to the New World: The Character of Early Massachusetts Immigration," William and Mary Quarterly, 3d ser., XXX (1973), 189-222.

* Perry Miller, Errand into the Wilderness, 1-15.

David Hall, "Understanding the Puritans," in Herbert Bass, ed., The State of American History, 330-49.

Michael Zuckerman, "Pilgrims in the Wilderness: Community, Modernity, and the Maypole at Merry Mount," New England Quarterly, L (1977), 255-77.

* Kenneth A. Lockridge, A New England Town: The First Hundred Years, 1-78.

T. H. Breen and Stephen Foster, "The Puritans' Greatest Achievement: A Study of Social Cohesion in Seventeenth-Century Massachusetts," Journal of American History, LX (1973), 5-22.

* Darrett B. Rutman, Winthrop's Boston: A Portrait of a Puritan Town, 1630-1649, 164-201.

PART THREE: CONTEMPORARY PERSPECTIVES

8   Old England

* Alan Macfarlane, The Origins of English Individualism 62-101, 165-88.

Lawrence Stone, "Social Mobility in England, 1500-1700," Past and Present, #33 (1966), 16-55.

E. A. Wrigley, "A Simple Model of London's Importance in Changing English Society and Economy 1650-1750," Past and Present, #37 (1967), 44-70.

E. E. Rich, "The Population of Elizabethan England," Economic History Review, 2d ser., II (1949-50), 247-65.

Robert Brenner, "The Social Basis of English Commercial Expansion, 1550-1650," Jo. Econ. Hist., XXXII (1972), 361-84.

PART THREE: Contemporary Perspectives   (cont'd.)

October   Old England

  8   Michael Walzer, "Puritanism as a Revolutionary Ideology,"
                 History and Theory, III (1963), 59-90.

 15   Ireland and Bermuda

                 Nicholas P. Canny, "The Ideology of English Colonization:
                   From Ireland to America," Wm. & Mary Qtly., 3d ser.,
                   XXX (1972), 575-98.

                 Karl S. Bottigheimer, "Kingdom and Colony: Ireland in the
                   Westward Enterprise 1536-1660," in Andrews, Canny, and
                   Hair, eds., Westward Enterprise, 45-64.

                 Nicholas Canny, "The Permissive Frontier: The Problem of
                   Social Control in English Settlements in Ireland and
                   Virginia, 1550-1650," in ibid., 17-44.

                 Aidan Clarke, "Colonial Identity in Early Seventeenth-Century
                   Ireland," in T. W. Moody, ed., Nationality and the Pursuit
                   of National Independence, 57-71.

 22   The Caribbean

                 Richard Pares, Merchants and Planters, 1-25.
                 F. C. Innes, "The Pre-Sugar Era of European Settlement
                   in Barbados," Journal of Caribbean History, I (1970),
                   1-22.

              * Richard S. Dunn, Sugar and Slaves: The Rise of the Planter
                   Class in the English West Indies, 1-83.

PART FOUR: TRANSFORMATIONS, 1660-1713

 29   The Chesapeake

              * Tate, Chesapeake in the Seventeenth Century, 126-296.

              * Morgan, American Slavery, American Freedom, 215-70.

              * Bernard Bailyn, "Politics and Social Structure in Virginia,"
                   in James M. Smith, ed., Seventeenth-Century America,
                   90-115.

                 Russell Menard, "From Servants to Slaves: The Transformation
                   of the Chesapeake Labor System," Southern Studies
                   XVI (1977), 355-390.

PART FOUR: Transformations, 1660-1713   (cont'd.)

November

 5   New England

    * Bernard Bailyn, The New England Merchants in the Seventeenth
       Century, 75-200.

    · Perry Miller, Nature's Nation, 14-49.

    * Kenneth Lockridge, New England Town, 79-143.

    * Paul Boyer and Stephen Nissenbaum, Salem Possessed: The
       Social Origins of Witchcraft, 1-109.

 12   No Class

 19   The Caribbean

    * Dunn, Sugar and Slaves, 117-341.

 26   Thanksgiving

PART FIVE: NEW MODELS OF COLONIZATION, 1660-1713.

December

 3   The Middle Colonies

    Gary B. Nash, Quakers and Politics: Pennsylvania 1681-1726,
       3-88.

    James T. Lemon, "The Weakness of Place and Community in
       Early Pennsylvania," in James R. Gibson, ed., European
       Settlement and Development in North America, 190-207.

    Thomas J. Archdeacon, New York City, 1664-1710: Conquest
       and Change, 1-96.

    Sung Bok Kim, Landlord and Tenant in Colonial New York, 1-43.

 10   The Carolinas

    Richard S. Dunn, "The English Sugar Islands and the Founding
       of South Carolina," South Carolina Historical Magazine,
       LXXII (1971), 81-93.

    * Peter H. Wood, Black Majority: Negroes in Colonial South
       Carolina from 1670 through the Stono Rebellion, 3-194.

History 358
Ames 321
Thursdays, 2-4

Sociology of Early Modern British
Colonization: The Eighteenth
Century

Professor Jack P. Greene

Spring Term 1982

This is a discussion and writing course. Each student will be expected
to read from 100 to 300 pages each week and to write a short two-page paper
on a sharply focused topic on the basis of that reading. These papers will
serve as a starting point for class discussions. There will be no
examinations.

All items on the reading list will be on reserve in the MSE Library.
Those marked by an asterisk are in paperback and should be available at the
JHU Book Center.

READING ASSIGNMENTS

January
28

Organization Meeting

PART ONE: ELABORATION AND CHANGE

February

4

The Golden Age of Sugar

Richard B. Sheridan, Sugar and Slavery: An Economic History
of the British West Indies, 140-47, 154-60, 164-83, 194-207,
216-33, 350-446.

Edward Brathwaite, Creole Society in Jamaica 1770-1832,
xiii-xvi, 9-39,105-75.

Winthrop D. Jordan, "American Chiaroscuro: The Status
and Definition of Mulattoes in the British Colonies,"
William and Mary Quarterly, 3d ser., XIX (1962), 183-200.

11

Transformation of the Chesapeake

Allan Kulikoff, "The Economic Growth of the Eighteenth-
Century Chesapeake Colonies," Journal of Economic History,
XXXIX (1979), 275-33.

Jacob M. Price, "The Economic Growth of the Chesapeake and
the European Market, 1697-1775," ibid., XXIV (1964),
496-511.

Aubrey C. Land, "Economic Base and Social Structure:
The Northern Chesapeake in the Eighteenth Century,"
ibid., XXV (1965), 639-54.

Rhys Isaac, The Transformation of Virginia, 1-142.

Daniel Blake Smith, Inside the Great House, 1-53.

April	
15	**Search for Identity**

* Richard Hofstadter, <u>America at 1750</u>, 180-293.

James A. Henretta, "Families and Farms: Mentalite in in Pre-Industrial America," <u>William and Mary Quarterly</u>, 3d ser., XXXV (1973), 3-32.

James T. Lemon, "Early Americans and their Social Environment," <u>Journal of Historical Geography</u>, VI (1980), 115-131.

C. Vann Woodward, "The Southern Ethic in a Puritan World," <u>William and Mary Quarterly</u>, 3d ser., XXV (1968), 343-70.

Jack P. Greene, "Search for Identity: An Interpretation of Selected Patterns of Social Response in Eighteenth-Century America," <u>Journal of Social History</u>, IV (1970), 189-220.

Philip Greven, <u>The Protestant Temperament</u>, 265-334.

22   **The Public World**

* Bernard Bailyn, <u>The Origins of American Politics</u>, 3-105.

Jack P. Greene, <u>Great Britain and the American Colonies</u>, xi-xlvii.

_____, "Political Mimesis: A Consideration of the Historical and Cultural Roots of Legislative Behavior in the British Colonies in the Eighteenth Century," <u>American Historical Review</u>, LXXIV (1969), 337-60.

Paul Lucas, "A Note on the Comparative Structure of Politics in Mid-Eighteenth-Century Britain and its American Colonies," <u>William and Mary Quarterly</u>, 3d ser., XXVIII (1971), 301-10.

Jack P. Greene, "The Growth of Political Stability: An Interpretation of Political Development in the Anglo-American Colonies, 1660-1760," in John Parker and Carol Urness, eds., <u>The American Revolution: A Heritage of Change</u>, 26-52.

March

Growth (cont'd.)

11   Jim Potter, "The Growth of Population in America, 1700-1860,"
in D. V. Glass and D.E.C. Eversley, eds., Population in
History: Essays in Historical Demography, 631-88.

Robert V. Wells, "Household Size and Composition in the
British Colonies in America, 1675-1775," Journal of
Interdisciplinary History, IV (1974), 543-69.

Jacob M. Price, "Economic Function and Growth of American
Port Towns in the Eighteenth Century," Perspectives in
American History, VIII (1974), 123-86.

James F. Shepherd and Gary M. Walton, "Trade, Distribution,
and Economic Growth in Colonial America," Journal of
Economic History, XXXII (1972), 128-45.

18   NO CLASS

25   SPRING VACATION

April

1   NO CLASS

8   Emergence of American Society

James T. Lemon and Gary B. Nash, "The Distribution of
Wealth in Eighteenth-Century America: A Century of Change
in Chester County, Pennsylvania, 1693-1802," Journal
of Social History, II (1968), 1-24.

Kenneth Lockridge, "Land, Population, and the Evolution
of New England Society, 1630-1790," Past and Present,
#39, 62-80.

Gary B. Nash, "Urban Wealth and Poverty in Pre-Revolutionary
America," Journal of Interdisciplinary History, VI, (1976),
545-84.

Duane F. Ball, "Dynamics of Population and Wealth in
Eighteenth-Century Chester County, Pennsylvania," ibid.,
621-44.

Darrett B. Rutman, "People in Process: The New Hampshire
Towns of the Eighteenth Century," Journal of Urban History,
I (1975), 268-92.

Alice Hanson Jones, Wealth of a Nation To Be, 50-69,
155-219, 258-72.

John M. Murrin, "The Legal Transformation: The Bench and
Bar of Eighteenth-Century Massachusetts," in Stanley N. Katz,
ed., Colonial America, 1st ed., 415-49.

Ira Berlin, "Time, Space, and the Evolution of Afro-American
Society on British Mainland North America," American
Historical Review, LXXXV (1980), 44-78.

February

18   Boom Times on the Rice Coast: The Colonies of the Lower
          South John J. McCusker and Russell R. Menard, The Economy
          of British America, 1607-1790, 105-19. (Only these pages
          of this unpublished work are available in the Reserve Room.)

          Ralph Gray and Betty Wood, "The Transition from Indentured
          to Involuntary Servitude in Colonial Georgia," Explorations
          in Economic History, XIII (1976), 353-70.

      * Carl Bridenbaugh, Myths and Realities, 54-118.

          John E. Crowley, "Family Relations and Inheritance in
          Early South Carolina," unpublished paper, MSE Reserve.

          Harry Roy Merrens, Colonial North Carolina in the
          Eighteenth Century, 85-141.

25   Embryo of the New American Order Douglas Greenberg,
          "The Middle Colonies in Recent American Historiography,"
          William and Mary Quarterly, XXXVI (1979), 396-427.

      * James T. Lemon, The Best Poor Man's Country, 1-71, 150-228.

      * Frederick B. Tolles, Meeting House & Counting House,
          45-62, 85-143.

      * Stephanie Grauman Wolf, Urban Village, 3-21, 287-337.

          Sung Bok Kim, Landlord and Tenant in Colonial New York,
          129-61, 235-80.

March

4   Crumbling of the Old Order

      * Richard L. Bushman, From Puritan to Yankee: Character and
          the Social Order in Connecticut, 1690-1765, 3-143, 267-88.

          Michael Zuckerman, "The Social Context of Democracy in
          Massachusetts," William and Mary Quarterly, 3d ser.,
          XXV, (1968), 523-44.

          Sidney James, Colonial Rhode Island, 156-85, 229-66.

      * Philip J. Greven, Four Generations: Population, Land,
          and Family in Colonial Andover, Massachusetts, 175-289.

          PART TWO: THE FORCES OF CONVERGENCE

11   Growth

          D. A. Farnie, "The Commercial Empire of the Atlantic,
          1607-1783," Economic History Review, XV (1962-63), 205-18.

          Ralph Davis, "English Foreign Trade, 1700-1774,"
          ibid., XV (1962), 285-303.

          Marc Egnal, "The Economic Development of the Thirteen
          Continental Colonies, 1720-1775," William and Mary
          Quarterly, 3d ser., XXXII (1975), 191-222.
                        (cont'd.)

44

History 246A
Professor Joyce Appleby
Fall 1982

Office: Bunche 6254
Hours: Monday, 10-11
Thursday, 11:30-
1:00

An Introduction to the Historical Literature of Early America

This course is designed to introduce you to the principal
scholarly works on seventeenth and eighteenth-century America.
In oder to uncover the rationale behind this body of historical
writing, we shall look at the various books as a part of scholarly
traditions. By looking at the history of historical writing,
we shall understand the questions the individual scholars addressed.
We should also get a better sense of how we have acquired an
intelligible, but highly selective account of our national past.

You will be asked to prepare six oral reports during the course
of the quarter and write one 15-20 page paper on a subject of
your choice. This paper should be suitable for submission as one
of your M.A. essays. A first draft of your paper is due
November 12 and the final draft, submitted in duplicate, is
due December 3.

Week 1 (September 30): The Historians' Questions About Slavery

Assigned readings:

    Oscar and Mary F. Handlin, "Origins of the Southern Labor
        System," William and Mary Quarterly, 7 (1950).
    Carl Degler, "Slavery and the Genesis of American Race
        Prejudice," Comparative Studies in Society and History 2
        (1959).

Week 2 (October 7): Coming to Terms with the Native American Presence

Assigned readings:

    Frances Jennings, The Invasion of America, 1975*
    Bruce Trigger, The Children of Aataentsic, 1976
        (first chapter of vol. I)

Reports:

    Trigger, The Children of Aataentsic, 1976, vols. I and II
    Karen Kupperman, Settling with the Indians, 1980.
    Calvin Martin, Keepers of the Game, 1978.
    Neil Salisbury, Manitou and Providence, 1982

Week 3 (October 14): Colonization and the Chesapeake Slave System

Assigned readings:

    Stanley M. Elkins and Eric McKitrick, "Institutions and the
        Law of Slavery," American Quarterly, 9(1957), pp. 3-21,
        159-79.

---

*All class members are asked to buy these books.

Frank Tannenbaum, "A Note on the Economic Interpretation of
History," _Political Science Quarterly_, 61 (1946).
Eugene Genovese, "Materialism and Idealism in the History
of Negro Slavery in the Americas," _Journal of Social
History_, 2 (1968).

Reports:

Richard Dunn, _Sugar and Slaves_, 1971.
Herbert Klein, _Slavery in the Americas_, 1967.
Winthrop Jordan, _White Over Black_, 1968.
Edmund Morgan, _American Slavery, American Freedom_, 1975.*
Peter Wood, _Black Majority_, 1974.

Week 4 (October 21): The Puritans and Their Lengthening Shadow

Assigned readings:

Perry Miller, "Errand in the Wilderness," _William and Mary
Quarterly_, 10 (1953).
Darret B. Rutman, "The Mirror of Puritan Authority," in
George A. Billias, Ed., _Law and Authority in Colonial
America_, 1965.

Reports:

Perry Miller, _The New England Mind: From Colony to Province_,
1953.
Robert Pope, _The Halfway Covenant_, 1969.
Robert Middlekauff, _The Mathers: Three Generations of Puritan
Intellectuals_, 1971.
Alan Heimert, _Religion and the American Mind_, 1966.
Nathan Hatch, _The Sacred Cause of Liberty_, 1977.

Week 5 (October 28): Men, Women and Children in a Family Context

Assigned readings:

Rhys Isaac, "Order and Growth, Authority and Meaning in
Colonial New England," _American Historical Review_, 76
(1971), pp. 728-37.
Daniel Blake Smith, "The Study of the Family in Early America:
Trends, Problems, and Prospects," _William and Mary Quarterly_,
39 (1982), pp. 3-28.

Reports:

Philip Greven, _Four Generations_, 1970.
Daniel Blake Smith, _Inside the Great House_, 1980.
Stephanie Grauman Wolfe, _Urban Village_, 1976.
Mary Beth Norton, _Liberty's Daughters_, 1980.
Lyle Koehler, _A Search for Power_, 1980.
Philip Greven, _The Protestant Temperament_, 1978.

Week 6 (**November 4**):   Explaining a Changing Colonial Society

Assigned readings:

> Richard Brown, "Modernization and the Modern Personality in
>   Early America, 1600-1865: A Sketch of a Synthesis,"
>   Journal of Interdisciplinary History, 2 (1972), pp. 201-28.
> James Henretta, "Families and Farms: Mentalite in Pre-
>   Industrial America," William and Mary Quarterly, 35 (1978),
>   pp. 3-32.

Reports:

> Gary Nash, The Urban Crucible, 1979.*
> Rhys Isaac, The Transformation of Virginia, 1982.
> David Konig, Law and Society in Puritan Massachusetts Essex
>   County, 1979.
> Richard Bushman, From Puritan to Yankee, 1967.
> James Henretta, The Evolution of American Society, 1973.

Week 7 (**November 11**):   Analyzing Imperial and Provincial Power
                            Structures

Assigned readings:

> Jack P. Greene, "Political Mimesis: A Consideration of the
>   Historical and Cultural Roots of Legislative Behavior in
>   the British Colonies in the Eighteenth Century," American
>   Historical Review, 75 (1969), pp. 337-60.
> Bernard Bailyn, "A Comment," Ibid., Greene, "Reply," Ibid.

Reports:

> Ian Steele, The Politics of Colonial Policy, 1968.
> Stephen Saunders Webb, The Governors-General, 1979.
> Jack P. Greene, The Quest for Power, 1963.
> Patricia Bonomi, A Factious People, 1971.
> Robert Zemsky, Merchants, Farmers and River Gods, 1971

Week 8 (**November 18**):   Interpreting the American Revolution

Assigned readings:

> Robert E. Shalhope, "Toward a Republican Synthesis," William
>   and Mary Quarterly, 29 (1972), pp. 49-80.
> Joyce Appleby, "The Social Origins of American Revolutionary
>   Ideology," Journal of American History, 64 (1978), pp.
>   935-58.

Reports:

> William Pencak, War, Politics & Revolution in Provincial
>   Massachusetts, 1981
> O.M. Dickerson, The Navigation Acts and the American Revolution,
>   1951.
> Edmund Morgan, The Stamp Act Crisis, 1953.

---

* All class members are asked to buy these books.

Robert E. Brown, <u>Middle-Class Democracy and the Revolution in Massachusetts</u>, 1955.
Bernard Bailyn, <u>The Ideological Origins of the American Revolution</u>, 1967.

<u>Week 9</u> (<u>December 2</u>): Economics and Ideology in the Framing of the Constitution

Assigned readings:

Richard Morris, The Confederation Period and the American Historian," <u>William and Mary Quarterly</u>, 13 (1956)
John P. Roche, "The Founding Fathers: A Reform Caucus in Action," <u>American Political Science Review</u>, 55 (1961), pp. 799-816.

Reports:

Charles A. Beard, <u>An Economic Interpretation of the Constitution of the United States</u>, 1913.
Forrest McDonald, <u>We the People</u>, 1958.
Jackson Turner Main, <u>Political Parties before the Constitution</u>, 1973.
H. James Henderson, <u>Party Politics in the Continental Congress</u>, 1974.
Jack Rakove, <u>The Beginnings of National Politics</u>, 1979.
Gordon Wood, <u>The Creation of the American Republic</u>, 1969.

<u>Week 10</u> (<u>December 9</u>): The Origins of Political Parties

Assigned readings:

Ira Berlin, "The Revolution in Black Life," in Alfred Young, ed., <u>The American Revolution</u>, 1976.
Frances Jennings, "The Indians' Revolution," in <u>Ibid</u>.
William W. Freehling, "The Founding Fathers and Slavery," <u>American Historical Review</u>, 77 (1972).

Reports:

Joseph Charles, <u>The Origins of the American Party System</u>, 1956.
William Nisbet Chambers, <u>Political Parties in a New Nation</u>, 1963.
Richard Hofstadter, <u>The Idea of a Party System</u>, 1969.
Rudolph Bell, <u>Party and Faction in American Politics</u>, 1974.
Drew McCoy, <u>The Elusive Republic</u>, 1980.

Prof. Appleby

Below is a list of statements which I would like you to assign
to the historical school which it characterizes.

Assign the statements listed below to the proper historical school
and write a sentence or two explaining what it is that gives
unity to the several statements you have identified with each
group of historians.

Patriotic Whig school represented by McLaughlin_____

_____

These assertions go together because _____

_____

_____

Progressive school represented by Beard _____

_____

These assertions go together because _____

_____

_____

Consensus school represented by Brown and Roche and the two Diamonds

_____

_____

Ideological school represented by Wood and Banning _____

_____

These assertions go together because _____

_____

1. Ideas transcend time and place and have a life of their own.
2. Ideas are only important historically when they are part of
   a coherent view of reality shared by a particular society.
3. Ideas are instruments which men use to attain their ends and
   often are employed to mask the true interests of those who
   profess them.
4. Americans cleave to the ideals of democracy and economic
   opportunity because their particular situation predisposed
   them to affirm these goals.
5. History presents us with the eternal conflict between progress
   and reaction, initiators of change and their opponents,
   dissent and consensus.

6. The economies of the past have produced diverse interest groups whose conflicts supply the principal influences affecting historical change.

7. Societies are knit together through shared values and beliefs which change only in response to external challenges which in turn are viewed through the cultural lenses of the society affected.

8. Americans created a set of institutions peculiarly suited to their needs and fought the American Revolution to conserve those institutions and drafted the US Constitution to perfect them.

9. Human beings are primarily social animals and receive their ideas and values from their society.

10. Human beings should be viewed as individuals seeing their own self-interest which they are capable of discerning on their own.

11. Human beings are slow to recognize the truth of new ideas and oppose them because their societies teach them to resist change.

12. Human beings basically desire freedom and opportunity and can achieve them with a fair degree of success when the situation is favorable because they have good common sense.

University of Connecticut
History 244
The Eighteenth-Century Colonies and the American Revolution
R.D. Brown

I. The Development of the English Colonies

1. The Colonies in 1700
2. Colonial Economic and Social Patterns
3. Immigration and Mobility
4. Great Awakening
5. Race Attitudes and Slavery
6. Imperial Government in America
7. English Politics
8. The French and Indian War
9. Discussion

II. The Imperial Crisis

10. English Reforms: Phase One
11. Patterns of American Resistance: The Stamp Act.
12. Variations on a Theme: The Townshend Acts
13. The Lull: Case Studies, 1770-1773
14. The Boston Tea Party
15. The Coercive Acts and the Continental Congress
16. Conspiracies
17. Discussion (Knox)
18. EXAM
19. Warfare in Massachusetts
20. Virginia Support
21. Mid-Atlantic Divisions
22. Discussion (Paine)
23. Independence (Discussion): Declaration of Independence; Hutchinson's Strictures

III. The Formation of the American Republic

24. Warfare: British Techniques of Counterinsurgency, 1775-1778
25. Saratoga and the French Alliance
26. Warfare: The Southern Strategy
27. Peace with Honor
28. Discussion
29. Social Consequences: Loyalists
30. Revolutionary Ideals and Slavery
31. Social Consequences: Women
32. State Politics and Constitutions
33. Articles of Confederation: A Balance-Sheet
34. Discussion
35. Constitutional Reform Efforts
36. The Constitution of 1787
37. Ratification
38. Discussion (Federalist nos. 10, 39; Warren)
39. Free Speech
40. American Nationalism
41. Discussion: Was There a Revolution in America?

READINGS

I. Development of the English Colonies

Bernard Bailyn, The Origins of American Politics (New York:
Vintage, 1968), entire (pp. 3-161).
Bernard Bailyn, The Ideological Origins of the American Revolution
(Cambridge, Mass.: Harvard University Press, 1968), chs. 1-3,
(pp. 1-93).
Charles S. Sydnor, American Revolutionaries in the Making, (New
York: Free Press, 1952), entire (pp. 13-118).
I.R. Christie, Crisis of Empire, (New York: Norton, 1967),
chs. 1, 2 (pp. 3-38).

II. Imperial Crisis

Christie, Crisis of Empire, chs. 3-7 (pp. 39-114)
Bailyn, Ideological Origins, ch. 4 (pp. 94-159)
Robert A. Gross, The Minutemen and Their World, (New York:
Hill and Wang, 1976), chs. Prologue - 5 (pp. 3-132)
Henry Knox, On American Taxation (Old South Leaflet, No. 210),
entire
Thomas Paine, Common Sense, entire
Thomas Hutchinson, Strictures Upon the Declaration of Independence
(Old South Leaflet, No. 227), entire
Declaration of Independence, any edition
Benjamin Quarles, The Negro in the American Revolution (New York:
Norton, 1961), chs. 1-2 (pp. 3-32)

III. Formation of the American Republic

Eric Robson, The American Revolution in its Political and Military
Aspects, (New York: Norton, 1966), chs. 5-7 (pp. 93-174)
Bailyn, Ideological Origins, chs. 5-6, (pp. 160-320)
Quarles, Negro in the American Revolution, chs. 3-10 (pp. 33-200)
Gross, Minutemen, chs. 6-7 (pp. 133-191)
Forrest McDonald, E PLURIBUS UNUM: The Formation of the American
Republic, 1776-1790 (Indianapolis, 1979), entire
Alexander Hamilton, et al., The Federalist Papers, No. 10, No. 39
Mercy Otis Warren, Observations on the New Constitution (Old South
Leaflet, No. 226)
Constitution and the first ten amendments, any edition

Discussions:

Students are expected to come to these classes fully prepared. Announcements
will advise you as to particular assignments. At the beginning of each
discussion you are required to hand in a short (1-2 p.) informal comment
on some aspect of the subject under consideration. Your work in discussions
can help your grade.

Papers:

Students are required to write a review essay on one of the assigned readings (5-8 p.). Prior consultation with the instructor is advised. All papers will be due on April 25. They will count for about 30 percent of your grade. If you wish to write on another book, see me for approval.

Exam:

There will be a one-hour essay exam on March 4. You are required to hand in one essay question and two identifications on March 2. The exam will count for about 20 percent of your grade. Prior to the final exam you are also required to hand in two essay questions and two identifications.

UNIVERSITY OF CALIFORNIA, IRVINE

Revolutionary America

Instructor: Christine Heyrman
Office: 300 D, Humanities Office Building
Office Hours: Monday and Wednesday, 2:00 - 3:30 p.m. or by
   appointment

Course Objectives:

The aim of History 130B is twofold. The first goal is to place
the American War for Independence within the context of colonial
demographic, economic, social, political and cultural development during the latter half of the eighteenth century. The
second objective is to acquaint class members with the historiography of the American Revolution, specifically, the ongoing
debate between "Consensus" and "New Left" historians. In other
words, we will be concernd 1) with the relationship between a
"revolutionary" movement and the processes of socio-political
change within the American colonies and 2) with the current status
of the debate among contemporary historians over the causes,
character and consequences of the War for Independence.

Course Readings:

All of the books listed below are available in the bookstore on
campus.

   Edmund Morgan, The Birth of the Republic
   Bernard Bailyn, The Ideological Origins of the American
      Revolution
   Edmund and Helen Morgan, The Stamp Act Crisis
   Pauline Maier, From Resistance to Revolution
   David Ammerman, In the Common Cause
   Robert Gross, The Minutemen and Their World
   Eric Foner, Tom Paine and Revolutionary America
   Jeffrey Crow and Larry Tise, eds., The Southern Experience
      in the American Revolution

The following articles and essays are on closed reserve at the
UCI library:

   Rhys Isaac, "Preachers and Patriots: Popular Culture and the
      Revolution in Virginia"
   Edward Countryman, "'Out of the Bounds of the Law': Northern
      Land Rioters in the Eighteenth Century"
   Edmund Morgan, "The Puritan Ethic and the American Revolution,"
      "Conflict and Consensus in the American Revolution"
   Thad Tate, "The Coming of the Revolution in Virginia: Britain's
      Challenge to Virginia's Ruling Class, 1763-1776
   Gary Nash, "The Stamp Act," in The Urban Crucible
   John Adams and Daniel Leonard, Massachusettensis and Novangius
   Thomas Paine, Common Sense
   James Chalmers, Plain Truth

54

Course Requirements:

1) Keep up with the reading. Assignments are due on the dates listed in the syllabus.

2) The take-home mid-term is due on May 10th at the beginning of class.

3) The take-home final is due on the last day of finals week, spring quarter.

A Note on Prerequisites for History 130B

I have designed History 130B as an advanced, upper-division history course that emphasizes reading and discussion. It is intended especially for the veterans of History 130A, Colonial America. History 130B IS NOT AN INTRODUCTORY COURSE, NOR DOES IT FULFILL THE REQUIREMENT FOR AMERICAN HISTORY AND INSTITUTIONS. If you have never taken a history course before (at the college level), you should probably not enroll in History 130B. If you are in doubt, talk to me.

Course Evaluation:

Class Participation 30%
Mid-Term Essay Examination: 30%
Final Essay Examination: 40%

Course Syllabus:

THE UNEASY CONNECTION: THE AMERICAN REVOLUTION
AS A COLONIAL WAR FOR INDEPENDENCE

Week One: British America in the Mid-Eighteenth Century

Reading: Edmund Morgan, The Birth of the Republic. This overview of the Revolution as a political and constitutional struggle should be completed by the end of this week, April 2.

Week Two: Republicanism as a Revolutionay Ideology

April 5, Reading: Bernard Bailyn, The Ideological Origins of the American Revolution, pp. 1-93.

April 7, Reading: Bailyn, Ideological Origins, pp. 94-159.

April 9, Reading: Pauline Maier, From Resistance to Revolution, Chapters I and II.

Week Three: The Imperial Controversy

April 12, Reading: Edmund and Helen Morgan, The Stamp Act Crisis, pp. 15-154.

April 14, Reading: Morgan and Morgan, The Stamp Act Crisis, pp. 157-262.

April 16, Reading: Maier, From Resistance to Revolution, Chs. III, IV.

Week Four: The Imperial Controversy

April 19, Reading: Gary Nash, "The Stamp Act," in The Urban
                    Crucible, on reserve in the UCI Library

April 21, Reading: Morgan and Morgan, The Stamp Act Crisis,
                    pp. 327-376.

April 23, Reading: Maier, From Resistance to Revolution, Chs.
                    V, VI, and VII

Week Five: The Crisis of Empire

April 26, Reading: David Ammerman, In the Common Cause (abt half)

April 28, Reading: Ammermann, In the Common Cause (the rest)

April 30, Reading: Maier, From Resistance to Revolution, VIII and IX.

Week Six: The Conflict of Loyalties

May 3, Reading: Morgan and Morgan, The Stamp Act Crisis, pp. 265-324

May 5, Reading: John Adams and Daniel Leonard, Massachusettensis
                  and Novanglus, on reserve in the UCI library

May 7, Reading: Thomas Paine, Common Sense and James Chalmers,
                  Plain Truth, on reserve in the UCI library.

WHO SHOULD RULE AT HOME? THE AMERICAN REVOLUTION
WITHIN AMERICA

Week Seven: The Revolution in the Rural North

May 10, Reading: Robert Gross, The Minutemen and Their World,
                    pp. 3-108.

May 12, Reading: Gross, The Minutemen, pp. 109-191

May 14, Reading: Edward Countryman, "'Out of the Bounds of the Law':
                    Northern Land Rioters in the Eighteenth Century,"
                    on reserve in the UCI library.

Week Eight: The Revolution in the Cities

May 17, Reading: Eric Foner, Tom Paine and Revolutionary America
                    pp. 1-106.

May 19, Reading: Foner, Tom Paine, pp. 107-144.

May 21, Reading: Foner, Tom Paine, pp. 145-209.

Week Nine: The Revolution in the Rural South

May 24, Reading: Jeffrey Crow and Larry Tise, eds., The Southern
                    Experience in the American Revolution, essay by

Jack Greene, and Rhys Isaac, "Preachers and Patriots: Popular Culture and the Revolution in Virginia," and Thad Tate, "The Coming of the Revolution in Virginia: Britain's Challenge to Virginia's Ruling Class, 1763-1776," both on reserve in the UCI library.

May 26, Reading: Crow and Tise, eds., The Southern Experience, essays by Kay and Cary and Shy.

May 28, Reading: Crow and Tise, eds., The Southern Experience, essays by Mullin, Wood and Norton.

Week Ten: Conflict, Consensus and American Culture in the Late Eighteenth Century

May 31, Reading: Edmund Morgan, "The Puritan Ethic and the American Revolution," and "Conflict and Consensus and the American Revolution," Bernard Bailyn, Ideological Origins, pp. 160-303. (Morgan articles on closed reserve, UCI library)

UNIVERSITY OF CALIFORNIA, LOS ANGELES

History 145B
Professor Joyce Appleby
Spring, 1983

Office: Bunche 6254
Hours: M 12-1:00
       W 11-12:00
       F 9-10:00

America in the Revolutionary Era

Our subject is the American revolutionary era which stretches from the initial resistance to the new British measures to tax the colonies through the movement towards independence, the revolutionary war, and the prolonged aftermath in which Americans of different persuasions conflicted over how best to secure the revolution's diverse goals. We shall focus upon the tangible events of colonial resistance, forming a confederation, drafting and ratifying the constitution, and splitting into opposing political camps. We shall also consider the intangible impact of revolution and nation-building: the troubling implications of the American creed of natural rights and the nationalizing effect of the Americans' involvement in an expansive commercial economy.

Calendar of Readings by Weeks:

April 4:   Gary Nash, The Urban Crucible, Cambridge, 1979, pp. 3-157.

April 11: Nash, Urban Crucible, pp. 159-291

April 18: Nash, Urban Crucible, pp. 292-417.

April 25: Charles Royster, A Revolutionary People at War, Chapel Hill, 1979,
           pp. 3-151.

May 2:   Royster, Revolutionary People, pp. 152-378.

May 9:   Jack N. Rakove, The Beginnings of National Politics, Baltimore, 1979,
           pp. 3-215.

May 16:   Rakove, Beginnings of National Politics, pp. 216-399.

May 23:   Saul K. Padover, The Living U.S. Constitution, New York, 1968, pp. 15-
           93, 97-123, 138-142, 185-192.

N.B.: Your essay is due today.

May 30:   Holiday, June 2: Forrest McDonald, The Presidency of George Washington,
           Lawrence, Kansas, 1974.

June 6:   Review.

Below is a list of books. Choose one to read and use as the basis of a 2,000-word essay. I have carefully avoided calling this assignment a book report, for I want it to be an essay with a theme of your choosing which will permit you to discuss the book in the context of what you are learning in the course as a whole. It is not necessary for you to do outside reading for this assignment.

Ira Berlin, Slaves Without Masters, New York, 1974.
Felix Gilbert, To the Farewell Address, Princeton, 1961.
Robert A. Gross, The Minutemen and Their World, New York, 1976.
Mary Beth Norton, Liberty's Daughters, Boston, 1980.

Howard B. Rock, Artisans of the New Republic, New York, 1979.
Gordon S. Wood, The Creation of the American Republic, 1776-1787, Chapel Hill, 1969.

Your grade will be based on the following division: 2,000-word essay, 25%; mid-term examination, 30%; final examination, 45%. No incompletes will be accepted without documented proof of need. All late papers will be marked down a half grade. Please come see if you have anything about the course that you would like to discuss.

Chronology of American Events, 1760-1800

1760 Accession of George III
1763 Peace of Paris ends Seven Years (French and Indian) War
      Proclamation of 1763
1764 Passage of the Sugar Act by Parliament
1765 Passage of the Stamp Act
      Calling of Stamp Act Congress
      Boston mobs rampage; stamp collectors in Connecticut, Pennsylvania, Rhode Island, Virginia, South Carolina, New York, New Hampshire and Georgia resign their commissions.

1766 Repeal of Stamp Act and passage of Declaratory Act
1767 Passage of Townshend Acts, creation of Board of Customs Commissioners, Quartering Act
1768 Adoption of Non-Importation Agreements
      Troops arrive in Boston
1769 Passage of Virginia Resolutions
      Revival of Statute of Henry VIII providing for English trial of colonists suspected of treason
1770 Boston Massacre
      Break-up of Non-importation agreements
      Partial repeal of the Townshend Acts
1771
1772 All's quiet on the Western (Atlantic) front
1773 Virginia sponsors general intercolonial committees of correspondence from Massachusetts model
      Passage of Tea Act
      Boston Tea Party
1774 Passage of Coercive Acts
      First Continental Congress meets in Philadelphia in September
      Adoption of the Continental Association
1775 Lord North's Conciliatory Propositions
      Battles of Lexington and Concord
      Second Continental Congress meets, continues as the Continental Congress
      Battle of Bunker Hill and siege of Boston
1776 Common Sense published
      Congress recommends formation of state governments
      Secret treaty with France negotiated
      Declaration of Independence
      British occupy New York
1777 British occupy Philadelphia
      Burgoyne surrenders at Saratoga
      Congress presents Articles of Confederation to the states

1778 France enters the war; alliance made public
1779 Spain enters war
1781 Virginia cedes western lands; Articles of Confederation approved
       Cornwallis surrenders at Yorktown
1783 Treaty of Paris signed
1786 Annapolis convention held
       Shays' Rebellion
1787 Continental Congress passes Northwest Ordinance
       Constitutional convention held
       Delaware, Pennsylvania and New Jersey ratify Constitution
1788 Georgia, Connecticut, Massachusetts, Maryland, South Carolina, New Hampshire,
       Virginia, New York ratify Constitution
1789 New federal government organized; Washington elected president
       North Carolina ratifies Constitution
1790 Rhode Island ratifies Constitution
1791 Bill of Rights (first ten amendments to Constitution) approved
1796 Adams elected president
1800 Jefferson elected president

FINAL EXAMINATION

Please write an essay in answer to a question from each of the three sections.
All three essays will be graded on the basis of the coherence, correctness
and comprehensiveness of your answer. Each essay will count for a third of
the grade assigned the final examination.

I

1. According to Jack Rakove, the national politics reflected in the decisions
of the Continental Congress were shaped by external constraints and shared
goals among the delegates than by partisan conflicts. How does Rakove support
this thesis?

2. The hero of Forrest McDonald's The Presidency of George Washington appears
to be Alexander Hamilton? What did Hamilton do to deserve this role and how
did his successes affect the history of the new American nation, according
to McDonald?

II

3. How did the Federalists and Jeffersonians perceive each other and how did
these perceptions influence the sequences of events after 1793?

4. What provisions of the U.S. Constitution justify considering it a capitalist,
a slave-holder's and a liberal document?

5. How did the American natural right ideology affect relations between the
citizens of the United States and black Americans and native Americans between
the Revolution and the early decades of the nineteenth century?

III

6. Participation in the Atlantic economy exercised a persistent influence
in the affairs of the Americans. Describe this influence as we find it in the
1760s and 70s and indicate how it changed after the American colonies had
formed the more perfect union represented in the U.S. Constitution.

7. When Americans turned from the rights of Englishmen to the rights of man
in defending their revolution they opened the way for a radical restructuring
of their institutions. Trace this change of ideas between 1764 and 1800 and
show how new beliefs and values affected politics during the same period.

8. The history we have studied this term opened up with the thirteen colonies
both traditional and British and closed with the new nation conspicuously
modern and American. What was involved in this transformation?

9. America was born free, rich and modern, according to some historians, and
its history through the last half of the eighteenth century represents a
realization of this birthright. Write an essay defending this position.

THE JOHNS HOPKINS UNIVERSITY

Department of History

Spring 1983

History 80:314:

Professor Jack P. Greene

The Causal Pattern of Revolutions
The American Revolution as a Case Study

All items on the reading list are on reserve in Milton S. Eisenhower Library.
Those items marked with an asterisk (*) have also been ordered for the book
store. It is not necessary to purchase any of these.

Reading List

January 27: The American Revolution?: Some Earlier Interpretations

Recommended Reading:

Charles M. Andrews, "The American Revolution: An Interpretation," American
    Historical Review, XXXI (1926), 41-52.
Arthur M. Schlesinger, Sr., "The American Revolution Reconsidered," Political
    Science Quarterly, vol. 34 (1919), 61-78.
* Edmund S. Morgan, "The American Revolution: Revisions in Need of Revising,"
    William and Mary Quarterly, 3d ser., XIV (1957), 51-77. (B-M reprint H-154).
* Jack P. Greene, "The Flight from Determinism: A Review of Recent Literature on
    the American Revolution," South Atlantic Quarterly, LXI (1962), 235-59.
    (B-M Reprint H-348).
* Bernard Bailyn, "The Central Themes of the American Revolution: An Interpretation,"
    in Stephen G. Kurtz and James H. Hutson, eds., Essays on the American
    Revolution, 3-31.

February 3: Concepts of Revolution? Frames of Reference

Required Reading:

Lawrence Stone, "Theories of Revolution," World Politics XVIII (1966), 159-76.
Perez Zagorin, "Theories of Revolution in Contemporary Historiography," Political
    Science Quarterly, LXXXVIII (1973), 23-52.
Isaac Kramnick, "Reflections on Revolution: Definition and Explanation in Recent
    Scholarship," History and Theory, XI (1972), 26-63.

February 17: Anglo-American Society in the Mid-Eighteenth Century?

Required Reading:

* Gordon S. Wood, "Rhetoric and Reality in the American Revolution," WMQ, 3d ser.,
    XXII (1966), 3-32.(B-M Reprint H-492).
Kenneth Lockridge, "Social Change and the Meaning of the American Revolution,"
    Journal of Social History, VI (1973), 403-99.

Jack P. Greene, "The Social Origins of the American Revolution," PSQ, LXXXVIII
    (1973), 1-22.
* Rowland Berthoff and John M. Murrin, "Feudalism, Communalism and the Yeoman
    Freeholder: The American Revolution Considered as a Social Accident,"
    in Kurtz and Hutson, eds., Essays on the American Revolution, 256-88.
James A. Henretta, The Evolution of American Society, 1700-1815, 119-55.
* Jack P. Greene and Pauline Maier, eds., Interdisciplinary Studies of the
    American Revolution, 9-108.
* Bernard Bailyn, The Origins of American Politics, 106-61.
Jack P. Greene, "The Growth of Political Stability: An Interpretation.
    Political Development in the Anglo-American Colonies, 1660-1760," in
    John Parker and Carol Urness, eds., The American Revolution: A Heritage
    of Change (Minneapolis, 1975), 26-52.
* Richard Buel, Jr., "Democracy and the American Revolution: A Frame of Reference,"
    WMQ, 3d ser., XXI (1964), 165-190. (B-M Reprint H-246).

February 24: The Relationship with Britain: Part One.

Required Reading:
Curtis P. Nettels, "British Mercantilism and the Economic Development of the
    Thirteen Colonies," in Jack P. Greene, ed., The Reinterpretation of the
    American Revolution, 76-86.
* Oliver N. Dickerson, The Navigation Acts and the American Revolution, 31-102,147-58.
* Robert Paul Thomas, "A Quantitative Approach to the Study of the Effects of
    British Imperial Policy upon Colonial Welfare: Some Preliminary Findings,"
    Journal of Economic History, XXV (1965), 615-38. (B-M Reprint H-479).
Marc Egnal and Joseph Ernst, "An Economic Interpretation of the American
    Revolution," WMQ, 3d ser., XXIX (1972), 3-32.
Jack P. Greene, "The Role of the Lower Houses of Assembly in Eighteenth-Century
    Politics," in Greene, ed., Reinterpretation, 86-109.
* Jack P. Greene, "Political Mimesis: A Consideration of the Historical Roots of
    Legislative Behavior in the British Colonies in the Eighteenth Century,"
    American Historical Review, LXXV (1969), 337-60. (B-M Reprint H-395).
* Bernard Bailyn, The Origins of American Politics, 59-105.

March 3: The Relationship with Britain: Part Two.

Required Reading:

* Jack P. Greene, "Search for Identity: An Interpretation of Selected Patterns of
    Social Response in Eighteenth-Century America," Journal of Social History,
    III (1970), 189-220. (B-M Reprint H-396).
* Edwin Burrows and Michael Wallace, "The American Revolution: The Ideology and
    Psychology of National Liberation," Perspectives in American History,
    VI (1972), 161-89.
Max Savelle, "Nationalism and Other Loyalties in the American Revolution,"
    American Historical Review, LXVII (1962), 901-23.
* Jack P. Greene, "An Uneasy Connection: An Analysis of the Preconditions of the
    American Revolution," in Kurtz and Hutson, eds., Essays on the American
    Revolution, 32-80.

March 10: Changing Relationships, 1748-1763

Required Reading:

Jack P. Greene, "'A Posture of Hostility': A Reconsideration of Some Aspects
        of the Origins of the American Revolution," American Antiquarian Society
        Proceedings, LXXXVII (1977), Part I, 5-46.

Marc Egnal, "The Economic Development of the Thirteen Continental Colonies,
        1720 to 1775," WMQ, 3d ser., XXXII (1975), 191-222.
J. M. Bumstad,"'Things in the Womb of Time: Ideas of American Independence,
        1663-1763'", WMQ, 3d ser., XXXI (1974), 533-64.
Jack P. Greene, "The Seven Years' War and the American Revolution: The Causal
        Relationship Reconsidered," Journal of Imperial and Commonwealth History,
        VIII (1980), 85-105.
* Bernhard Knollenberg, Origins of the American Revolution, 1-171.
* Lawrence H. Gipson, "The American Revolution as an Aftermath of the Great War
        for Empire," PSQ, LXV (1950), 86-104. (B-M Reprint H-268).

March 17: The Stamp Act Crisis

Required Reading:

* Edmund S. Morgan and Helen M. Morgan, The Stamp Act Crisis.
P.D.G. Thomas, British Politics and the Stamp Act Crisis, 185-252, 364-71.
Edmund S. Morgan, "Colonial Ideas of Parliamentary Power," in Greene,
        Reinterpretation, 151-81.
David L. Lovejoy, "Right Imply Equality: The Case Against Admiralty Jurisdiction
        in America," ibid., 181-206.

March 31: Britain and the Colonies, 1766-1774

Required Reading:

* Jack P. Greene, "The Plunge of Lemmings: A Consideration of Recent Writings on
        British Politics and the American Revolution," South Atlantic Quarterly,
        LXVII (1968), 141-75. (B-M Reprint H-397).
Paul Langford, "The Rockingham Whigs and America, 1767-1773," in Anne Whiteman,
        J. S. Bromley and P.G.M. Dickson, eds., Statesmen, Scholars and Merchants,
        135-52.
Paul Langford, "Old Whigs, Old Tories, and the American Revolution," Journal
        of Imperial and Commonwealth History, VIII (1980), 106-30.
Ira D. Gruber, "The American Revolution as a Conspiracy: The British View,"
        WMQ, 3d ser., XXVI (1969), 360-72.
Benjamin W. Labaree, "The Idea of American Independence: The British View,
        1774-1776," Massachusetts Historical Society Proceedings, LXXXII (1970),
        3-20.

April 14: The Colonies and Britain, 1766-1774.

Required Reading:

* Bernard Bailyn, Ideological Origins of the American Revolution, 22-159.
Edmund S. Morgan, "The Puritan Ethic and the American Revolution," in Greene,
        Reinterpretation, 235-51.

Perry Miller, "The Moral and Psychological Roots of Resistance," in _ibid._, 251-74.
Gerald Stourzh, "William Blackstone: Teacher of Revolution," _Jahrbuch für Amerikastudien_ (Heidelberg, 1970), 184-200.
W. Paul Adams, "Republicanism in Political Rhetoric Before 1776," _Political Science Quarterly_, LXXXV (1970), 397-421.
Jack P. Greene, "Social Context and the Causal Pattern of the American Revolution: A Preliminary Consideration of New York, Virginia, and Massachusetts," _La Révolution Américaine et L'Europe: Colloque Internationaux du Centre National de la Recherche Scientifique_, #577 (1979), 25-63.

April 21: _Independence, 1774-1776._

Required Reading:

* Benjamin W. Labaree, _The Boston Tea Party_, 80-145.
* David Ammerman, _In the Common Cause._
Burrows and Wallace, "The American Revolution," 190-306.
Pauline Maier, "The Beginnings of American Republicanism," in _Development of a Revolutionary Mentality_, 99-117.
Winthrop D. Jordan, "Familial Politics: Thomas Paine and the Killing of the King, 1776," _Journal of American History_, LX (1973), 294-308.
Jack N. Rakove, "The Decision for American Independence: A Reconstruction," _Perspectives in American History_, X (1976), 217-78.
Jack P. Greene, "Paine, America, and the 'Modernization' of Political Consciousness," _Political Science Quarterly_, XCIII (1978), 73-92.

UNIVERSITY OF CALIFORNIA, LOS ANGELES

History 101
Professor Joyce Appleby
Spring, 1983

Office: Bunche 6254
Office Hours:
  Monday, 12-1
  Wednesday, 11-12
  Friday, 9-10

Undergraduate seminar

"Remember, gentlemen, we aren't here just to draft a constitution. We're here to draft the best damned constitution in the world."

A Historiographical inquiry into the drafting of the United States Constitution

In this seminar we shall study the theory behind historical writing and the methods historians use in their research. Past events have completely vanished, leaving behind only memories, consequences, and tangible objects like newspapers, public records and buildings. These form the evidence which historians draw upon when they reconstruct the past. It is important to realize that all of our historical knowledge began as a question in someone's mind. This means that the study of history as a disciplined inquiry involves looking at both the historians who ask the questions and the evidence which enables them to arrive at answers.

Because historical writing deals with the meaning and significance of facts about the past, it is also interpretive. Historians offer us interpretations of what happened in the past based upon assessments of evidence. Their interpretations also involve assumptions about society and human nature which go beyond the evidence itself. Hence historical proof is never absolute. Rather historians persuade us to believe their accounts by developing an argument.

We will consider these aspects of historical scholarship by addressing a single question throughout the quarter: how American historians have interpreted the drafting of the U.S. Constitution.

Below is a calendar of class assignments. Each student will contribute to one group project, give one oral report and write a 12-to-16 page paper. In addition to these formal assignments, we shall have weekly discussions and occasional papers on assigned readings. Students are expected to attend all class sessions and be prepared to talk about the readings. The final grade will be based on class participation (20%), group reports (20%), the oral report (15%), and the individual term paper (45%). Incompletes will be granted for documented medical reasons only. All late work will be marked down a half grade.

66

April 4: Carl Becker, "What are Historical Facts?" Assignment of group projects. Discussion of historical questions.

April 11: For discussion in class: Lance Banning, "Republican Ideology and the Constitution," William and Mary Quarterly, 31 (1974)* and Gordon S. Wood, "Democracy and the Constitution," and Ann Stuart Diamond, "Decent, Even Thought Democratic," in Robert A. Goldwin and William A. Schambra, eds., How Democratic Is the Constitution?, Washington, 1980. Please write a 500-word essay with footnotes in as correct a form as you can manage on a subject of your choosing taken from these readings. Review of library resources for historical research.

April 18: For discussion in class: Patrick Gardiner, The Nature of Historical Explanation, Oxford, 1961, pp. 1-112. Write a 500-word essay with footnotes on a subject taken from The Nature of Historical Explanation. We will also discuss John P. Roche, "The Founding Fathers: A Reform Caucus in Action," American Political Science Review, 55 (1961)* and Martin Diamond, "Democracy and the Federalist: A Reconsideration of the Framers' Intent," Ibid., 53 (1959)*

April 25: For discussion in class: Patrick Gardiner, The Nature of Historical Explanation, pp. 113-39; Robert E. Brown, "Economic Democracy Before the Constitution," American Quarterly, 7 (1955);* and Michael Parenti, "The Constitution as an Elitist Document" and Alfred F. Young, "Conservatives, the Constitution and the 'Spirit of Accommodation,'" in Goldwin and Schambra, eds., How Democratic Is the Constitution?

May 2: Group A presents its findings. For discussion in class: Charles Beard, An Economic Interpretation of the Constitution of the United States, New York, 1913.

May 9: Group B presents its findings. Continuing discussion of Beard's Economic Interpretation of the Constitution.

May 16: Group C presents its findings. For discussion in class: Andrew McLaughlin, The Foundations of American Constitutionalism, New York, 1918.

May 23: Group D presents its findings. For discussion in class: Federalist Papers Nos. 1-25, 39 and 51. The United States Constitution in Sauld K. Padover, The Living U.S. Constitution, New York, 1968.

June 6: A summing up.

June 10: Individual papers due.

*This article is at the reserve room of Powell library and the Graduate Reading Room of the University Research Library. You can also find it in the bound volume of the periodical on the shelves of both libraries and (perhaps) the History Department Library.

NINETEENTH CENTURY AMERICA

This course is partly chronological and partly topical in its
organization. In addition to lectures (ordinarily three per week),
there will be discussion meetings on the dates indicated (d).

Required readings are available at the Book Store and on library
reserve.

There is no term paper in the course, but two short written reports
are required, one on your reading of a newspaper and the other on
your reading of a novel. Details are on the following page.

There will be two intra-quarter examinations, one on Thursday,
January 27, and the second on Thursday, February 17. Makeup
examinations will be given only on the day of the final examination at 8:15 AM. The final, a two-hour examination, will be
given on Thursday, March 17, at 9:30 AM.

Office: 209. Monday, 10:00 to 10:30
              Tuesday, 10:00 to 10:30
              Wednesday, 1:00 to 2:00

Calendar

January 4, 5: Introduction

January 10, 11, 12, 13d: Jeffersonian America

January 17, 18, 19, 20d: The Age of Jackson

January 24, 25, 26: Conquest of the Continent

January 27: Examination

January 31, February 1, 2, 3d: Race and Slavery

February 7, 8, 9, 10d: The Reform Impulse

February 14, 15, 16: The Civil War and Reconstruction

February 17: Examination

February 21: Holiday

February 22, 23, 24d: The Ethnic Multitude

February 28, March 1, 2, 3d: The Industrial Nation

March 7, 8, 9: Politics and Protest

March 10: Conclusion

March 17: Final examination

Newspaper Report

In order to spread out use of microfilm machines, due dates are staggered according to first letters of last names:

A-F: January 17   N-R: January 31
G-M: January 24   S-Z: February 7

Spend several hours surveying one 19th-century year of an American newspaper. Write a brief report (300-500 words) indicating some of the knowledge gained about the quality of life and the character of the people. Be sure to give some attention to editorials, local news, and advertisements. Here are some of the newspapers available in long runs:

Boston Daily Advertiser   Chicago Tribune
Cincinnati Gazette   Mobile Register
New Orleans Picayune   New York Times
Richmond Enquirer   New York Herald
San Francisco Chronicle   New York Tribune
Sacramento Union   Washington Post
          Washington National Intelligencer

Book Report

Due: March 7

Read one of the novels listed below and write a short essay (500-1000 words) discussing what it says or implies about American history and culture in the 19th century:

Henry Adams, Democracy
Edward Bellamy, Looking Backward
George W. Cable, The Grandissimes
Willa Cather, My Antonia
Cather, O Pioneers
James Fenimore Cooper, Homeward Bound
Cooper, Home as Found
John William De Forest, Miss Ravenel's Conversion
Ignatius Donnelly, Caesar's Column
Edward Eggleston, The Hoosier School-Master
Hamlin Garland, A Son of the Middle Border
Nathaniel Hawthorne, The Blithedale Romance
William Dean Howells, A Hazard of New Fortunes
Howells, The Rise of Silas Lapham
Howells, A Traveler from Altruria
Henry James, The Bostonians
James, Washington Square
John Pendleton Kennedy, Swallow Barn
Herman Melville, The Confidence-Man
Melville, White Jacket
Frank Norris, The Octopus
Ole E. Rolvaag, Giants in the Earth
Harriet Beecher Stowe, Old Town Folks
Stowe, Uncle Tom's Cabin
Mark Twain and Charles Dudley Warner, The Gilded Age
Albion W. Tourgee, A Fool's Errand
Edith Wharton, The Age of Innocence

Introduction

January 4: Looking Back to the Nineteenth Century
        5: The United States in 1800

Required reading:
  Marshall Smelser, The Democratic Republic, chapters 1-2

Recommended reading:
  Don E. Fehrenbacher, The Era of Expansion, chapters 1, 8
  James MacGregor Burns, The Vineyard of Liberty, chapters 3-4
  John C. Miller, The Federalist Era
  Morton Borden, Parties and Politics in the Early Republic, chapter 1

I
Jeffersonian America

January 10: Rounding Out the Constitution
        11: The European Connection
        12: The Jefferson Tradition
        13: Discussion

Required reading:
  Smelser, chapters 3-15

Recommended reading:
  Fehrenbacher, chapter 2
  Burns, chapters 5-7
  Daniel J. Boorstin, The Lost World of Thomas Jefferson
  Borden, chapter 2
  Richard Hofstadter, The American Political Tradition, chapter 2
  Merrill D. Peterson, The Jefferson Image in the American Mind
  Adrienne Koch, Jefferson and Madison: The Great Collaboration
  Harry L. Coles, The War of 1812
  James Sterling Young, The Washington Community
  George Dangerfield, The Awakening of American Nationalism

Vocabulary items:

Tertium quids	Macon's Bill No. 2	Burr trial
strict construction	judicial review	Albert Gallatin
Virginia dynasty	Chesapeake affair	George Clinton
caucus system	Fletcher v. Peck	Jay's Treaty
36° 30'	Hartford Convention	right of deposit
Tippecanoe	Bank of United States	Barbary wars

Discussion questions:
  1. Which was the most significant characteristic of the Jeffersonian party? Its constitutional principles, its agrarian outlook, its Southernness, or its expansionism?

  2. "All men claim to be Jeffersonians today," says Marshall Smelser. Which has the better claim, a modern liberal or a modern conservative?

  3. Jefferson's second term was much less successful than his first. Was this an accident of history or is such decline a common characteristic of the American presidency?

II
The Age of Jackson

January 17: The Maturing Political System
        18: Sectional Strains and Party Politics
        19: The Democratic Society: Reality and Myth
        20: Discussion

Required reading:
  Glyndon G. Van Deusen, The Jacksonian Era, chapters 1-10, 13

Recommended reading:
  Burns, chapters 9-10, 12
  Fehrenbacher, chapter 5
  Hofstadter, 3-4
  Douglas T. Miller, The Birth of Modern America
  Robert V. Remini, The Revolutionary Age of Andrew Jackson

Vocabulary items:
  removal of deposits   locofocos   programmatic party
  tariff of abominations   nullification   Schlesinger thesis
  corrupt bargain   kitchen cabinet   Roger B. Taney
  Anti-Masonry   Maysville veto   gag rule
  two-thirds rule   Barnburners   Specie Circular

Discussion questions:
  1. In explaining the difference between Whigs and Democrats,
     which should be emphasized most: ideology, class, geography?

  2. In what ways was Jackson representative of his age and in
     what ways unrepresentative?

III
Conquest of the Continent

January 24: The Expansion of National Sovereignty
        25: The Westward Movement as a Social Process
        26: The Frontier and American Character

Required reading:
  Ray A. Billington, The Far Western Frontier

Recommended reading:
  Van Deusen, chapters 11-12
  Fehrenbacher, chapters 3, 7
  Billington, ed., The Frontier Thesis
  William T. Hagan, American Indians
  Roy M. Robbins, Our Landed Heritage
  Richard A. Bartlett, The New Country
  Robert Hine, The American West

Vocabulary items:
  safety-valve thesis   rendezvous system   Santa Fe Trail
  placer mining   manifest destiny   Trail of Tears
  line of semi-aridity   keelboat   54° 40' or fight
  National Road   public domain   Dawes Act

Discussion questions:
  1. It has been said that the Turner thesis is wrong, not for
     what it says, but for what it omits. Comment.

  2. What policy should the United States government have adopted
     with respect to the American Indian?

IV
Race and Slavery

January 31: The Idea of Race
February 1: The Increasingly Peculiar Institution
         2: Slavery in the American Constitutional System
         3: Discussion

Required reading:
  Allan Weinstein, et al., eds., American Negro Slavery (3rd ed.)

Recommended reading:
  Winthrop Jordan, White Over Black, chapters 12-15
  George M. Fredrickson, The Black Image in the White Mind
  Leon Litwack, North of Slavery
  Kenneth M. Stampp, The Peculiar Institution
  Don E. Fehrenbacher, Slavery, Law, and Politics, chapters 1-8
  Ira Berlin, Slaves Without Masters

Vocabulary items:
  three-fifths clause   polygenesis   nonintervention
  romantic racialism   colonization   Prigg v. Pennsylvania
  Herrenvolk democracy   Sambo thesis   George Fitzhugh
  diffusion theory   Creole affair   slave codes

Discussion questions:
  1. In what ways, if any, did the institution of slavery change
     between the Revolution and the Civil War?

  2. Did social class make a difference in the racial attitudes
     of white Americans in the 19th century?

V
The Reform Impulse

February 7: The Varieties of Reform
         8: The Discovery of Social Evil   February 10: Discussion
         9: The Antislavery Crusade

Required reading:
  Ronald Walters, American Reformers

Recommended reading:
  Fehrenbacher, Era of Expansion, pp. 103-13
  Clifford Griffin, The Ferment of Reform
  Alice Felt Tyler, Freedom's Ferment
  David B. Davis, ed., Ante-Bellum Reform
  Timothy L. Smith, Revivalism and Social Reform
  James Stewart, Holy Warriors

Vocabulary items:
  benevolent societies   Washingtonians   Sylvester Graham
  perfectionism   immediatism   Dorothea Dix
  millenialism   Maine Law   Fourierism
  Seneca Falls   Oneida   Phillips-Spooner debate

Discussion questions:
  1. Antebellum social reform has been viewed variously as conserva-
     tive and repressive, as liberal and democratic, and as radical
     and utopian. Which is closest to the truth?

  2. Of all the antebellum reform movements, abolitionism was the
     a) most successful; b) most typical; c) most respectable

VI
Disunion and Reunion

February 14: The Sectional Conflict
    15: The Long Road to Appomattox
    16: The Aftermath

Required reading:
 David Herbert Donald, Liberty and Union

Recommended reading:
 Fehrenbacher, Slavery, Law, and Politics, chapters 9-10
 David M. Potter, The Impending Crisis
 Eric Foner, Free Soil, Free Labor, Free Men
 Bruce Catton, This Hallowed Ground
 LaWanda Cox, Lincoln and Black Freedom
 Emory M. Thomas, The Confederate Nation
 Kenneth M. Stampp, The Era of Reconstruction

Vocabulary items:
Lecompton constitution	Trent affair	Anaconda plan
Freeport doctrine	scalawags	Peninsular campaign
Crittenden compromise	Vicksburg	Wade-Davis bill
Wilmot Proviso	draft riots	Civil Rights cases

Discussion questions:
1. What important questions did the Civil War settle and what new questions did it raise?

2. Which one of the following would you be most disposed to label "inevitable"? The coming of the Civil War; the defeat of the Confederacy; the failure of Radical Reconstruction.

VII
The Ethnic Multitude

February 22: Changing Patterns of Immigration
    23. The Immigrant in American Society
    24. Discussion

Required reading:
 Oscar Handlin, The Uprooted

Recommended reading:
 Maldwyn Jones, American Immigration, chapters 3-9
 John Higham, Strangers in the Land
 Ray A. Billington, The Protestant Crusade
 Robert Ernst, Immigrant Life in New York City
 Philip Taylor, The Distant Magnet

Vocabulary items:
shock of alienation	Cahenslyism	Dillingham Commission
Potato Famine	melting pot	Denis Kearney
Mr. Dooley	Maria Monk	Turnverein
American Party	A.P.A.	literacy test
Castle Garden	steerage	new immigration

Discussion questions:
1. Can one draw meaningful comparisons between immigration from Europe and the westward movement within the United States?

2. How does one explain the fact that immigrants have fared better than Indians and blacks in American society?

VIII
The Industrial Nation

February 28: The Railroad Century
   March 1: Machines, Money, and Men
       2: The Rise of the City
       3: Discussion

Required reading:
  Carl N. Degler, The Age of Economic Revolution, chapters 1-3
  John Kasson, Civilizing the Machine

Recommended reading:
  Fehrenbacher, Era of Expansion
  George R. Taylor, The Transportation Revolution
  Robert Higgs, The Transformation of the American Economy
  Andrew Callow, American Urban History, parts 4-7
  Gunther Barth, City People

Vocabulary items:
Lowell system	gross national product	balloon-frame house
robber barons	take-off thesis	Edward Bellamy
machine tools	limited liability	Knights of Labor
rebates	Crystal Palace	dumb-bell tenement

Discussion questions:
1. "Although Ralph Waldo Emerson and Mark Twain were both ambiva-
   lent in their attitudes toward technology, Twain was less
   consciously so." Comment.

2. Did the American political system impede or accelerate or
   otherwise affect the great economic expansion of the second
   half of the 19th century?

IX
Politics and Protest

March 7: Government in the Gilded Age
     8: The Crisis of the Nineties
     9: Manifest Destiny Again
    10: Conclusion

Required reading:
  Degler, chapters 4-6
  Lawrence Goodwyn, The Populist Moment

Recommended reading:
  Robert D. Marcus, Grand Old Party
  John G. Sproat, The Best Men
  Robert Wiebe, The Search for Order
  Walter LaFeber, The New Empire

Vocabulary items:
social Darwinism	Omaha Platform	crop-lien system
social gospel	shadow movement	Haymarket riot
mugwumps	free silver	Greenback Party
Tom Watson	De Lome letter	Aguinaldo

Discussion questions:
1. Was there a decline in public virtue and political leadership
   from the days of Jefferson to the days of Bryan? If so, why?

2. Abolitionism and Populism were both sectional movements. Were
   comparable in any other significant ways?

GRADUATE SEMINAR

PRINCETON UNIVERSITY
Department of History
History 588

Spring, 1982   Profs. McPherson/
(1st Seven Weeks)   Rodgers
READINGS IN AMERICAN HISTORY, 1815-1877

Wednesday, 9:30 a.m. in Graduate Seminar Room, Firestone

The purpose of this seminar is to acquaint students with some of the important
works on the political, social, and economic history of the Jacksonian, Antebellum,
and Civil War/Reconstruction eras of American history. Class discussions each
week will be based on the general assignment and on student-written review essays
of additional books. Suggested books for review essays will be listed in this
syllabus, but students may select non-listed books for review with the permission
of the instructors. The review essays should be no more than six typewritten
pages in length. They should both summarize the thesis and factual content of a
book and appraise the author's handling and interpretation of the subject. Review
essays must be typed and reproduced either by ditto or Xerox and copies made
available to the instructors and other students by the Monday before the seminar
meeting. Each student will be expected to write 3 review essays during the
semester.

Books for review have not been placed on reserve, so reviewers will be responsible for hunting them out of the stacks. All books and articles listed
as assigned readings have been placed on reserve in the graduate study room,
except for articles in the American Historical Review, a set of which is
available in the graduate study room. Except for articles in the AHR, assigned
articles have been Xeroxed and one copy of each placed on the reserve shelf in
the graduate study room. Books marked with an asterisk are available at the
University Store, and students are urged to purchase them.

SCHEDULE

Feb. 3:   Introduction and Organization

Feb. 10:   The Transformation of the Economy (I)

Assignment:

   E. A. Wrigley, "The Process of Modernization and the Industrial Revolution
   in England," Journal of Interdisciplinary History, 3 (1972), 225-59.

   Richard D. Brown, "Modernization and the Modern Personality in Early America,
   1600-1865," Journal of Interdisciplinary History, 2 (1972), 480-539.

   *George R. Taylor, The Transportation Revolution, 1815-1860, chaps. 1-3, 5,
   7-11, 14-17.

   *Morton J. Horwitz, The Transformation of American Law, 1780-1860, chaps.1-4,8.

   Charles J. McClain, Jr., "Legal Change and Class Interests: A Review Essay on
   Morton J. Horwitz's The Transformation of American Law," California Law
   Review, 68 (1980), 383-97.

Feb. 10 (continued)

Review Essays:

> Daniel J. Boorstin, The Americans: The National Experiment
> Peter Temin, ed., The New Economic History
> J. E. Crowley, This Sheba, Self: The Conceptualization of Economic Life in Eighteenth-Century America AND Drew McCoy, The Elusive Republic.
> J. Willard Hurst, Law and the Conditions of Freedom in the Nineteenth-Century United States.

Feb. 17:   The Transformation of the Economy (II)

Assignment:

> Edward Pessen, "The Egalitarian Myth and American Social Reality: Wealth, Mobility, and Equality in the 'Era of the Common Man,'" AHR, 76 (1971), 989-1031.
> Michael B. Katz, et al., "Migration and the Social Order in Erie County, New York,: 1855," Journal of Interdisciplinary History,8 (1978), 669-701.
>
> John Modell, "The Peopling of a Working-Class Ward: Reading, Pennsylvania, 1850," Journal of Social History, 5 (1971), 71-95.
>
> *Paul E. Johnson, A Shopkeeper's Millenium: Society and Revivals in Rochester, New York, 1815-1837.
>
> Daniel J. Walkowitz, Worker City, Company Town: Iron and Cotton-Worker Protest in Troy and Cohoes, New York, 1855-1884.
>
> Herbert G. Gutman, "The Worker's Search for Power: Labor in the Gilded Age," in H. Wayne Morgan, ed., The Gilded Age.
>
> Herbert G. Gutman, Work, Culture, and Society in Industrializing America, Chap. 1.

Review Essays:

> Alan Dawley, Class and Community: The Industrial Revolution in Lynn
> Anthony F. C. Wallace, Rockdale
> Thomas Dublin, Women at Work: Work and Community in Lowell, Massachusetts.
> John R. Commons, History of Labour in the United States.

Feb. 24:   The Political Culture of the Jacksonian Era

Assignment:

> Charles G. Sellers, "Andrew Jackson versus the Historians," Mississippi Valley Historical Review, 44 (1958), 615-34
>
> Ronald P. Formisano, "Toward a Reorientation of Jacksonian Politics: A Review of the Literature, 1959-1975," Journal of American History, 63 (1976), 42-65.
>
> Richard P. McCormick, "Political Development and the Second Party System," in William N. Chambers and Walter D. Burnham, eds., The American Party Systems, 90-116.
>
> Marvin Meyers, "The Jacksonian Persuasion," American Quarterly, V (Spring 1953), 3-15.
>
> *Lee Benson, The Concept of Jacksonian Democracy: New York as a Test Case, esp. chaps. 1, 2, 3, 5, 7, 8, 9, 13, 14, 15.

Feb. 24   Assignment continued:

Herbert Ershkowitz and William Shade, "Consensus or Conflict: Political Behavior in the State Legislatures During the Jacksonian Era," Journal of American History,58 (1971), 591-621.

David Grimsted, "Rioting in Its Jacksonian Setting," American Historical Review, 77 (1972), 361-97.

Richard H. Brown, "The Missouri Crisis, Slavery, and the Politics of Jacksonianism," South Atlantic Quarterly, 55 (1966), 55-72

John M. McFaul, "Expediency vs.Morality: Jacksonian Politics and Slavery," Journal of American History, 62 (1975), 24-39.

Major Wilson, "The Concept of Time and the Political in the United States," American Quarterly, 19 (1967), 619-44

*Daniel W. Howe, The Political Culture of the American Whigs, esp. chaps. 1, 2, 3, 5, 6, 7, 8, 9.

Review Essays:

Frederick Jackson Turner, The Rise of the New West, 1815-1829, and/or Turner, The United States, 1830-1850.
Arthur M. Schlesinger, Jr., The Age of Jackson
Michael P. Rogin, Fathers and Children: Andrew Jackson and the Subjugation of the American Indian
Ronald P. Formisano, The Birth of Mass Political Parties: Michigan, 1827-1861
William G. Shade, Banks or No Banks: The Money Issue in Western Politics, 1832-1865

March 3:   Shaping a Bourgeois Society

Assignment:

Mary P. Ryan, Cradle of the Middle Class: The Family in Oneida County, New York, 1790-1865

Carroll Smith-Rosenburg, "The Female World of Love and Ritual: Relations between Women in Nineteenth-Century America," Signs, 1 (1975), 1-29

Alan Dawley and Paul Faler, "Working-Class Culture and Politics in the Industrial Revolution: Sources of Loyalism and Rebellion," Journal of Social History, 9 (1976), 466-80.

Michael B. Katz, "The Origins of Public Education: A Reassessment," History of Education Quarterly, 16 (1976), 381-407.

Carl Kaestle and Maris Vinovskis, Education and Social Change in Nineteenth Century Massachusetts

Ronald G. Walters, "The Erotic South: Civilization and Sexuality in American Abolitionism," American Quarterly, 25 (1973), 177-201.

David B. Davis, "The Emergence of Immediatism in British and American Antislavery Thought," Mississippi Valley History Review,49 (1962), 209-30

*Stanley M. Elkins, Slavery: A Problem in American Institutional and Intellectual Life, chap. 4.

David B. Davis, The Problem of Slavery in the Age of Revolution, 1770-1823 pp. 343-73, 453-68.

March 3: (continued)

Review Essays:

Kathryn Sklar, Catharine Beecher
Ann Douglas, The Feminization of American Culture
Michael B. Katz, The Irony of Early School Reform
Alice F. Tyler, Freedom's Ferment

March 10:   Slavery

Assignment:

David Brion Davis, "Slavery and the Post-World War II Historians," Daedalus, 103 (1974), 1-16.

*Stanley M. Elkins, Slavery, 3rd ed. (1976), chaps. 1-3, 5-6.

Laura Foner and Eugene D. Genovese, eds., Slavery in the New World, pp. 38-59, 238-55, 202-10.

Carl N. Degler, "Slavery in Brazil and the United States: An Essay in Comparative History," American Historical Review, 75 (1970), 1004-28.

Kenneth M. Stampp, "Rebels and Samboes: The Search for the Negro's Personality in Slavery," Journal of Southern History, 37 (1971), 367-92

*Robert W. Fogel and Stanley L. Engerman, Time on the Cross: The Economics of American Negro Slavery, vol. I, Prologue and chaps. 1, 2, 4, 6.

*Paul A. David et al, Reckoning With Slavery, Introduction (Stampp), Part I (all essays), and chap. 6 (Sutch) of Part II.

Willie Lee Rose, Slavery and Freedom, pp. 18-48.

Eugene D. Genovese, Roll, Jordan, Roll, 202-84.

Review Essays:

Ulrich B. Phillips, American Negro Slavery
Kenneth M. Stampp, The Peculiar Institution
Eugene D. Genovese, Roll, Jordan, Roll
Herbert G. Gutman, The Black Family in Slavery and Freedom
Mark Tushnet, The American Law of Slavery, 1810-1860

March 24:   Slavery and the Southern Economy

Assignment:

*Eugene D. Genovese, The Political Economy of Slavery
*Fogel and Engerman, Time on the Cross, vol. I, chaps. 3,5.
*David et al., Reckoning With Slavery, chaps. 5, 7.

March 24:

Assignment: (continued)

Alfred H. Conrad et al., "Slavery as an Obstacle to Economic Growth in
the South: A Panel Discussion," Journal of Economic History, 27 (1967),
518-60.

Robert E. Gallman and Ralph V. Anderson, "Slaves as Fixed Capital: Slave Labor
and Southern Economic Development," Journal of American History, 64 (1977),
24-46.

Morton Rothstein, "The Antebellum South as a Dual Economy: A Tentative
Hypothesis," Agricultural History, 41 (1967), 373-82.

Gavin Wright, "'Economic Democracy' and the Concentration of Wealth in
the Cotton South," Agricultural History, 44 (1970), 62-99.

Eugene D. Genovese, "Yeoman Farmers in a Slaveholders' Democracy,"
Agricultural History, 49 (1975), 331-42.

Forrest McDonald and Grady McWhiney, "The Antebellum Southern Herdsman:
A Reinterpretation," Journal of Southern History, 41 (1975), 147-66.

Forrest McDonald and Grady McWhiney, "The South from Self-Sufficiency
to Peonage: An Interpretation," Edward Pessen, "How Different from Each
Other were the Antebellum North and South?" and AHR Forum: Antebellum
North and South in Comparative Perspective: A Discussion," all in
American Historical Review, 85 (Dec. 1980), 1095-1163.

Review Essays:

Frank L. Owsley, Plain Folk of the Old South, and Fabian Linden, "Economic
Democracy in the Slave South: An Appraisal of Some Recent Views,"
Journal of Negro History, 31 (1946), 140-89.

Fred BAteman and Thomas Weiss, A Deplorable Scarcity: The Failure of Industrialization in the Slave Economy

Dickson D. Bruce, Jr., Violence and Culture in the Antebellum South

Harold D. Woodman, King Cotton and His Retainers

William R. Taylor, Cavalier and Yankee: The Old South and National
Character

(to be continued)

JM/DR/lah 1/12/82 (35)

March 31: Manifest Destiny and Sectionalism

Assignment:

   *Frederick Merk, <u>Manifest Destiny and Mission in American History</u>, chaps. 1-9.

   Reginald Horsman, "American Indian Policy and the Origins of Manifest Destiny," <u>University of Birmingham Historical Journal</u>, 11 (1968), 127-40

   *Michael Holt, <u>The Political Crisis of the 1850's</u>, chaps. 1-4

   David M. Potter, <u>The Impending Crisis 1845-1861</u>, chaps. 1-5

   Joel Silbey, "The Civil War Synthesis in American Political History," <u>Civil War History</u>, 10 (1964), 130-40

   Charles W. Ramsdell, "The Natural Limits of Slavery Expansion," <u>Mississippi Valley Historical Review</u>, 16 (1929), 151-71.

   Harry Jaffa, "The 'Natural Limits' of Slavery Expansion," in Jaffa, <u>The Crisis of the House Divided</u>, 387-99.

Review Essays:

   Joel Silbey, <u>The Shrine of Party: Congressional Voting Behavior, 1841-1852</u>

   Michael F. Holt, <u>Forging a Majority: The Formation of the Republican Party in Pittsburgh</u>

   William R. Brock, <u>Parties and Political Conscience: American Dilemmas 1840-1850</u>

   Frederick J. Blue, <u>The Free Soilers: Third Party Politics 1848-1854</u>

   William J. Cooper, <u>The South and the Politics of Slavery 1828-1856</u>

   Chaplain W. Morrison, <u>Democratic Politics and Sectionalism: The Wilmot Proviso Controversy</u>

   Kinley J. Brauer, <u>Cotton Versus Conscience: Massachusetts Whig Politics and Southwestern Expansion 1843-1848</u>

April 7: The 1850's and the Breakdown of Comity

Assignment:

Potter, _Impending Crisis_, chaps. 6-16

Michael Holt, "The Politics of Impatience: The Origins of Know-Nothingism," _Journal of American History_, 60 (1973), 309-31.

*Holt, _Political Crisis of the 1850's_, chaps. 5-8

*Eric Foner, _Free Soil, Free Labor, Free Men: The Ideology of the Republican Party before the Civil War_, esp. chaps. 1-3, 7-9.

Don E. Fehrenbacher, "Roger B. Taney and the Sectional Crisis," _Journal of Southern History_, 43 (1977), 555-66.

Review Essays:

John McCardell, _The Idea of a Southern Nation: Southern Nationalists and Southern Nationalism 1830-1860_

Don E. Fehrenbacher, _The Dred Scott Case_

Avery Craven, _The Coming of the Civil War_

Stanley W. Campbell, _The Slave Catchers: Enforcement of the Fugitive Slave Law 1850-1860_

Thomas D. Morris, _Free Men All: The Personal Liberty Laws of the North 1780-1861_

Robert E. May, _The Southern Dream of a Caribbean Empire, 1854-1861_

George B. Forgie, _Patricide in the House Divided: A Psychological Interpretation of Lincoln and His Age_.

April 14: Secession and the Meaning of War

Assignment:

*Hans Trefousse, ed., _The Causes of the Civil War_

Eric Foner, _Politics and Ideology in the Age of the Civil War_, 3-53

Potter, _Impending Crisis_, chaps. 17-20

81

April 14 Assignment continued:

Barrington Moore, "The American Civil War: The Last Capitalist
Revolution," in Moore, Social Origins of Dictatorship and Democracy,
111-55

Herbert Aptheker, The American Civil War (pamphlet)

James M. McPherson, "Dimensions of Counterrevolution and Revolution
in the American Civil War," unpublished paper.

James M. McPherson, Ordeal By Fire: The Civil War and Reconstruction,
chaps. 16, 20, 21, 22

Emory Thomas, The Confederacy as a Revolutionary Experience,
chaps. 2-8

Kenneth Stampp, "The Southern Road to Appomattox," in Stampp,
The Imperiled Union, 246-69

James Roark, Masters Without Slaves, chap. 3

John S. Rosenberg, "Toward a New Civil War Revisionism,"
American Scholar, 38 (1969) 250-72.

George Fredrickson, "Blue Over Gray: Sources of Success and
Failure in the Civil War," in Fredrickson, ed., A Nation
Divided, 57-80

Review Essays:

Steven Channing, Crisis of Fear: Secession in South Carolina

William Barney, The Secessionist Impulse: Alabama and Mississippi
in 1860

Michael P. Johnson, Toward a Patriarchal Republic: Secession
in Georgia

Paul D. Escott, After Secession: Jefferson Davis and the Failure
of Confederate Nationalism

George M. Fredrickson, The Inner Civil War: Northern Intellectuals
and the Crisis of the Union

James H. Moorhead, American Apocalypse: Yankee Protestants and the
Civil War 1860-1869

Peyton McCrary, Abraham Lincoln and Reconstruction: The Louisiana
Experiment

Willie Lee Rose, Rehearsal for Reconstruction: The Port Royal
Experiment

Louis Gerteis, From Contraband to Freedman: Federal Policy Toward
Southern Blacks 1861-1865

April 21: Reconstruction and Historiography

Assignment

> William A. Dunning, <u>Reconstruction: Political and Economic</u>,
> <u>or</u> Walter L. Fleming, <u>The Sequel of Appomattox</u>

> *Kenneth M. Stampp, <u>The Era of Reconstruction</u>

> W. E. B. Du Bois, "Reconstruction and Its Benefits,"
> <u>American Historical Review</u>, 15 (1910), 781-99

> Bernard A. Weisberger, "The Dark and Bloody Ground of
> Reconstruction Historiography," <u>Journal of Southern History</u>,
> 25 (1959), 427-47

> Larry G. Kincaid, "Victims of Circumstance: An Interpretation
> of Changing Attitudes Toward Republican Policy Makers and
> Reconstruction," <u>Journal of American History</u>, 57 (1970), 48-66

> Herman Belz, "The New Orthodoxy in Reconstruction Historiography,"
> <u>Reviews in American History</u>, 1 (1973), 106-13

> Michael Les Benedict, "Equality and Expediency in the
> Reconstruction Era: A Review Essay," <u>Civil War History</u>,
> 23 (1977), 322-35

> Gerald Grob, "Reconstruction: An American Morality Play," in
> George A. Billias and Gerald Grob, eds., <u>American History</u>:
> <u>Retrospect and Prospect</u>, 191-231

> William G. Shade, "'Revolutions May Go Backwards': The American
> Civil War and the Problem of Political Development," <u>Social</u>
> <u>Science Quarterly</u>, 55 (1974), 753-67

Review Essays:

> Carl Degler, <u>The Other South: Southern Dissenters in the</u>
> <u>Nineteenth Century</u>

> James S. Allen, <u>Reconstruction: The Battle for Democracy</u>

> W. E. B. Du Bois, <u>Black Reconstruction in America</u>

> E. Merton Coulter, <u>The South During Reconstruction</u>

> Morton Keller, <u>Affairs of State: Public Life in Late</u>
> <u>Nineteenth Century America</u>

April 28: The Politics of Reconstruction

<u>Assignment</u>:

Read <u>one</u> of the following:

    Eric McKitrick, <u>Andrew Johnson and Reconstruction</u>

    LaWanda and John Cox, <u>Politics, Principle, & Prejudice 1865-66</u>

    William R. Brock, <u>An American Crisis, Congress and Reconstruction</u>

    Michael Les Benedict, <u>A Compromise of Principle: Congressional Republicans and Reconstruction, 1863-1869</u>

plus:

    C. Vann Woodward, "Seeds of Failure in Radical Race Policy," in Woodward, <u>American Counterpoint</u>, 163-83

    LaWanda and John Cox, "Negro Suffrage and Republican Politics: The Problem of Motivation in Reconstruction Historiography," <u>Journal of Southern History</u>, 33 (1967), 303-80

    Glenn M. Linden, "A Note on Negro Suffrage and Republican Politics," <u>Journal of Southern History</u>, 36 (1970), 411-20

    James M. McPherson, <u>Ordeal By Fire</u>, chaps. 30, 32

    C. Vann Woodward, <u>Origins of the New South</u>, chap. 2

    Allan Peskin, "Was There a Compromise of 1877?" and C. Vann Woodward, "Yes, There Was a Compromise of 1877," both in <u>Journal of American History</u>, 60 (1973), 63-73 and 215-23.

    Michael Les Benedict, "Southern Democrats in the Crisis of 1876-1877: A Reconsideration of Reunion and Reaction," <u>Journal of Southern History</u>, 46 (1980), 489-524.

<u>Review Essays</u>:

    Michael Perman, <u>Reunion Without Compromise: The South and Reconstruction 1865-1868</u>

    William Gillette, <u>The Right to Vote: Politics and Passage of the Fifteenth Amendment</u>

    William Gillette, <u>Retreat From Reconstruction: A Political History</u>, 1867-1878

April 28   Review Essays continued:

> Thomas Holt, <u>Black Over White: Negro Political Leadership in South Carolina during Reconstruction</u>
>
> Keith I. Polakoff, <u>The Politics of Inertia: The Election of 1876 and the End of Reconstruction</u>

May 5: Social and Economic Reconstruction

Assignment:

> *Roger Ransom and Richard Sutch, <u>One Kind of Freedom: The Economic Consequences of Emancipation</u>
>
> Ransom and Sutch, "Growth and Welfare in the American South of the Nineteenth Century," <u>Explorations in Entrepreneurial History</u>, 16 (1979), 207-35
>
> Harold D. Woodman, "Sequel to Slavery: The New History Views the Postbellum South," <u>Journal of Southern History</u>, 43 (1977), 523-54
>
> Jonathan Wiener, Robert Higgs, and Harold Woodman, "Class Structure and Economic Development in the American South, 1865-1955," <u>American Historical Review</u>, 84 (1979), 970-1006
>
> J. William Harris, "Plantations and Power: Emancipation on the David Barrows Plantation," unpublished paper.
>
> C. Vann Woodward, <u>Origins of the New South</u>, chaps. 1, 6
>
> James Tice Moore, "Redeemers Reconsidered: Change and Continuity in the Democratic South, 1870-1900," <u>Journal of Southern History</u>, 44 (1978), 357-78

Review Essays:

> Allen W. Trelease, <u>White Terror: The Ku Klux Klan Conspiracy and Southern Reconstruction</u>
>
> Jonathan M. Wiener, <u>Social Origins of the New South: Alabama 1860-1885</u>
>
> Leon Litwack, <u>Been in the Storm So Long: The Aftermath of Slavery</u>
>
> Donald G. Nieman, <u>To Set the Law in Motion: The Freedman's Bureau and the Legal Rights of Blacks 1865-1868</u>

May 5 Review Essays continued:

Jacqueline Jones, Soldiers of Light and Love: Northern
Teachers and Georgia Blacks 1865-1873

Lawrence N. Powell, New Masters: Northern Planters During
the Civil War and Reconstruction

JM/DR/cs 3/22/82 (40)

University of Virginia
HIUS 358: THE SOUTH SINCE 1865
Upper Division Undergraduates

Paul M. Gaston
205 Levering Hall
924-7939

Spring '1980

Office Hours:
Tu, 2-4; Th, 2-3;
and by appointment

REQUIRED READING

The following books, all required reading, are available at the Newcomb Hall Bookstore, in paperback editions, and are also on two-day reserve in Alderman Library:

Agee, James. Let Us Now Praise Famous Men
Carter, Dan T. Scottsboro: A Tragedy of the American South
Faulkner, William. Absalom, Absalom!
Moody, Anne. Coming of Age in Mississippi
Percy, William Alexander. Lanterns on the Levee
Smith, Lillian. Killers of the Dream
Woodward, C. Vann. Origins of the New South, 1877-1913
Woodward, C. Vann. The Strange Career of Jim Crow, 3rd revd. ed.

COURSE PLAN

We will meet on Tuesdays and Thursdays from 12:30 to 1:45; each meeting should combine lecture and class discussion. In the "Calendar of Class Meetings and Reading Assignments" that follows you will note the dates by which each reading assignment should be completed. Following this calendar should help to make each class meeting more successful for you. In addition to the common reading I will ask each of you to select a U. S. History textbook account of Reconstruction to read. During the course of the semester I will suggest articles and books that you might look at to follow up on particular interests. There will be one mid term test, on March 4, and two papers: a short essay on Absalom, Absalom! due January 24, and a longer review essay, due in April. I will hold office hours every Tuesday and Thursday after class and welcome the chance to talk to you about the course.

CALENDAR OF CLASS MEETINGS AND READING ASSIGNMENTS

Jan 17 Teaching and Learning History

22 Themes and Burdens in Southern History

24 Yoknapatawpha: The South in Microcosm?
Faulkner, Absalom, Absalom!, should be completed by this time; submit a short essay (4-5 typed pages) on the meaning of southern history that you find in the novel.

29 On Reconstructing the South
Start reading a U. S. History textbook account of Reconstruction

31 Reconstruction: Myths, Realities, Home Truths
Finish reading a U. S. History textbook account of Reconstruction

87

Feb 5 Redemption & Redeemers: Contours of a New South
         Woodward, _Origins_, chs. 1-2

      7 New South Politics and Priorities
         Woodward, _Origins_, chs. 3-4

     12 The Poverty of New South Progress
         Woodward, _Origins_, chs. 5-8

     14 The Populist Alternative
         Woodward, _Origins_, chs. 9-11

     19 White Supremacy Progressivism
         Woodward, _Origins_, chs. 12-17

     21 Jim Crow: Continuity, Change, and the Historian's Role
         Woodward, _Jim Crow_, chs. 1-3

     26 Negro Protest: "Of Mr. Booker T. Washington and Others"

     28 Race, Rape, and the Southern Lady
         Carter, _Scottsboro_, to be completed by this time

Mar 4 MID TERM EXAMINATION

      6 Southern Poverty: The Nation's #1 Economic Problem

     18 Darker Phases of Southern Life

     20 Dixie's Demagogues

     25 Life on the Farm: Three Tenant Families
         Agee, _Famous Men_, to be completed by this time

     27 The Savage South

Apr 1 The Southern Gentleman and the Meaning of Paternalism
         Percy, _Lanterns on the Levee_, to be completed by this time

      3 The Southern Awakening: Journalism and Scholarship

      8 The Southern Awakening: Letters and Politics

     10 Encounters with the Invisible Man--and Woman
         Smith, _Killers of the Dream_, to be completed by this time

     15 Simple Justice
         Woodward, _Jim Crow_, ch. 4

     17 Growing up in the Closed Society
         Moody, _Coming of Age_, to be completed by this time

HIUS 358, p. 3

Apr 22 Movement Culture: Black & White Together
        Woodward, *Jim Crow*, ch. 5

    24 Stateways and Folkways
        Woodward, *Jim Crow*, ch. 6

    29 Sutpen's Door: New Myths, Old Realities

May 5 FINAL EXAMINATION

REVIEW ESSAY

Each of you is to write one review essay on a combination of three books chosen from the list that follows. You will combine two books not on the required reading list with one book of required reading. Your essay should be no fewer than eight typewritten pages, no more than ten. Most of the books are on two-day reserve in Alderman Library; some are in the open stacks; and some are available in paperback in the west wing of the Newcomb Hall Bookstore.

More than a book review, but less than a term paper, your essay should be one that informs and interests us as an original contribution on a topic of your own choosing inspired by the books under review. At the same time, it should describe and analyze the unique characteristics of each of the books. The paper is an important part of the course, and should be written with great care. If you submit it by April 10 you will get it back with detailed comments at the next class meeting. You will then have the option of revising it, in light of the criticism, and submitting it a second time for the final grade. All papers are due by April 24.

Choose your combination from any one of the eight groups that follow. Select the first book listed (which is required reading for everyone) and any two others in the group you choose. (Consult me about substitutions.)

FAULKNER, WILLIAM. *ABSALOM, ABSALOM!*
Cash, W. J. *The Mind of the South*
Woodward, C. Vann. *The Burden of Southern History*
Davenport, F. Garvin. *The Myth of Southern History*
Twelve Southerners, *I'll Take My Stand: The South and the Agrarian Tradition*
O'Brien, Michael. *The Idea of the American South, 1920-1941*
Warren, Robert Penn. *All the King's Men*

WOODWARD, C. VANN. *ORIGINS OF THE NEW SOUTH*
Wright, Gavin. *The Political Economy of the Cotton South*
Mandle, Jay. *The Roots of Black Poverty*
Wiener, Jonathan. *Social Origins of the New South: Alabama, 1860-1885*
Hackney, Sheldon. *Populism to Progressivism in Alabama*
Gaston, Paul M. *The New South Creed: A Study in Southern Mythmaking*
Kousser, J. Morgan. *The Shaping of Southern Politics*

89

CARTER, DAN T. SCOTTSBORO: A TRAGEDY OF THE AMERICAN SOUTH
Ellison, Ralph. Invisible Man
Faulkner, William. Light in August
Rosengarten, Theodore. All God's Dangers
Scott, Ann F. The Southern Lady
Hall, Jacquelyn D. Revolt Against Chivalry
Kluger, Richard. Simple Justice

WOODWARD, C. VANN. THE STRANGE CAREER OF JIM CROW
Kousser, J. Morgan, The Shaping of Southern Politics
Rabinowitz, Howard N. Race Relations in the Urban South, 1865-1890
Coles, Robert. Children of Crisis, I: A Study of Courage and Fear
Kluger, Richard. Simple Justice
Brauer, Carl M. John F. Kennedy and the Second Reconstruction
Raines, Howell. My Soul is Rested

AGEE, JAMES. LET US NOW PRAISE FAMOUS MEN
Rosengarten, Theodore. All God's Dangers
Twelve Southerners. I'll Take My Stand: The South and the Agrarian Tradition
Gaston, Paul M. The New South Creed: A Study in Southern Mythmaking
Green, James R. Grass Roots Socialism
Coles, Robert. Children of Crisis, II: Migrants, Sharecroppers, Mountaineers
Goodwyn, Lawrence C. The Populist Moment

PERCY, WILLIAM ALEXANDER. LANTERNS ON THE LEVEE
Roark, James. Masters without Slaves
Wright, Gavin. The Political Economy of the Cotton South
Rosengarten, Theodore. All God's Dangers
Coles, Robert. Children of Crisis, II: Migrants, Sharecroppers, Mountaineers
Morris, Willie. North Toward Home
Goodwyn, Lawrence C. The Populist Moment

SMITH, LILLIAN. KILLERS OF THE DREAM
Hall, Jacquelyn D. Revolt Against Chivalry
Lumpkin, Katharine DuPre. The Making of a Southerner
Boyle, Sarah Patton. The Desegregated Heart
Sosna, Morton. In Search of the Silent South
Campbell, Will D. Brother to a Dragonfly
McGill, Ralph. The South and the Southerner

MOODY, ANNE. COMING OF AGE IN MISSISSIPPI
Wright, Richard. Black Boy
Murray, Albert. Train Whistle Guitar
Silver, James W. Mississippi: The Closed Society
Morris, Willie. North Toward Home
Watters, Pat, and Reese Cleghorn. Climbing Jacob's Ladder
Raines, Howell. My Soul is Rested

The South in American History

History 368 - Graduate Supplement

Vernon Burton

This syllabus follows a topical approach to the history and culture of the American South and is based primarily on the way in which I organize my lecture course (368) on the South in American History.

The readings are divided into two groups. Group A includes essential readings. Students should read all items in Group A. Group B has particularly relevant works to the topics. Students should be familiar with the major themes of the books in Group B. There are several ways to become familiar with books, but what I have in mind encompasses more than leisurely leafing through the pages of these important works. This bibliography is deliberately selective. When students wish to go beyond my suggested readings, they should first consult the excellent bibliographical essays in Arthur Link and Rembert Patrick (eds.) Writing Southern History and James M. McPherson, et. al., Blacks in America.

The South

         I   The Culture of the South
        II   When and Why the Old South
       III   Plantation Slavery
        IV   Comparative Slavery and Slave Revolts
         V   Social Structure and Cause of the Civil War
        VI   The Civil War and Reconstruction
       VII   The New South
      VIII   Populism and Progressivism
        IX   Modernization
         X   The Nadir of Race Relations
        XI   Turning Toward the Apogee?
       XII   The Contemporary South

I. The Culture of the South

A. Common Reading:

Francis B. Simkins, THE EVERLASTING SOUTH, Ch. II.
C. Vann Woodward, THE BURDEN OF SOUTHERN HISTORY. Chs. I,II,IX,X.
T. Harry Williams, ROMANCE AND REALISM IN SOUTHERN POLITICS, pp. 1-16.
D.Grantham (ed.), THE SOUTH AND THE SECTIONAL IMAGE, Chs. I, X, and XI.
Frank Vandiver (ed.), THE IDEA OF THE SOUTH, pp. 43-56.
David Potter, THE SOUTH AND THE SECTIONAL CONFLICT, Chs. I,II, AND III.
Frederick J. Turner, THE SIGNIFICANCE OF SECTION IN AMERICAN HISTORY
      (title essay)
Charles G. Sellers, THE SOUTHERNER AS AMERICAN, Chs. VI & VII.

B.

Howard Odum, et al., SOUTHERN REGIONS OF THE UNITED STATES
Donald Davidson, THE ATTACK ON LEVIATHAN
W. J. Cash, THE MIND OF THE SOUTH
David Bertelson, THE LAZY SOUTH
Twelve Southerners, I'LL TAKE MY STAND
Rupert Vance, THE HUMAN GEOGRAPHY OF THE SOUTH
W. T. Couch, THE CULTURE OF THE SOUTH
Howard Odum and Howard E. Moore, AMERICAN REGIONALISM

B. (cont.)

John Hope Franklin, THE MILITANT SOUTH
Allison Davis, & Burleigh and Mary Gardner, DEEP SOUTH
John Dollard, CASTE AND CLASS IN SOUTHERN TOWN
Merrill Jensen, REGIONALISM IN AMERICA
Earl E. Thorpe, EROS AND FREEDOM IN SOUTHERN LIFE AND THOUGHT
Louis D. Rubin, Jr.& James J. Kilpatrick(eds.), THE LASTING SOUTH
Willie Morris (ed.) THE SOUTH TODAY

II. When and Why the Old South

A. Common Readings:

From Link and Patrick (eds.), WRITING SOUTHERN HISTORY:

1. Hugh F. Rankin, "The Colonial South"
2. Charles G. Sellers, "The American Revolution"
3. Ernest M. Lander,Jr., "The 'Critical Period'"
4. Malcolm C. McMillan, "Jeffersonian Democracy and the Origins of
   Sectionalism"

Staughton Lynd, "Beyond Beard," in Barton J. Bernstein (ed.)
    TOWARDS A NEW PAST
John R. Alden, THE FIRST SOUTH
Jesse T. Carpenter, THE SOUTH AS A SELF CONSCIOUS MINORITY

B.

1. William R. Taylor, CAVALIER AND YANKEE
2. Rollin Osterweiss, ROMANTICISM AND NATIONALISM IN THE OLD SOUTH
3. William W. Freehling, PRELUDE TO CIVIL WAR
4. Wesley Frank Craven, WHITE, RED, AND BLACK: THE SEVENTEENTH-CENTURY
   VIRGINIANS

III. Plantation Slavery

A. Common Reading:

Meier and Rudwick, FROM PLANTATION TO GHETTO, 47-64.
Weinstein and Gatell (eds.), AMERICAN NEGRO SLAVERY, 37-63,98-111,221-33,259-93,.
Stanley Elkins, SLAVERY, 1-139,22 -3   335-41.
    "The Question of Sambo," NEWBERRY LIBRARY BULLETIN, V (Dec.1958),14-40.
Eugene Genovese, "Rebelliousness and Docility in the Negro Slave:
    A Critique of the Elkins Thesis," and George M. Fredrickson and
    Christopher Lasch, "Resistance to Slavery," in CIVIL WAR HISTORY, XIII
    (December, 1967), 293-329.
Eugene Genovese, "Race and Class in Southern History: An Appraisal of the
    Work of Ulrich Bonnell Phillips," AGRICULTURAL HISTORY XLI (October,
    1967), 345-58.
E Franklin Frazier, THE NEGRO FAMILY IN THE UNITED STATES (abridged edition
    1966), 17-69.
Ophelia Settle, "Social Attitudes during the Slave Regime: Household Servants
    Versus Field Hands," in Meier and Rudwick (eds.), THE MAKING OF BLACK
    AMERICA, I, 148-52.
John Blassingame, THE SLAVE COMMUNITY

B.

1. U. B. Phillips, AMERICAN NEGRO SLAVERY
2. Kenneth Stampp, THE PECULIAR INSTITUTION
3. Richard Wade, SLAVERY IN THE CITIES
4. Eugene Genovese, ROLL JORDAN ROLL
5. Robert McColley, SLAVERY IN JEFFERSONIAN VIRGINIA
6. Gerald W. Mullen, FLIGHT AND REBELLION
7. Peter H. Wood, BLACK MAJORITY

IV. Comparative Slavery and Slave Revolts

A. Common Reading:

David B. Davis, "Slavery," in C. Vann Woodward (ed.), THE COMPARATIVE APPROACH
    TO AMERICAN HISTORY, 121-34.
Frank Tannenbaum, "The Negro in the Americas," in M. Drimmer(ed.), BLACK HISTORY
    56-75.
Weinstein & Gatell(eds.), AMERICAN NEGRO SLAVERY, 25-34,199-218, 310-332.
Arnold Sio, "Society, Slavery and the Slave," SOCIAL AND ECONOMIC STUDIES,
    XVI (September, 1967), 330-344.
Laura Foner & Eugene Genovese, SLAVERY IN THE NEW WORLD
Raymond A. & Alice H. Bauer, "Day to Day Resistance to Slavery," JOURNAL OF
    NEGRO HISTORY, XXVII (October, 1942), 388-419.
Harvey Wish, "American Slave Insurrections before 1861," JOURNAL OF NEGRO
    HISTORY, XXII (July, 1937), 299-320.
Herbert Aptheker, "Slave Guerrilla Warfare," in Aptheker (ed.), TO BE FREE:
    STUDIES IN AMERICAN NEGRO HISTORY, 11-30.
Meier and Rudwick, THE MAKING OF BLACK AMERICA, I, 165-197.
Richard Wade, "The Vesey Plot: A Reconsideration," JOURNAL OF SOUTHERN HISTORY
    XXX (May 1964), 143-161.
Eugene Genovese, "The World the Slaveholders Made" and "The Legacy of Slavery
    and the Roots of Black Nationalism," plus the comments by Aptheker,
    Woodward, and Kofsky, and Genovese's reply in STUDIES ON THE LEFT, VI
    (November-December, 1966), 3-65.

B:

1. Herbert Klein, SLAVERY IN THE AMERICAS
2. Herbert Aptheker, AMERICAN NEGRO SLAVE REVOLTS
3. William S. Drewry, THE SOUTHAMPTON INSURRECTION,and John W. Lofton,
    INSURRECTION IN SOUTH CAROLINA: THE TURBULENT WORLD OF DENMARK VESEY.
4. Carl Degler, NEITHER BLACK NOR WHITE

V. Social Structure and the Cause of the Civil War

A. Common Reading:

From Link and Patrick, WRITING SOUTHERN HISTORY:
    Edwin A. Miles, "The Jacksonian Era"
    James C. Bonner, "Plantation and Farm"
    Herbert J. Doherty,Jr., "The Mind of the Antebellum South"
    Charles E. Cauthen, "The Coming of the Civil War"

Eugene Genovese, THE POLITICAL ECONOMY OF SLAVERY
Eugene Genovese, "Marxian Interpretations of the Slave South" in Barton J.
    Bernstein (ed.), TOWARDS A NEW PAST.

A. (cont.)

James McPherson, "Slavery and Race: A Review Essay," in HARVARD PERSPECTIVES
    IN AMERICAN HISTORY 1971
Lee Benson, "An Approach to the Scientific Study of American Civil War
    Causation," in THE SCIENTIFIC STUDY OF AMERICAN HISTORY
Thomas J. Pressly, AMERICANS INTERPRET THEIR CIVIL WAR
Robert Fogel and Stanley Engerman, TIME ON THE CROSS
James M. Banner,Jr., "The Problem of South Carolina," in THE HOFSTADTER
    AEGIS, ed. by Stanley Elkins & Eric McKitrick, 60-93.

B.

1. Frank L. Owsley, PLAIN FOLK OF THE OLD SOUTH, and Fabian Linden,
    "Economic Democracy in the Slave South: An Appraisal of Some Recent
    Views," JOURNAL OF NEGRO HISTORY XXXI (April, 1946, 140-189, and
    Randolph B. Campbell, "Planters and Plain Folk," JOURNAL OF SOUTHERN
    HISTORY, vol. XL (August 1974), pp. 369-398.
2. Charles S. Sydnor, GENTLEMEN FREEHOLDERS:Carl Bridenbaugh, MYTHS AND
    REALITIES, Robert E. and Katherine B. Brown, VIRGINIA, 1705-1786:
    DEMOCRACY OR ARISTOCRACY: and relevant portions of Jackson T. Main,THE SO-
    CIAL STRUCTURE OF REVOLUTIONARY AMERICA.
3. Ralph Wooster, THE SESSION CONVENTIONS OF THE SOUTH: Bernard Bailyn,
    "Politics and Social Structure in Virginia," in James M. Smith (ed.),
    SEVENTEENTH CENTURY AMERICA, 90-115; Barrington Moore, THE SOCIAL
    ORIGINS OF DICTATORSHIP AND DEMOCRACY; and Louis Hartz, THE LIBERAL
    TRADITION IN AMERICA.
4. Relevant portions of Ray Allen Billington, AMERICA'S FRONTIER HERITAGE:
    Stanley Elkins and Eric McKitrick, "A Meaning for Turner's Frontier,"
    POLITICAL SCIENCE QUARTERLY, LXIX, pp. 321-353 (July 1954), and
    pp. 562-602 (December 1954); Thomas P. Abernethy, "Democracy and the
    Southern Frontier," JOURNAL OF SOUTHERN HISTORY, IV (February 1938),
    3-13; Robert Dykstra, THE CATTLE TOWNS.

VI. The Civil War and Reconstruction

    A. Common Reading:

    From Link and Patrick, WRITING SOUTHERN HISTORY:
        Mary Elizabeth Massey, "The Confederate States of America: The Homefront"
        John G. Barrett, "The Confederate States of America at War on Land
            and Sea"
        Vernon L. Wharton, "Reconstruction"

    Kenneth Stampp, RECONSTRUCTION
    David Donald (ed.), WHY THE NORTH WON THE CIVIL WAR.
    Meier and Rudwick, FROM PLANTATION TO GHETTO, Ch. 4.
    C. Vann Woodward, in Harold Hyman (ed.), NEW FRONTIERS OF THE AMERICAN
        RECONSTRUCTION.
    Issue of CIVIL WAR HISTORY, December 1974.

    B.

    Willie Lee Rose, REHEARSAL FOR RECONSTRUCTION
    James McPherson, THE STRUGGLE FOR EQUALITY
    William S. McFeely, YANKEE STEPFATHER
    William A. Dunning, RECONSTRUCTION, POLITICAL AND ECONOMIC
    Joel Williamson, AFTER SLAVERY

B. (cont.)

C. Vann Woodward, THE STRANGE CAREER OF JIM CROW
John Hope Franklin, "History of Racial Segregation in the United States,"
    in Meier and Rudwick, THE MAKING OF BLACK AMERICA, II, 3-13.
John and LaWanda Cox, POLITICS, PRINCIPLE AND PREJUDICE
Eric McKitrick, ANDREW JOHNSON AND RECONSTRUCTION
Peter Kolchin, FIRST FREEDOM, AND W.E.B. Dubois, BLACK RECONSTRUCTION

VII. The New South

A. Common Reading:

From Link and Patrick, WRITING SOUTHERN HISTORY
    Paul M. Gaston, "The New South."
C. Vann Woodward, ORIGINS OF THE NEW SOUTH, Chs. 1-6.
Paul Buck, THE ROAD TO REUNION
Allen Trelease, "Who Were the Scalawags?" JOURNAL OF SOUTHERN HISTORY,
    XXIX (November 1963), 445-468.
Thomas B. Alexander, "Persistent Whiggery in the Confederate South,"
    JOURNAL OF SOUTHERN HISTORY, XXVII (August 1961), 324-25;
    "Persistent Whiggery in Alabama and the Lower South," ALABAMA REVIEW,
    XII (January 1959), 35-52; "The Basis of Alabama's Ante-Bellum
    Two-Party System" ALABAMA REVIEW, XIX (October 1966), 243-276.
David Donald, "The Scalawag in Mississippi Reconstruction," JOURNAL OF
    SOUTHERN HISTORY, X (November 1944), 447-46?.
Sheldon Hackney, "ORIGINS OF THE NEW SOUTH in Retrospect," JOURNAL OF SOUTHERN
    HISTORY, XXXVIII (May 1972), 191-216.

B.

1. William B. Hesseltine, CONFEDERATE LEADERS IN THE NEW SOUTH
2. Allen Going, BOURBON DEMOCRACY IN ALABAMA
3. Vincent DeSantis, REPUBLICANS FACE THE SOUTHERN QUESTION, or Stanley
   Hirshon, FAREWELL TO THE BLACK SHIRT
4. Paul Gaston, THE NEW SOUTH CREED

VIII. Populism and Progressivism

A. Common Reading:

From Link and Patrick, WRITING SOUTHERN HISTORY
    Allen J. Going, THE AGRARIAN REVOLT.
    Dewey W. Grantham, Jr., THE TWENTIETH-CENTURY SOUTH

Robert Durden, THE CLIMAX OF POPULISM
C. Vann Woodward, ORIGINS OF THE NEW SOUTH
Arthur S. Link, "The Progressive Movement in the South, 1870-1914,"
    NORTH CAROLINA HISTORICAL REVIEW, XXIII (April 1946), 172-195.
C. Vann Woodward, "The Populist Heritage and the Intellectual in THE BURDEN
    OF SOUTHERN HISTORY, Symposium on Populism, Agricultural History,
    XXXIX (April 1965).
Theodore Saloutos, "The Professors and the Populists," Agricultural History,
    XL (October 1966), 235-254.
Herbert Shapiro, "The Populists and the Negro: A Reconsideration," in
    Meier and Rudwick, THE MAKING OF BLACK AMERICA, II, 27-36.
Jack Abramowitz, "The Negro in the Populist Movement," JOURNAL OF NEGRO
    HISTORY, XXXVIII (July 1953), 257-289.
Sheldon Hackney, ed. POPULISM: THE CRITICAL ISSUES

B.

1. Sheldon Hackney, POPULISM TO PROGRESSIVISM IN ALABAMA
2. Albert D. Kirwan, THE REVOLT OF THE REDNECKS
3. Norman Pollack, THE POPULIST MIND
4. M. P. Rogin, THE INTELLECTUALS AND McCARTHY.
5. C. Vann Woodward, TOM WATSON: AGRARIAN REBEL and Francis B. Simkins,
   PITCHFORK BEN TILLMAN, and William J. Cooper, THE CONSERVATIVE REGIME

IX. Modernization, Social and Economic

A. Common Reading:

George Tindall, THE EMERGENCE OF THE NEW SOUTH
Allen Sindler, CHANGE IN THE CONTEMPORARY SOUTH
Avery Leiserson, THE SOUTH IN THE 1960's

B.

1. (a) Thomas D. Clark, THE EMERGING SOUTH
   (b) Calvin B. Hoover and Benjamin U. Ratchford, ECONOMIC RESOURCES AND
       POLICIES OF THE SOUTH
2. (a) William H. Nicholls, SOUTHERN TRADITION AND REGIONAL PROGRESS
   (b) Robert A. Lively, THE SOUTH IN ACTION
3. (a) John F. Stover, RAILROADS OF THE SOUTH
   (b) Broadus Mitchell and George Mitchell, THE INDUSTRIAL REVOLUTION IN
       THE SOUTH

X. The Nadir of Race Relations

A. Common Reading:

C. Vann Woodward, THE STRANGE CAREER OF JIM CROW
August Meier, NEGRO THOUGHT IN AMERICA
Leslie H. Fishe, Jr., "The Negro in the New Deal," WISCONSIN MAGAZINE OF
   HISTORY, XLVIII (Winter 1964-65).

B.

1. Hylan G. Lewis, BLACKWAYS OF KENT
2. Gunnar Myrdal, AN AMERICAN DILEMMA
3. Louis Harlen, SEPARATE AND UNEQUAL
4. Vernon Lane Wharton, THE NEGRO IN MISSISSIPPI, and George Brow Tindall,
   SOUTH CAROLINA NEGROES, 1877-1900
5. Pete Daniel, THE SHADOW OF SLAVERY

XI. Turning Toward the Apogee?

A. Common Reading:

Benjamin Muse, TEN YEARS OF PRELUDE and THE NEGRO REVOLUTION
Allen Sindler, "The Unsolid South," in Allen Westin (ed.), THE USES OF POWER
DAEDULUS, "The Negro American," (Fall 1965 and Winter 1966).

B.

1. Donald R. Mathews and James Prothro, NEGROES AND THE NEW SOUTHERN POLITICS
2. Elizabeth Sutherland, LETTERS FROM MISSISSIPPI, and James Foreman,
   SAMMY YOUNGE
3. Howard Zinn, SNCC: THE NEW ABOLITIONISTS
4. Theodore Rosengarten, ALL GOD'S DANGERS.

UNIVERSITY OF VIRGINIA

HIUS 309   The Age of Jefferson and Jackson: The U.S. 1787-1845   Fall 1978

Mr. Michael F. Holt
Office: 203 Randall Hall
Phone: 924-7146

This course will focus primarily, but not exclusively, on American political development from the writing of the Constitution to the emergence of the
slavery extension problem in the 1840s. Aside from completing the reading
and attending lectures, students will have three main requirements: a midterm
and then a final examination that will cover both the reading and lectures
and a six-to-eight page paper on one of the topics to be listed later. The
midterm will be on Monday, October 16th. The midterm and paper will each
count 30% of the final grade; the final examination will count 40%. Due dates
for the paper will depend upon the topic chosen, but the purpose of each topic
is to force you to be more precise and analytical in your approach to the
required texts.

Except where noted, all of the books listed below are available in paperback editions at the Newcomb Hall Bookstore. The other assignments are on
reserve at the Alderman Library. The order of readings is as follows:

Week of

Sept. 4   Forrest McDonald, The Presidency of George Washington
           Paul Goodman, "The First American Party System," in William N.
           Chambers and Walter Dean Burnham, eds., The American Party Systems.
           (RESERVE)

Sept. 11   Richard Buel, Securing the Revolution: Ideology and American Politics
           1789-1815

Sept. 18   Richard Ellis, The Jeffersonian Crisis: Courts and Politics in the
           Young Republic

Sept. 25   James S. Young, The Washington Community, 1800-1828

Oct. 2   Don E. Fehrenbacher, The Era of Expansion, 1800-1848

Oct. 9   Alexis de Tocqueville, Democracy in America, Vol. II, pp. 3-352.

Oct. 16   Midterm exam on Monday, October 16. No additional assignment.

Oct. 23   James C. Curtis, Andrew Jackson and the Search for Vindication

Oct. 30   Arthur M. Schlesinger, Jr., The Age of Jackson (Omit Chapter 25,
           28-29, 31-36)

Nov. 6   Lee Benson, The Concept of Jacksonian Democracy: New York as a Test
           Case

-2-

Week of

Nov. 13   William W. Freehling, <u>Prelude to Civil War. The Nullification</u>
          <u>Controversy in South Carolina</u>

Nov. 20   Eugene Genovese, <u>The Political Economy of Slavery</u>, Introduction
          and Chapters 1 and 10 (RESERVE)

Nov. 27   James B. Stewart, <u>Holy Warriors: The Abolitionists and American</u>
          <u>Slavery</u>

          The following are the topics for papers and the dates on which each
is due. Students should choose ONE of these topics.

1. Compare and contrast the arguments of Richard Buel and Richard Ellis
    about the nature, role, and impact of Revolutionary ideology or republi-
    canism on political development before 1815. Do they mean the same thing
    by republicanism? Are the books complementary or contradictory?

    Due: Friday, September 29.

2. Precisely how do Lee Benson and Arthur Schlesinger, Jr. differ in their
    accounts of New York politics in the Jacksonian period? What explains
    the differences, if any, in their interpretations? Which book do you
    find more persuasive and why?

    Due: Friday, November 10.

3. "Alexis de Tocqueville was both a remarkably accurate observer and an
    astute prophet. A careful reading of <u>Democracy in America</u> allows one
    to isolate or define all the issues of political conflict in the
    Jacksonian period and to predict the contours that conflict took."

    Evaluate the accuracy of this assertion on the basis of the reading you
    have done. Remember that the Nullification crisis is in the Jacksonian
    period.

    Due: Monday, November 27.

GRADUATE CENTER, CITY UNIVERSITY OF NEW YORK
History U751 Jacksonian Democracy   1983

Course Description

Discussion of the important developments that shaped society
in the United States during the second quarter of the 19th century.
and the historical literature on these developments. As the very
title of the course makes clear, historians often treat the period
as though national politics is the key to understanding it. The
premise of the course is that there are many keys to understanding.
Politics on the local and state as well as the national level will
not be neglected. But equally central were the diverse economic,
social, demographic, religious, and intellectual trends that the
course also examines. A term paper, analytical and historiographical,
will be required, on a theme that the student has discussed with
the instructor.

Topics

1 An overview of American society, 1820-1850
2 The historians' controversy over the nature of the era
3 Changes in agriculture and industry
4 "Revolutions" in transportation, commerce, and banking
5 Labor
6 The growth of cities: new institutions, new problems
7 Opportunity, equality, social mobility and social structure
8 Blacks slave and free
9 "The female appendage": women in Jacksonian America
10 Religious developments
11 The democratization of politics
12 The Great Men of National Politics
13 Jacksonian Democrats, Whigs, and Party Conflict
14 The minor parties
15 Reform

There is of course a vast literature on the period. A
comprehensive treatment is Edward Pessen, Jacksonian America:
Society, Personality, and Politics, revised edition (Dorsey Press,
1978). The course outline contains the readings for each topic.

History U751 Jacksonian Democracy

Course Outline

Topics and readings

1 An overview of American society, 1820-1850

Edward Pessen, Jacksonian America: Society, Personality, and
    Politics, revised edition (Dorsey Press, 1978)

2 The historians' controversy over the nature of the era

Ronald P. Formisano, "Toward a Reorientation of Jacksonian Politics:
A Review of the Literature, 1959-1975," Journal of American History,
    64 (June 1976), 42-65
Alfred A. Cave, Jacksonian Democracy and the Historians (U of Florida
    Press 1964)
Charles G. Sellers, Jr., "Andrew Jackson versus the Historians,"
    Mississippi Valley Historical Review, 44 (March 1958), 615-634
E. Pessen, Jacksonian America, Bibliographical essay, 329-367

3 Changes in agriculture and industry

    Gavin Wright, The Political Economy of the Cotton South
(Norton 1978)
    Stanley L. Engerman, "A Reconsideration of Southern Economic
Growth, 1770-1860," Agricultural History, 49 (1975), 343-361
    Paul W. Gates, The Farmers' Age: Agriculture, 1815-1860
(Holt, R & W 1967
    Alan Dawley, Class and Community: The Industrial Revolution in
Lynn (Harvard 1976)

4 "Revolutions" in transportation, commerce, and banking

    George R. Taylor, The Transportation Revolution, 1815-1860
(Holt 1951)
    Robert G. Albion, The Rise of New York Port (NY 1939)
    Bray Hammond, Banks and Politics in America from the Revolution
to the Civil War (Princeton 1957)
    Walter B. Smith, Economic Aspects of the Second Bank of the
United States (Harvard 1953)

5 Labor

    Walter Hugins, Jacksonian Democracy and the Working Class
(Stanford 1960)
    Edward Pessen, Most Uncommon Jacksonians: The Radical Leaders
of the Early American Labor Movement (State Univ. of NY Press, 1967)
    Alan Dawley, Class and Community
    Paul G. Faler, Mechanics and Manufacturers in the Early American
Industrial Revolution, 1780-1860 (State U of NY Press, 1981)
    Bruce Laurie, Working People of Philadelphia, 1800-1850
(Temple University Press 1980)

6 The growth of cities: new institutions, new problems

Sam Bass Warner, Jr., The Private City: Philadelphia in Three
Periods of Its Growth (Phila. 1968)
Richard C. Wade, The Urban Frontier (Harvard 1959)
Leonard P. Curry, "Urbanization and Urbanism in the Old South:
A Comparative View," Journal of Southern History, 40 (1974), 43-60
Edward Pessen, "The Social Configuration of the Antebellum City,"
Journal of Urban History, 2 (May 1976), 267-306
Kathleen N. Conzen, Immigrant Milwaukee, 1836-1860 (Harvard 1976)

7 Opportunity, equality, social mobility and social structure

Edward Pessen, Riches, Class, and Power Before the Civil War
(D.C. Heath 1973)
R.B. Campbell and R.G. Lowe, Wealth and Power in Antebellum
Texas (College Station, Texas 1977)
Robert Doherty, Society and Power: Five New England Towns,
1800-1860 (U of Amherst Press 1977)
E. Pessen, "The Egalitarian Myth and the American Social Reality:
Wealth, Mobility, and Equality in the "Era of the Common Man,""
American Historical Review, 76 (October 1971), 989-1034
E. Pessen, "Who Has Power in the Democratic Capitalistic
Community? Reflections on Antebellum New York City," New York
History, LVIII (April 1977), 129-155
E. Pessen, "How Different From Each Other Were the Antebellum
North and South?" AHR, 85 (December 1980), 1119-1149

8 Blacks slave and free

Stanley Elkins, Slavery (U of Chicago 1959)
Eugene D. Genovese, Roll Jordan Roll: The World the Slaveowners
Made (New York 1974)
Lawrence W. Levine, Black Culture and Black Consciousness:
Afro-American Folk Thought From Slavery to Freedom, (NY 1977)
John W. Blassingame, The Slave Community: Plantation Life in
the Antebellum South (NY 1972)
Herbert G. Gutman, The Black Family in Slavery and Freedom,
1750-1825 (New York 1976)
Leon Litwack, North of Slavery: The Negro in the Free States,
1790-1860 (U of Chicago Press 1961)
Ira Berlin, Slaves Without Masters: The Free Negro in the
Antebellum South (NY 1974)

9 "The female appendage": women in Jacksonian America

Barbara Welter, Dimity Convictions: the American Woman in the
19th Century (U of Ohio Press 1976)
Nancy F. Cott, The Bonds of Womanhood: Woman's Sphere in New
England, 1780-1835 (Yale 1977)
Carroll Smith-Rosenberg, "Beauty, the Beast, and the Militant
Woman," American Quarterly, 73 (October 1971), 562-584
Ann Douglas Wood, "The 'Fashionable Diseases': Women's Complaints
and Their Treatment in 19th Century America," Journal of Interdsicip-
linary History, 4 (Summer 1973), 25-52
Mary P. Ryan, Cradle of the Middle Class: The Family in Oneida
County, NY, 1790-1865 (Cambridge U Press 1981)

10 Religious developments

   T.L. Smith, Revivalism and Social Reform (Harper 1957)
   Whitney R. Cross, The Burned-Over District (Cornell 1950)
   Clifford S. Griffin, Their Brothers' Keepers: Moral Stewardship in the United States, 1800-1865 (Rutgers 1960)
   Paul E. Johnson, A Shopkeeper's Millenium: Society and Revivals in Rochester, New York, 1815-1837 (Hill and Wang 1978)
   Jay P. Dolan, The Immigrant Church: New York's Irish and German Catholics, 1815-1865 (Johns Hopkins 1975)

11 The   Democratization of politics

   Richard P. McCormick, The Second American Party System: Party Formation in the Jacksonian Era (U of North Carolina 1966)
   Arthur M. Schlesinger Jr., The Age of Jackson (Little Brown 1945)
   Marvin Meyers, The Jacksonian Persuasion (Stanford 1957)
   G.G. Van Deusen, The Jacksonian Era, 1828-1848 (Harper 1959)
   L.D. White, The Jacksonians: An Administrative History (NY 1954)

12 The Great Men of National Politics

   James C. Curtis, Andrew Jackson and the Search for Vindication (Little Brown 1976)
   Robert V. Remini, Andrew Jackson and the Course of American Freedom (Harper 1981)
   Irving H. Bartlett, Daniel Webster (Norton 1978)
   Charles M. Wiltse, John C. Calhoun (Indianapolis, 1944-1951)
   Charles G. Sellers, Jr., James K. Polk, 2 vol. (Princeton, 1957, 1966)

13 Jacksonian Democrats, Whigs, and Party Conflict

   Lee Benson, The Concept of Jacksonian Democracy: New York As a Test Case (Princeton 1961)
   John M. McFaul, The Politics of Jacksonian Finance (Cornell 1972)
   Michael P. Rogin, Fathers and Children: Andrew Jackson and the Subjugation of the American Indian (New York 1975)
   J. Mills Thornton III, Politics and Power in a Slave Society: Alabama, 1800-1860 (Lousiana State U Press 1978)
   Herbert Ershkowitz and William G. Shade, "Consensus or Conflict? Political Behavior in the State Legislatures During the Jacksonian Era," Journal of American History, 58 (December 1971), 591-621
   Daniel Walker Howe, The Political Culture of the American Whigs (Univ. of Chicago Press 1979)

14 The minor parties

Edward Pessen, "The Working Men's Party Revisited," Labor History, IV (Fall 1963), 203-226)
Frank Gerrity, "The Masons, the Anti-Masons, and the Pennsylvania Legislature, 1834-1836," Pa. Magazine of History and Biography, 99 (April 1975), 180-206
Ronald P. Formisano with Kathleen Kutolowski, "Antimasonry and Masonry: The Genesis of Protest, 1826-1827," American Quarterly, (Summer 1977) 139-165
Walter Hugins, Jacksonian Democracy and the Working Class
Leo Hershkowitz, "The Loco-Foco Party of New York: Its Origins and Career, 1835-1847," New-York Historical Society Quarterly, 46 (July 1962), 305-329

15 Reform

David J. Rothman, The Discovery of the Asylum: Social Order and Disorder in the New Republic (Boston 1971)
Michael B. Katz, The Irony of Early School Reform (Harvard 1968)
Lois W. Banner, "Religious Benevolence as Social Control: A Critique of an Interpretation," Journal of American History, 60 (June 1973), 23-41
Carroll Smith-Rosenberg, Religion and the Rise of the American City: The New York City Mission Movement (Cornell 1971)
Martin Duberman, ed, The Antislavery Vanguard (Princeton 1965)
Aileen Kraditor, Means and Ends in American Abolitionism: William Lloyd Garrison and His Critics, 1834-1850 (New York 1969)

COLUMBIA UNIVERSITY

DEPARTMENT OF HISTORY
611 Fayerweather Hall

History W3121x
Fall 1982

Professor Eric Foner
502 Fayerweather Hall

The United States in the Nineteenth Century: 1815-1850

The Age of Jackson: 1815-1840

(America in 1815; The Rise of the West; Missouri Compromise
and Monroe Doctrine; Tocqueville's America; Creation of the
Democratic Party; Jacksonian Democracy; The Second Party
System; The Bank War; Workingmen and Workingwomen in the Age
of Jackson; The Panic of 1837 and Depression)

Required Readings:

Richard Hofstadter, The American Political Tradition, chs. 1-3
Frederick Jackson Turner, Frontier and Section (ed. Ray
        Billington), ch. 3
George Dangerfield, The Awakening of American Nationalism,
        chs. 4, 8-9, 11-12
Alexis deTocqueville, Democracy in America (Vintage edition),
        I, 180-205, 246-297; II, 172-202, 256-279
Richard Hofstadter, The Idea of a Party System, pp. 170-252
Marvin Meyers, The Jacksonian Persuasion, chs. 1-3
Glyndon Van Deusen, The Jacksonian Era, chs. 2-7
Bray Hammond, Banks and Politics in America, ch. 12
Arthur Schlesinger, Jr., The Age of Jackson, chs. 7-11, 14-15,
        24-26
Lee Benson, The Concept of Jacksonian Democracy, chs. 1, 4,
        8-9
William Freehling, Prelude to Civil War, Chs. 4-5, 9
Harry Watson, Jacksonian Democracy and Community Conflict,
        chs. 1, 4-7
Ronald P. Formisano, The Birth of Mass Political Parties, chs. 1,
        3-4, 6-7
Thomas Cochran, Frontiers of Change, chs. 3-6
Anthony Wallace, Rockdale, chs. 6-7
Frank O. Gatell, ed., Essays on Jacksonian America, chs. 3, 8,
        15, 18, 20

Midterm Date: October 21

Slavery, the Old South, and the Roots of Revolution

(Origins of the Slave Labor System; the Slave Community;
Resistance to Slavery; the Planter Class; the Economics of
Slavery; the Emergence of Pro-Slavery Thought; the Free Black;
Antebellum Reform; Abolitionism; the Politics of Reform and
Expansionism; Free Soil and the Compromise of 1850)

Required Readings:

Kenneth Stampp, The Peculiar Institution, chs. 2-5
Stanley Elkins, Slavery, chs. 2-4
Frederick Douglass, The Life and Times of Frederick Douglass,
    chs. 1-15
Eugene D. Genovese, Roll, Jordan, Roll, pp. 3-25, 161-284,
    365-88
Herbert Gutman, The Black Family in Slavery and Freedom, chs.
    1-2, 6-7
James Oakes, The Ruling Race, chs. 2-5, 7
Eugene D. Genovese, The Political Economy of Slavery, chs. 1,
    6-7
Robert Fogel and Stanley Engerman, Time on the Cross, I, chs.
    1-4, 6-7
Leon Litwack, North of Slavery, chs. 3, 5
Ira Berlin, Slaves Without Masters, chs. 6-9
Paul Johnson, A Shopkeepers' Millennium, chs. 3-7
Eleanor Flexner, Century of Struggle, pt. I
Ronald Walters, The Antislavery Appeal, chs. 1,2,5,7
David J. Rothman, The Discovery of the Asylum, chs. 4,6,10
David Donald, Lincoln Reconsidered, ch. 2
Richard Hofstadter, The American Political Tradition, ch. 4
James B. Stewart, Holy Warriors, chs. 1-6
Vincent Harding, There Is a River, chs. 3-7
Glyndon Van Deusen, The Jacksonian Era, chs. 8-13
David Potter, The Impending Crisis, chs. 4-5

HIUS 729   Recent Literature in 19th Century American Political History
    Fall 1982

Mr. Michael F. Holt
Office: 203 Randall Hall
Telephone: 924-6418
Office Hours: M.W. 10-12 and by appointment

    This colloquium will consider some of the more interesting recent
literature on American political history from about 1830 to 1880. Books and
articles have been selected because they illustrate different approaches to
the writing of political history, because of the importance of their
interpretations, and because they provide an introduction to newer
methodologies. All of the books and articles have been placed on reserve in
Clemons Library. I have also ordered copies of all the books to be placed on
sale at the Newcomb Hall Bookstore with the exception of Benedict's Compromise
of Principle which is out of print. Students are urged to buy as many of
these as possible, but they should be warned that because the books are
relatively new, many of them are available only as rather expensive hardbacks.

    For each week's discussion all students in the colloquium are expected to
prepare a three-page critical evaluation of the readings to be discussed.
This paper should summarize the author's thesis, place it in an
historiographical context if possible, and point out the major strengths and
weaknesses of the book. Here the book's evidence, methodology, and
conclusions must be assessed. Then, at the beginning of each session, I shall
call on one student to read his paper to launch class discussion.

    What follows is a schedule of the weekly assignments.

Sept. 8 Introductory Meeting. No Assignment.

Sept. 15 Rush Welter, The Mind of America, 1820-1860

Sept. 22 Alternative Approaches to the Political Ideology of the Middle Period

            Daniel Walker Howe, The Political Culture of the American Whigs

                            or

            George Forgie, Patricide in the House Divided: A Psychological
            Interpretation of Lincoln and His Age

Sept. 29 William R. Brock, Parties and Political Conscience: American
            Dilemmas 1840-1850

Oct. 6 The Nature of Antebellum Southern Politics

        J. Mills Thornton III, Politics and Power in a Slave Society:
        Alabama 1800-1860

                    or

        William J. Cooper, Jr., The South and the Politics of Slavery,
        1828-1856

Oct. 13 The Secession Crisis

        Michael Johnson, Toward a Patriarchial Republic: The Secession
        of Georgia

                    or

        William Barney, The Secessionist Impulse: Alabama and
        Mississippi in 1860

All students should also read the following articles:

Peyton McCrary et. al., "Class and Party in the Secession Crisis: Voting
Behavior in the Deep South, 1856-1860," Journal of Interdisciplinary History,
8 (Winter 1978), 429-457.

Daniel J. Crofts, "The Union Party of 1861 and the Secession Crisis,"
Perspectives in American History, 11 (1977-78), 327-376.

Oct. 20 The Causes of the Civil War I

David M. Potter, The Impending Crisis 1848-1861; Eric Foner, "The Causes
of the American Civil War: Recent Interpretations and New Directions," Civil
War History, 20 (Sept. 1974), 197-214; Eric Foner, "Politics, Ideology, and
the Origins of the American Civil War," in George Frederickson (ed.), A Nation
Divided, pp. 15-34.

Oct. 27 The Causes of the Civil War II and the Nature of Antebellum Northern
          Politics

Michael F. Holt, The Political Crisis of the 1850s; Kevin Sweeney, "Rum,
Romanism, Representation, and Reform: Coalition Politics in Massachusetts,
1847-1853," Civil War History, 22 (June 1976), 116-137; Dale Baum, "Know
Nothingism and the Republican Majority in Massachusetts: The Political
Realignment of the 1850s," Journal of American History, 64 (March 1978),
959-986; Kenneth Greenberg, "Civil War Revisionism," Reviews in American
History, (June 1979), 202-208.

Nov. 3 Civil War Politics and Emancipation

Herman Belz, Emancipation and Equal Rights: Politics and Constitutionalism in the Civil War Era; La Wanda Cox, Lincoln and Black Freedom: A Study in Presidential Leadership.

Nov. 10 Reconstruction I

Michael Les Benedict, A Compromise of Principle; Michael Les Benedict, "Preserving the Constitution: The Conservative Basis of Radical Reconstruction," Journal of American History, 61 (June 1974), 65-90.

Nov. 17 Reconstruction II

Thomas Holt, Black over White: Negro Leadership in South Carolina during Reconstruction

Nov. 24 Reconstruction III

William Gillette, Retreat from Reconstruction

Dec. 1 An Overview I

Paul Kleppner, The Third Electoral System, 1853-1892

Students should also read one of the following articles:

Richard L. McCormick, "Ethno-cultural Interpretations of American Voting Behavior," Political Science Quarterly, 89 (June 1974), 351-377.

James E. Wright, "The Ethnocultural Model of Voting: A Behavioral and Historical Critique," American Behavioral Scientist, 16 (May-June 1973), 35-56.

James R. Green, "Behavioralism and Class Analysis: A Review Essay on Methodology and Ideology," Labor History, 13 (Winter 1972), 89-106.

Dec. 8 An Overview II

Paul Kleppner et. al., The Evolution of American Electoral Systems

Richard L. McCormick, "The Party Period and Public Policy: An Exploratory Hypothesis," Journal of American History, 66 (Sept. 1979), 279-298.

Richard L. McCormick, Review article on realignments in the Journal of Interdisciplinary History (summer 1982)

PRINCETON UNIVERSITY
Department of History

History 584

SLAVERY, ANTISLAVERY, CIVIL WAR AND RECONSTRUCTION

Fall Term, 1983-84   Prof. McPherson

History Seminar Room, C Floor, Firestone Library, Wednesday, 9:00 - 12:00 A.M.

History 584 is offered this year as a reading/research seminar focusing on important themes of sectional conflict and its resolution, 1830-1877. The seminar is designed to complement History 588 by enabling students to read intensively and to carry out research projects in selected topics covered more broadly in that course. Although students will not have yet taken History 588, their previous work as undergraduates or graduate students should have provided them with adequate background. Nevertheless, the seminar will begin with five weeks of concentrated reading to prepare the ground for the research papers that will follow. Since some students may have already read some of the assigned material, supplemental readings are suggested for those who wish to explore the subjects further.

The pattern of class meetings will be divided into three parts. The first six meetings (including the organizational session) through October 19 will be devoted to discussion of assigned readings and of student oral reports. At each of these meetings (excluding the first), one or two students will make a brief oral report summarizing the main issues raised by the readings and suggesting possible questions for further research. Out of the discussion provoked by the readings and the reports may come some good ideas for student seminar research papers.

By the end of October each student should have worked out, at least in general terms, the topic of a research paper and should have begun the bibliographical work for the research. There will be no class meetings during November. Students should use this period to do research for their papers. In the early part of December there will be at least two class meetings at which each student will submit a brief prospectus outlining the subject of his or her research, the questions the paper will address, and the kinds of sources being used.. Class discussion of these prospectuses should provide advice and criticism useful to the authors when they undertake to write their papers. During January, two or three class sessions will be scheduled for discussion of the research papers.

Students are free to select topics of their own choice for research papers, so long as the topics fall within the general chronological and thematic limits of the course. The only requirement is that the scope and length of the paper (20-30 pages) be such that the research can be completed at Princeton or within a reasonable distance and the papers written for seminar presentation by mid-January. For a brief list of bibliographical and finding aids and of guides to sources available at Princeton and elsewhere, see the end of this syllabus.

The assigned readings in the first part of the course are designed to introduce students to certain kinds of sources and to the ways in which historians have used these sources. So far as possible, the assignment each week pairs a selection of primary sources with selections from the writings of historians based on these and similar sources. Some of the readings also discuss the problems of reliability and utilization of sources.

The titles marked below with an asterisk are available for purchase in paperback editions at the University Store. Students are encouraged to buy them. The Reserve Desk of the library has promised to put a single copy of each title listed for assigned reading on reserve in the Graduate Study Room. Further information on the availability of certain titles will be made available as the course proceeds.

Sept. 14: Introduction and Organization

Sept. 21: Slavery

Assigned Readings:

David Brion Davis, "Slavery and the Post-World War II Historians," Daedalus, 103 (1974), 1-16.

*Paul D. Escott, Slavery Remembered: A Record of Twentieth-Century Slave Narratives, chaps 1-4 (pp. 3-118) plus Appendices, pp. 183-199

Norman R. Yetman, ed., Life Under the "Peculiar Institution: Selections from the Slave Narrative Collection. Read the Introduction (pp. 1-6) and browse in the narratives.

John W. Blassingame, ed., Slave Testimony: Two Centuries of Letters, Speeches, Interviews, and Autobiographies. Read the Introduction (pp. xvii-lxv) and browse in the documents.

Gilbert Osofsky, ed., Puttin' On Ole Massa. Read the Introduction (pp. 9-44) and browse in the narratives.

Willie Lee Rose, ed., A Documentary History of Slavery in North America. Read the Introduction (pp. 3-12) and browse in the documents.

Suggested Supplemental Readings:

Ulrich B. Phillips, American Negro Slavery
Kenneth M. Stampp, The Peculiar Institution
Stanley M. Elkins, Slavery
Anne J. Lane, Ed., The Debate Over Slavery
John W. Blassingame, The Slave Community
Robert Fogel and Stanley Engerman, Time on the Cross
Paul A. David, et al., Reckoning With Slavery: A Critical Study in the Quantitative History of American Negro Slavery
George P. Rawick, From Sundown to Sunup: The Making of the Black Community
Charles H. Nichols, Many Thousand Gone: The Ex-Slaves' Account of Their Bondage and Freedom
Herbert Gutman, The Black Family in Slavery and Freedom
Lawrence W. Levine, Black Culture and Black Consciousness: Afro-American Folk Thought From Slavery to Freedom
Eugene Genovese, Roll, Jordan, Roll: The World the Slaves Made

Leslie Howard Owens, This Species of Property: Slave Life and Culture in the Old South
Willie Lee Rose, Slavery and Freedom

Sept. 28: Slavery and Ideology

Assigned Readings:

*Hugh Hawkins, ed., The Abolitionists: Means, Ends, and Motivation (2nd ed.)
Lewis Perry and Michael Fellman, ed., Antislavery Reconsidered: New Perspectives
 on the Abolitionists, pp. vii-xvi, 3-23.
*Drew Gilpin FAust, ed., The Ideology of Slavery: Proslavery Thought in the
 Antebellum South. Read the Introduction and as many of the selections as
 possible, with special attention to selections IV, V, and VII (Hammond,
 Nott, and Fitzhugh).

Suggested Supplemental Readings:

Gilbert Hobbs Barnes, The Anti-Slavery Impulse
Aileen Kraditor, Means and Ends in American Abolitionism
Merton L. Dillon, The Abolitionists: The Growth of a Dissenting Minority
Gerald Sorin, Abolitionism: A New Perspective
James B. Stewart, Holy Warriors: The Abolitionists and American Slavery
Ronald Walters, The Antislavery Appeal
Martin Duberman, ed., The Antislavery Vanguard
Richard H. Sewell, Ballots for Freedom: Antislavery Politics in the U.S.
David Brion Davis, The Problem of Slavery in the Age of Revolution, 1770-1823
William H. Pease and Jane Pease, eds., The Antislavery Argument
Benjamin Quarles, Black Abolitionists
Jane H. Pease and William H. Pease, They Who Would Be Free
William S. Jenkins, Pro-Slavery Thought in the Old South
Eugene D. Genovese, The Political Economy of Slavery
Eugene D. Genovese, The World The Slaveholders Made
James Oakes, The Ruling Race: A History of American Slaveholders
Catherine Clinton, The Plantation Mistress: Woman's World in the Old South

Oct 5: Causes of the Civil War

Assigned Readings:

*Edwin C. Rozwenc, ed., The Causes of the American Civil War (2nd ed.)
*Kenneth M. Stampp, ed., The Causes of the Civil War (1974 rev. ed.)
Joel Silbey, "The Civil War Synthesis in American Political History," Civil War
 History, 10 (June 1964), 130-40.
Eric Foner, "The Causes of the American Civil War: Recent Interpretations and
 New Directions," Civil War History, 20 (Sept. 1974), 197-214.

Suggested Supplemental Readings:

David M. Potter, The Impending Crisis 1848-1861
Eric Foner, Free Soil, Free Labor, Free Men
Don E. Fehrenbacher, The Dred Scott Case
Thomas J. Pressly, Americans Interpret Their Civil War
Michael Holt, The Political Crisis of the 1850's
Avery Craven, The Coming of the Civil War
William Barney, The Road to Secession
David M. Potter, Lincoln and His Party in the Secession Crisis
Kenneth M. Stampp, And The War Came
Steven A. Channing, Crisis of Fear: Secession in South Carolina
William L. Barney, The Secessionist Impulse: Alabama and Mississippi in 1860
Michael P. Johnson, Toward a Patriarchal Republic: The Secession of Georgia
Alan Nevins, The Ordeal of the Union (2 vols) and The Emergence of Lincoln (2 vols.)

Oct. 12: Emancipation

Assigned Readings:

*Leon Litwack, Been in the Storm So Long: The Aftermath of Slavery, chaps. 1-6
James M. McPherson, ed., The Negro's Civil War (Copies will be distributed
    gratis by the instructor).

Suggested Supplemental Readings:

Bell I. Wiley, Southern Negroes 1861-1865
Willie Lee Rose, Rehearsal for Reconstruction
Benjamin Quarles, The Negro in the Civil War
Benjamin Quarles, Lincoln and the Negro
James M. McPherson, The Struggle for Equality
Robert Cruden, The Negro in Reconstruction
Louis Gerteis, From Contraband to Freedman
Edward Magdol, A Right to the Land: Essays on the Freedmen's Community
William McFeely, Yankee Stepfather: O.O. Howard and the Freedmen
Roger L. Ransom and Richard Sutch, One Kind of Freedom: The Economic
    Consequences of Emancipation

LaWanda Cox, Lincoln and Black Freedom
Robert F. Durden, ed., The Gray and the Black: The Confederate Debate on Emancipation
Ira Berlin et al., eds., Freedom: A Documentary History of Emancipation: Series II,
    The Black Military Experience

Oct. 17: Reconstruction

Assigned Readings:

*Litwack, Been in the Storm So Long, chaps. 7-10
William Dusinberre,

*Kenneth M. Stampp and Leon Litwack, ed., Reconstruction: An Anthology of Revision -
    ist Writings
*Hans Trefousse, ed., Reconstruction: America's First Effort at Racial Democracy
J. Morgan Kousser and James M. McPherson, eds., Region, Race, and Reconstruction,
    pp. 283-416

Suggested Supplemental Readings:

Kenneth M. Stampp, The Era of Reconstruction
John Hope Franklin, Reconstruction
James S. Allen, Reconstruction: The Battle for Democracy
W.E.B. Du Bois, Black Reconstruction in America
Eric McKitrick, Andrew Johnson and Reconstruction
William R. Brock, An American Crisis: Congress and Reconstruction
Michael Les Benedict, A Compromise of Principle:Congressional Repub-
    licans and Reconstruction
Allen W. Trelease, White Terror: The Ku Klux Klan Conspiracy and
    Southern Reconstruction
C. Vann Woodward, Reunion and Reaction: The Compromise of 1877 and the
    End of Reconstruction
Vincent DeSantis, Republicans Face the Southern Question, 1877-1897
Stanley P. Hirshson, Farewell to the Bloody Shirt: Northern
    Republicans and the Southern Negro, 1877-1893
William Gillette, Retreat from Reconstruction, 1869-1879
Terry L. Seip, The South Returns to Congress: Men, Economic Measures, and Inter-
    sectional Relationships, 1868-1879
Otto Olsen, ed., Reconstruction and Redemption in the South

BIBLIOGRAPHICAL GUIDES AND RESEARCH AIDS

The following is a brief, selective list of bibliographical and finding aids to historical sources. All of these guides are available at the Firestone Library, most of them in the reference room. They are listed in the card catalog. No effort is made here to specify every relevant research aid, for many of them (e.g. THE READER'S GUIDE TO PERIODICAL LITERATURE) have been familiar to you since high school. The focus here is on guides to the kinds of material covered in this course, especially slavery, abolition, black history, the Civil War, Reconstruction, etc. For a far more thorough guide to sources for these and all other aspects of American history, consult Part I of Frank Freidel, ed., Harvard Guide to American History (rev. ed., Harvard Univ. Press, 1974), a handbook which despite its cost should be owned by all graduate students in American history. But above all, do not forget that the best guide to materials available in Firestone Library consists of the subject headings in the card catalog (e.g. slavery; abolition; Negro; United States; Civil War; etc) In addition, Firestone Library possesses a special collection (the Pierson Collection) of 19th-century books, pamphlets, and other materials, many of them quite rare and valuable, dealing with slavery, antislavery, the sectional conflict, and the war. All of the works in this collection are listed under author, title, and subject in the card catalog; in addition, the shelf-list in the Order and Cataloging Division of the library provides a convenient card index to the entire collection. Other special guides to collections in the Princeton University Libraries are listed in Part C, below.

A. Guides to Secondary (and some Primary) Sources

Frank Freidel, Ed., HARVARD GUIDE TO AMERICAN HISTORY, 2 vols., rev. ed.
William H. Cartwright and Richard L. Watson, Jr., eds., The Reinter-
    pretation of American History and Culture (1973).
Don E. Fehrenbacher, ed., Manifest Destiny and the Coming of the Civil
    War (Goldentree Bibliographies in American History)
David Donald, ed., The Nation in Crisis, 1861-1877 (Goldentree Biblio-
    graphies in American History).
Allan Nevins, James J. Robertson, Jr., and Bell Wiley, eds., Civil
    War Books: A Critical Bibliography (2 vols., 1967, 1969).
James G. Randall and David Donald, The Civil War and Reconstruction,
    "Bibliography" (1969)
James M. McPherson et al., Blacks in America: Bibliographical Essays
    (1971)
The Annual volumes of Writings in American History (1904-1959), with
    a cumulative index for all volumes through 1940. (Each volume
    is an exhaustive listing of articles and books published each year)
America: History and Life (1964-   ). A quarterly publication with
    annual indexes containing abstracts of articles on American history
    published in scholarly periodicals.
The quarterly or annual lists of articles, under subject headings, in
    the American Historical Review, Journal of American History,
    Journal of Southern History, Civil War History, and other scholarly
    journals are also invaluable .

Warren F. Kuehl, ed., Dissertations in History: An Index to History
    Dissertations in American Universities, 2 vols.
Earl H. West, ed., A Bibliography of Doctoral Research on the Negro,
    1933-1966.
Doctoral Dissertations Accepted by American Universities, annual
    volumes, superseded by Dissertation Abstracts: Abstracts of
    Dissertations and Monographs on Microfilm.

B. Guides to Primary (and some Secondary) Sources

The Union List of Serials
The Union List of Newspapers (Gregory's)
Newspapers on Microfilm
Negro Newspapers on Microfilm
Richard W. Hale, ed., Guide to Photocopied Historical Materials in
    the United States and Canada
Philip M. Hamer, ed., Guide to Archives and Manuscripts in the
    United States
The National Union Catalog of Manuscript Collections (several
    volumes, ongoing)
U. S. Superintendent of Documents, Checklist of United States Public
    Documents, 1789-1970
Comprehensive Guide to the National Archives
Kenneth W. Munden and Henry Putney Beers, Guide to Federal Archives
    Relating to The Civil War
Catalog of National Archives Microfilm Publications
Walter Schatz, ed., Directory of Afro-American Resources
Dictionary Catalog of the Schomburg Collection of Negro Literature
    and History (3 vols.)
Black Studies: Select Catalog of National Archives and Records
    Service Microfilm Publications
American Missionary Association Archives, Author and Added Entry
    Catalog (3 vols.)

C. Special Guides to Princeton University Resources, and Misc.

Princeton University Library, Microform Holdings of Historical
    Interest (1968), and Supplement (1970)
Some Special Libraries of Princeton University Library and Notes on
    Certain Holdings of the Center for Research Libraries
Princeton University Library, The Manuscript Collections of the
    Princeton University Library: An Introductory Survey, by
    Alexander P. Clark, and Additions to Manuscript Collections.
Louise G. Anderson,"A Finding List of Slave Narratives in Firestone Library"

The Office of Survey Research at Princeton is a member of the Inter-
university Consortium for Political Research, and possesses on
computer tape all of the electoral and congressional roll-call data
plus other material available from the Consortium at Ann Arbor. This
material is available to students and faculty in the Department of
History without cost. A complete list of all material available is
at the Office for Survey Research.

The Department of History provides to all of its undergraduate majors
a booklet that may be of value to graduate students as well. It is
entitled "A Guide to Independent Work, History Department, Princeton
University," and copies are available from the undergraduate secretary
of the History Department.

COLUMBIA UNIVERSITY   DEPARTMENT OF HISTORY
                                       611 Fayerweather Hall

                        History G8677x

            THE CIVIL WAR AND RECONSTRUCTION

Professor Eric Foner
Fall, 1982

September 13: Introductory Session

September 20: Fighting the Civil War

                    T. Harry Williams, Lincoln and His Generals

September 27: The Politics of Emancipation

                    V.J. Voegeli, Free But Not Equal
                    Hans L. Trefousse, The Radical Republicans,
                       chs. 6-8
                    George Fredrickson, ed., A Nation Divided,
                       35-56

October 4: The Confederate Experience

                    Emory Thomas, The Confederate Nation
                    William Chambers and Walter D. Burnham, eds.,
                       The American Party System, ch. 5
                    Fredrickson, ed., A Nation Divided, 57-80

October 11: Emancipation: The Black Response

                    Leon F. Litwack, Been in the Storm So Long
                    Orville V. Burton and Robert C. McMath, Jr.,
                       eds., Towards A New South?, 71-102

October 18: Black Reconstruction -- An Overview

                    W.E.B. DuBois, Black Reconstruction in
                       America, chs. 1-2, 4, 7, 9, 14-17
                    Francis B. Simkins, "New Viewpoints of
                       Southern Reconstruction," Journal of
                       Southern History, V (February, 1939),
                       49-61

October 25: Andrew Johnson, the Radicals, and Reconstruction

                    Eric L. McKitrick, Andrew Johnson and Re-
                       construction

                        115

November 8: The Decline of Radicalism

> David Montgomery, Beyond Equality, chs. 2,
> 5-7, 9
> Ellen C. DuBois, Feminism and Suffrage, chs. 2,
> 3, 6
> John G. Sproat, "The Best Men", chs. 1-3

November 15: Planter and Laborer

> Jonathan Wiener, Social Origins of the New
> South, pts. I-III
> Eric Foner, Politics and Ideology in the
> Age of the Civil War, chs. 6-7
> Burton and McMath, eds., Toward a New South?,
> pp. 246-64
> Joseph D. Reid, Jr., "Sharecropping as an
> Understandable Market Response," Journal
> of Economic History, XXXIII (March, 1973),
> 106-30
> Thomas F. Armstrong, "From Task Labor to Free
> Labor: The Transition Along Georgia's Rice
> Coast, 1820-1880," Georgia Historical Quar-
> terly, LXIV (Winter, 1980), 432-47

November 22: Carpetbaggers and Scalawags in Reconstruction

> Otto Olsen, ed., Reconstruction and Redemption
> in the South, chs. 3-6
> David Donald, "The Scalawag in Mississippi
> Reconstruction," Journal of Southern History,
> X (November, 1944), 447-60
> J. Morgan Kousser and James M. McPherson, eds.,
> Region, Race and Reconstruction, 51-88, 315-
> 94
> Lawrence Powell, "The American Land Company and
> Agency," Civil War History, XXI (December,
> 1975), 293-308

November 29: The Case of South Carolina

> Thomas Holt, Black Over White
> Joel Williamson, After Slavery, chs. 9-13
> Vernon Burton, "Race and Reconstruction:
> Edgefield County, South Carolina," Journal
> of Social History, XII (Fall, 1978), 31-56

December 6: <u>Reconstruction in Comparative Perspective</u>

> George M. Fredrickson, <u>White Supremacy</u>, chs.
> 4-5
> David Sansing, ed., <u>What Was Freedom's Price?</u>,
> 93-114
> Sidney W. Mintz, "Slavery and the Rise of
> Peasantries," <u>Historical Reflections</u>, VI
> (Summer, 1979), 213-42
> Kousser and McPherson, eds., <u>Region, Race and
> Reconstruction</u>, 283-314
> Frederick Cooper, "Peasants, Capitalists and
> Historians: A Review Article," <u>Journal of
> Southern African Studies</u>, VII (April, 1981),
> 285-314

December 13: <u>1877 and After</u>

> C. Vann Woodward, <u>Origins of the New South</u>,
> chs. 1-8, 12-13
> William B Hesseltine, "Economic Factors in the
> Abandonment of Reconstruction," <u>Mississippi
> Valley Historical Review</u>, XII (September,
> 1935), 191-210
> George C. Rable, "Southern Interests in the
> Election of 1876: A Reappraisal" <u>Civil War
> History</u>, XXVI (December, 1980), 347-61

YALE UNIVERSITY

HISTORY 140a

THE AMERICAN WEST TO 1850

INSTRUCTOR: Bill Cronon, 409 Calhoun.
  Phones: 436-0738 (office); 562-1187 (home). Please, no calls to
    either of these numbers after 8:00 P.M.
  Office Hours: 2:00-4:00 Thursdays. Please DO NOT stop by my office at times
    other than these unless you have first called for an appointment.

LECTURES will be held on Tuesdays and Thursdays, ordinarily running from 11:30 to
12:20. I will occasionally lecture for a full hour, however, so that we will
sometimes finish at 12:30.

SECTIONS will be announced on Tuesday, September 14, and will be held for the
first time either on Thursday or Friday of that week. They are required for all
students.

A NOTE ON THE READINGS:

  Readings for the course are extensive but not difficult, averaging from 150 to
200 pages per week; I have tried to reduce the reading load at key points in the
semester when papers or exams fall due. Readings are designed to provide a core
set of issues for discussion sections and to supplement the themes of the lectures
with both primary and secondary materials.

  The central "text" will be Howard Lamar's Reader's Encyclopedia of the American
West (henceforth referred to as REAW), a recently published volume that is one of
the good things of western history. Unlike an ordinary textbook, which is
traditionally written as a chronological narrative, the Encyclopedia is just that:
an alphabetical listing of names, places, and topics. You should refer to it
often. Because the book can easily become overwhelming, I've listed a number of
possible subjects for reading under each lecture topic. Those in CAPITALS are
required reading; those marked with an asterisk are important but less essential;
and others are listed just in case you want to do some exploring on your own. Try
to take an hour every week or two simply to wander through REAW more or less
randomly, following topics as they catch your eye, or tracing one reference to
another. Part of "doing history" is being willing to follow your curiosity, and
learning how to find answers to questions you didn't realize you had when you
started out. Wandering through the REAW--and then using its references to move on
to other sources--is much more akin to what historians actually do than is reading
a textbook narrative. Try to create your own stories and problems from the
fragments it provides. Quite frankly, you could probably do reasonably well in
this course even if you never looked at REAW, but you'd enjoy yourself a lot
less--the book is one I hope you'll want to return to long after the course is
over.

  One comment on expenses: I realize that the total cost of books for this course
is substantial, and strongly encourage you to share books or use Cross Campus
reserve copies whenever you can. REAW in particular usually costs $24.95,
although there are a number of copies at the Co-op which I was able to obtain at
$9.98: buy now while the supply lasts, because additional copies will cost over
twice as much. Buy REAW if you possibly can, but, if this is too difficult for
your budget, remember that there are several copies in CCL, and none of the weekly

118

assignments in it should take more than a couple of hours. A word of advice: read REAW after lectures in order to reinforce main points and make your wandering more productive. This syllabus provides a very detailed outline of what will be happening in the course, and I strongly advise you to refer to it often as you plan your studying.

Required readings are listed below. You will not necessarily be reading each volume in its entirety. Titles marked with an asterisk (*) have been used before at Yale, so you may be able to find used copies either at the Co-op or the Atticus Sales Annex.

Thomas Hariot, Brief and True Report of...Virginia
*Francis Jennings, The Invasion of America
*Charles Gibson, Spain in America
*W. J. Eccles, The Canadian Frontier
John Jakle, Images of the Ohio Valley
*Ray Allan Billington, The Far Western Frontier
*Black Hawk, Autobiography
*John Mack Faragher, Women and Men on the Overland Trail

In addition to the above titles, you are required to own (and use frequently) a high-quality map of the United States which shows both political and physiographic features. The Co-op has copies of Rand McNally's "Contemporary" map available for purchase at the text information desk, but if you own a good atlas or map already, don't bother to buy another. You will be expected to read William Strunk and E. B. White's Elements of Style before writing your mid-term paper; the book is worth its weight in gold and I'd recommend that you own a copy. The mid-term paper assignment requires you to read one of the following three books:

*Timothy Flint, Biographical Memoir of Daniel Boone
*Caroline Kirkland, A New Home--Who'll Follow?
*James Fenimore Cooper, The Prairie

The Co-op also has copies of Henry Nash Smith's Virgin Land, which you may find helpful in writing both of your two papers. Finally, if you feel you would like a good textbook survey of American western history to supplement these readings and the lectures, the Co-op has copies of Ray Allan Billington's Westward Expansion, the standard survey of the subject. It is particularly good for its massive annotated bibliography, and if you're thinking about doing a senior essay in western history, you may want to become familiar with it.

PAPERS AND EXAMINATIONS:

Aside from the readings listed above, there will be two papers and two examinations (a mid-term and an abbreviated final that will cover only the second half of the course). The first paper (4-6 pages) will be on the image of the frontier as presented by one of three books written about the West in the years before 1840 (see list above). The second paper (8-12 pages) will involve reading one or two overland trail diaries and discussing what they tell us about the social history of the frontier in the mid-nineteenth century, in part as a test and critique of Faragher's Women and Men on the Overland Trail.

Final grades will be taken as the average of the two tests (20% each), the two writing assignments (15% and 25% respectively), and classroom discussion (20%). Late papers will not be greeted enthusiastically, and will be marked down by at least one-third of a grade.

WEEKLY OUTLINE OF LECTURES AND ASSIGNMENTS:

(Note: Numbers in parentheses after the section reading indicate how many pages of non-REAW reading are required during that week. Again, REAW assignments are indicated as follows: CAPITALS are required; asterisked items are important but not crucial; and all other listings are purely optional.)

WEEK 1: INTRODUCTORY

Sept. 7: Why is the West at Yale?
REAW: collectors and collections of Western Americana, FRONTIER THEORY, manifest destiny, *noble savage concept, FREDERICK JACKSON TURNER.

Sept. 9: North America--An Introduction to the Continent
Study a good quality map of the U.S. before and after lecture.
REAW: Arkansas R, cartography, Colorado R, Columbia R, Cumberland Gap, Gila R, Great American Desert, Imperial Valley, Mississippi R, Pecos R, PHYSIOGRAPHY (most important section), Platte R, Red River of the North, Rio Grande, Sacramento R, Salinas R, San Joaquin R, Snake R, *vegetation, *wildlife (see also separate sections on key animals you may be interested in, such as beaver, buffalo, deer, fisheries, horse, etc.), Willamette R.

WEEK 2: ANTHROPOLOGIZING INVADERS AND INVADED

Sept. 14: Indian Prehistory
REAW: ARCHEOLOGY OF THE NORTH AMERICAN INDIANS, *Indian Languages.

Sept. 16: Indians and Europeans at Contact
REAW: There are many entries for most of the chief groups of Indians, so spend some time wandering. Key entries which you should definitely browse through, if not read closely, are Apache, Cheyenne and Arapaho, Comanche, Five Civilized Tribes, Hopi, *Horse, Huron, INDIANS AND WHITE DISEASES, Indians of California, Indians of the Great Basin, Indians of the Northwest Coast, Iroquois Confederacy, Navaho, Pueblo, Siouan Tribes, etc.

SECTION: Hariot, Brief and True Report of...Virginia (all, pp 1-91);
Jennings, Invasion of America, (pp 32-104).   (163pp)

WEEK 3: SPANISH DAWN OF EMPIRE

Sept. 21: Spanish Beginnings
REAW: *Cabeza da Vaca, Cabrillo, *Coronado, de Soto, EXPLORATION (SPANISH), Florida, Narvaez, Ponce de Leon.

Sept. 23: Across the Rio Grande
REAW: Adobe, *Anza, Guevavi, KINO, NEW MEXICO, *New Mexico Missions, Old Spanish Trail, Palace of the Governors, *Roman Catholic Missionaries, *Serra, Texas.

SECTION: Gibson, Spain in America, (all).   (215pp)

WEEK 4: LINEAR EMPIRES OF THE NORTH

Sept. 28: France and the Beaver
REAW: BEAVER, FRONTIER (CANADA), FUR TRADE (IN THE COLONIES), HURON, IROQUOIS CONFEDERACY, Francis Parkman, Ribault.

Sept. 30: French Exploration and Settlement
    REAW: *Chouteau, EXPLORATION (FRENCH), French Dialects, *French
    Heritage, Iberville, Illinois (settlement of), LaClede, LaSalle,
    *Mississippi Valley (French and Spanish Rivalry), New Orleans, Roman
    Catholic Missionaries.
SECTION: Eccles, The Canadian Frontier, (all). (191pp)

WEEK 5: THE ENGLISH COLONIES IN AMERICA
Oct. 5: Virginia and New England--The Earliest Years
    REAW: *Connecticut, EXPLORATION (ENGLISH), FUR TRADE (IN THE COLONIES),
    Iroquois, *Massachusetts (settlement of), NEW ENGLAND (SETTLEMENT OF), New
    Haven (settlement of), Opechancanough, Plymouth Colony, Powhatan, Rhode
    Island (settlement of), *Virginia (settlement of).
Oct. 7: Patterns of Settlement
    REAW: headright system, LAND POLICY (IN THE COLONIES), LAND SYSTEM
    (SOUTHERN), Maine (settlement of), Negroes on the Frontier, New Jersey
    (settlement of), New York (settlement of), North Carolina (settlement of),
    Pennsylvania (settlement of), South Carolina (settlement of), VIRGINIA
    (SETTLEMENT OF).
SECTION: Jennings, Invasion of America, (pp 128-45, 177-326). (166pp)

WEEK 6: EUROPEANS AND INDIANS AT TRADE AND WAR
OCT. 12: The Colonial Wars
    REAW: Brant, Cherokee War, COLONIAL WARS, Cornstalk, Fort Stanwik (1768
    treaty of), HUDSON'S BAY COMPANY, INDIAN-WHITE RELATIONS (1763-75),
    IROQUOIS CONFEDERACY, Johnson (William), King Philip's War, McGillivray
    (Alexander), Lord Dunmore's War, Natchez War, Pontiac's Rebellion,
    Protestant Missionaries, *American Revolution, *British Administrative
    Policy, Clark (George Rogers), forts (revolutionary), *Franklin
    (Benjamin), Paris (Treaties of 1763, 1783), Regulators of North Carolina,
    Sullivan-Clinton Campaign.
  Oct. 14: MID-TERM EXAM
NO SECTION THIS WEEK.

WEEK 7: NEW NATION, NEW WEST
Oct. 19: Kentucky Images (Guest Lecture by Howard Lamar)
    REAW: DANIEL BOONE, James Fenimore Cooper, Davy Crockett, Timothy Flint,
    Harrod, INDIAN CAPTIVITY NARRATIVES, *Kentucky Frontier Stations,
    *Kentucky Rifle.
Oct. 21: Trans-Appalachian West
    REAW: Articles of Confederation, BURR CONSPIRACY, *Fallen Timbers,
    Franklin (State of), Harrod, Henderson, *Jay's Treaty, KENTUCKY
    (SETTLEMENT OF), LAND COMPANIES, LAND POLICY (TO 1850), NORTHWEST
    ORDINANCE, OHIO (SETTLEMENT OF), Old West, PUBLIC DOMAIN, Scotch Irish,
    Spanish Conspiracy, Tennessee (Settlement of), TERRITORIAL SYSTEM,
    Washington (George), Watauga Association, Whiskey Rebellion, *Wilkinson.
SECTION: Jakle, Images of the Ohio Valley, (all). (174pp)

WEEK 8: ACROSS THE MISSISSIPPI
Oct. 26: The Great Explorations
    REAW: CLARK (WILLIAM), LEWIS (MERRIWETHER), LEWIS AND CLARK EXPEDITION,
    LOUISIANA PURCHASE, LOUISIANA TERRITORY, Mississippi River (source of),
    Nootka Sound (controversy of), PIKE (ZEBULON), *Sacagawea, San Ildefonso
    (treaty of), Schoolcraft (Henry), LONG (STEPHEN).

Oct. 28: Mountain Men
    REAW: There are many entries on explorations and the fur trade, so again, do some wandering on your own. Key entries include *American Fur Co., ASHLEY, ASTOR, CHOUTEAU, EXPLORATION (U.S.), FUR TRADE (IN THE U.S.), fur trading forts, Mackenzie (Kenneth), *Missouri Fur Co., *Northwest Co., *Rocky Mountain Fur Co., SMITH (JEDEDIAH), trappers.

SECTION: Three reports to be given by volunteers on the books by Flint, Cooper, and Kirkland. You are expected to have read the book you will be writing on for your mid-term paper by this time. You should also have read Billington, Far Western Frontier, pp 41-68. (27pp + book)

WEEK 9: SPANISH BORDERLANDS

Nov. 2: Santa Fe
    REAW: BENT BROTHERS, BENT'S FORT, forts (1812 to the Mexican War), Glenn-Fowler Expedition, Gregg, Magoffin, MEXICAN-AMERICANS, MULE, SANTA FE (NM), Santa Fe and the Chihuahua Trail.

Nov. 4: Texas
    REAW: EMPRESARIO SYSTEM, HOUSTON, San Jacinto (battle of), TEXAS.

SECTION: MID-TERM PAPERS ARE DUE IN CLASS!! Discussion will revolve around the papers, but you are also expected to have read Billington, Far Western Frontier, pp 1-40, 116-42. (66pp)

WEEK 10: THE PASSING FRONTIER, ACT I

Nov. 9: Trail of Tears (Guest Lecture by George Miles)
    REAW: BLACK HAWK, BLACK HAWK WAR, INDIAN WARS (1789-1865), INDIAN-WHITE RELATIONS (1789-1865), *Andrew Jackson, Keokuk, Osceola, Prairie du Chien (treaty of), Red Bird, Ross (John), Dancing Rabbit Creek Treaty, New Echota (treaty of), Boudinot (Elias).

Nov. 11: From Northwest Towards Middle West
    REAW: American System, *banking and currency, Benton (Thomas Hart), *canal era, Henry Clay, *cities, diseases, doctors, *English language and the westward movement, *frontier life (to 1850), gambling, humor, Illinois, Indiana, *internal improvements, Iowa, law and order, *lead mining, Michigan (settlement of), Missouri (to 1850), *national roads, *Old Northwest, *Old Southwest, Protestant Churches, revivalism, *taverns and hotels, *transportation on the Great Lakes, *transportation on the Mississippi River system, *utopian colonies.

SECTION: Black Hawk, Autobiography, (pp 41-160) (119pp)

WEEK 11: ROMANTICS AND VISIONARIES

Nov. 16: Farmers and Missionaries--Oregon
    REAW: Bidwell, Gray, LEE, MCLOUGHLIN, Ogden, OREGON, Oregon Controversy, OREGON TRAIL, PROTESTANT MISSIONARIES, Ross, Washington, Webster-Ashburton Treaty, WHITMAN.

Nov. 13: Zion in Utah--The Mormons
    REAW: Deseret, LATTER DAY SAINTS, Mormon Trail, polygamy, Salt Lake City, JOSEPH SMITH, Utah, Walkara, YOUNG (BRIGHAM).

NO SECTION THIS WEEK. You are encouraged to take Faragher, Women and Men on the Overland Trail, along with you over Thanksgiving if you have not already read it; your final paper project on overland trail diaries should be under way by now.

WEEK 12: THANKSGIVING BREAK, NO CLASSES

WEEK 13: TO THE PACIFIC

Nov. 30: War for American Empire--1846
        REAW: Bear Flag Rebellion, boundary commissions, forts (Mexican War),
        Guadalupe Hidalgo, MANIFEST DESTINY, MEXICAN WAR, MONROE DOCTRINE, TEXAS
        (ANNEXATION OF), TEXAS, *Texas Rangers.

Dec. 2: California Gold
        REAW: CALIFORNIA, CALIFORNIA TRAIL, *Donner Party, Donner Trail,
        *emigrants' guidebooks, American River, forty-niners (trail of), FREMONT,
        GOLD AND SILVER RUSHES, McCulloch, Hartnell & Co.

SECTION: FINAL PAPERS ARE DUE IN CLASS!! Discussion will be on the papers, and
you are expected to have read Faragher, Women and Men on the Overland Trail,
(all), and Billington, Far Western Frontier, pp 143-92, 218-42.

WEEK 14: THE SUMMING UP

Dec. 7: The West in 1850

YALE UNIVERSITY

HISTORY 141b

THE AMERICAN WEST SINCE 1850

Lectures: Bill Cronon, 409 Calhoun. Office phone: 436-0738.
    Home phone: 562-1187. (Please, no calls at home after 8:00 P.M.)

Discussions: Kathy Morrissey

Lectures will be held on Monday, Wednesday, and Friday of the first two
weeks of term (through 22 January), and on Monday and Wednesday thereafter.
Discussion sections will meet on Friday, starting 29 January. Assignments
to section will be made on Wednesday, 27 January.

A Note on the Readings

Readings for the course are extensive but not difficult. They are
designed to provide a core set of issues for the discussion sections and
to supplement both the themes and factual details of the lectures.
Movies and writing assignments are also geared toward promoting discussion
in section.

The central "text" will be Howard Lamar's Reader's Encyclopedia of the
American West (henceforth referred to as REAW), a recently published
volume which is one of the good things of western history. Unlike an
ordinary textbook, which is traditionally arranged as a chronological
narrative, the Encyclopedia is just that: an alphabetical listing of
names, places, and topics. You should refer to it often. Because the
book can easily become overwhelming, I've listed a number of subjects
for reading under each lecture topic. Those underlined and with an
asterisk are must reading; those simply underlined are very important
for you to look at; and others are there just in case you want to do
some additional reading. Try to take an hour every week or two to
wander through REAW more or less randomly, following topics as they
catch your eye, or tracing one reference to another. Part of "doing
history" is being willing to follow your curiosity, and learning how
to find answers to questions you didn't realize you had when you
started out. Wandering through the REAW--and then using its references
to move on to other sources--is much more akin to what historians really
do than is reading a textbook narrative. Try to create your own stories
and problems from the fragments it provides.

One comment on costs: I realize that the total cost of books for this
course is substantial, and strongly encourage you to share books or
use Cross Campus reserve copies whenever you can. REAW in particular
usually costs $24.95, although I have been able to obtain (at the Co-op)
a number of remaindered copies at $9.95--a real bargain. Buy REAW if
you possibly can, but, if this is too difficult for your budget, remember
that there are several reserve copies at CCL, and none of the weekly
assignments in it should take more than a couple of hours. A bit of
advice: read the REAW after lectures in order to reinforce main points.
This syllabus provides a very detailed outline of what will happen in
the course, and I strongly advise you to refer to it often in planning
your studying.

Required readings are listed below. You will not necessarily be reading
each volume in its entirety. Titles marked with an asterisk (*) have
been used before at Yale, so you may be able to find used copies at
bookstores such as Atticus, Whitlocks, or the Paperback Trader.
    *David Potter, The Impending Crisis
    *Rodman Paul, Mining Frontiers of the Far West
     Andrew Garcia, Tough Trip Through Paradise
     Albert Camarillo, Chicanos in a Changing Society
    *Charles Siringo, A Texas Cowboy
     John Ise, Sod and Stubble
     Maisie & Richard Conrat, The American Farm (photographs)
     George Tindall, A Populist Reader
     Bill Haywood, Autobiography
    *Samuel Hays, Conservation and the Gospel of Efficiency
    *John McPhee, Coming Into the Country
     William Strunk & E. B. White, The Elements of Style
In addition to the above titles, you are required to own (and use
frequently) a good quality map of the United States which shows both
political and physiographic features. The Co-op has copies of Rand
McNally's inexpensive "Contemporary" map available for purchase at the
text information desk, but if you own a good atlas or map, don't bother
to buy another. The final paper assignment requires you to read one
of the following pairs of books, about which more in a moment:

    Andy Adams, Log of a Cowboy
    Owen Wister, The Virginian

    Mary Hallock Foote, A Victorian Gentlewoman in the Far West
    *Wallace Stegner, Angle of Repose

    *John G. Neihardt, Black Elk Speaks
    *Thomas Berger, Little Big Man

    Georgina Binnie-Clark, Wheat and Woman
    O. E. Rölvaag, Giants in the Earth

    *John Steinbeck, Grapes of Wrath
    O. E. Rölvaag, Giants in the Earth

Finally, copies of six additional books are available at the Co-op as
recommended titles. Frederick Merk's History of the Westward Movement
is an inexpensive paperback text which covers most of the themes of
the course and which may prove helpful is you want a more traditional
narrative text to back up the REAW and the lectures. Gerald Nash's
The American West in the Twentieth Century tends to be a bit dry, but
is the only available book covering that portion of the course.
If you are interested in pursuing the role of women in the American
West, two books may prove useful: Julie Roy Jeffrey's Frontier Women,
1840-1880, a general history of the subject; and Christiane Fischer's
Let Them Speak for Themselves, a collection of primary documents
relating to women's experiences in the West. Finally, much of the
course will focus on the image of the West in American culture.
Jack Nachbar's Focus on the Western contains a series of essays on the
western as a film genre. Henry Nash Smith's Virgin Land is a brilliant
exposition of symbols and ideologies related to the west and the frontier;
you may find it very helpful in tackling the final paper assignment.

Films

Because a major theme of the course is the role of the West in American popular culture, a number of movies will be shown both to exemplify certain aspects of the course and to trace the development of the western genre in film. These will be shown in the evenings at a place and time yet to be determined, in _five_ separate screenings, and _are a required activity of the course_. Movies to be shown are:

Siringo (documentary)
The Plow that Broke the Plains (documentary)
Grapes of Wrath (based on the Steinbeck novel about Dust Bowl migration)
The Great Train Robbery (first western ever made)
The Battle of Elderbush Gulch (D.W. Griffith's classic silent)
Stage Coach (_the_ classic John Ford western, John Wayne's first)
The Lone Ranger (a radio adventure)
Settlers Valley (a Hopalong Cassidy "B" short)
High Noon (Stanley Kramer overturns a number of western conventions)
Giant (James Dean's last film, about the coming of Texas oil)

Papers and Examinations

Aside from the readings and films listed above, there will be two papers and two one-hour examinations (a mid-term and an abbreviated final covering the second half of the course). The first paper (3-5 pages) will be a discussion of the major themes in one of two required books, Siringo's _Texas Cowboy_ or Ise's _Sod and Stubble_. Half the class will do Siringo, half Ise, and discussion sections will focus on the papers.

The second paper is more complicated, and two class sections will be devoted to discussing its results. It asks that you read two books, one more or less a primary document narrating some aspect of the West, and the other a novel covering comparable themes. Your essay (7-10 pages) should deal not only with comparisons and contrasts between the two books, but with the general problem of historical fiction and its relation to historical fact. The paper will be due a week before the end of term in order to avoid the rush, and you are advised to choose and think about your two books during the spring break.

Final grades will be taken as the average of the two tests (20% each), the two writing assignments (15% and 25% respectively), and classroom discussion (20%). _Note that discussion sections are mandatory!_ You are also warned that excuses for late papers will be given only under extreme circumstances, and that _late assignments will be marked down by at least 1/2 grade_. Please take this seriously.

Weekly Outline of Lectures and Assignments

Remember: the topics listed under REAW are sometimes required, sometimes recommended, and sometimes simply there for the sake of wandering. Read them less for their specific detail than for the connections they suggest. Don't let yourself be overwhelmed by the mass of facts, a common problem for historians: look for the patterns and then attach the crucial facts to those patterns.

Week 1: Introductory
  Jan 11: Defining the Frontier
    REAW: collectors and collections of Western Americana; *frontier theory, manifest destiny; noble savage concept; safety-valve theory; Frederick Jackson Turner.
  Jan 13: A Tour of the West
    *Study a good quality map of the U.S. before and after the lecture.
    REAW: Read *physiography of the U.S. and *vegetation. Then spend some time wandering among the following: Arkansas R, cartography, Colorado R, Columbia R, Gila R, Great American Desert, Imperial Valley, Mississippi R, Pecos R, Platte R, Red River of the North, Rio Grande, Sacramento R, Salinas R, San Joaquin R, Snake R, wildlife (also note separate sections on key animals such as beaver, buffalo, deer, fisheries, horse, mule, etc., if you're interested), Willamette R.
  Jan 15: Towards War
    REAW: John Brown; Civil War; *Compromise of 1850; *Stephen Douglas; *elections of 1852, 1856, 1860; Free-Soil Party; Jayhawkers; Kansas; *Kansas-Nebraska issue; Know-Nothing Party; Abraham Lincoln; Missouri Compromise; *popular sovereignty.

Week 2: Underground West
  Jan 18: Empire of the Sierra
    REAW: David Broderick; California; Dame Shirley; Dan DeQuille; James G. Fair; *gold and silver rushes; Great Diamond Hoax; William Gwin; Jewish immigration; Denis Kearny; John W. MacKay; *mining, metal; *mining law; *mining towns; Lola Montez; Nevada; prospector; *prostitution; William C. Ralston; saloon; San Francisco; Adolph Sutro; Virginia City, Nevada.
  Jan 20: The Coming of Corporate Mining
    REAW: Aspen; *boom towns; Central City; William A. Clark; Colorado; *copper mining; Marcus Daly; Deadwood; Denver; Douglas Family; Emma Mine; Mary Hallock Foote; *Geological Survey; ghost towns; William Gilpin; Ferdinand Hayden; Nathaniel P. Hill; Idaho; Clarence King; Lead, SD; lead mining; Leadville; *mining engineer; *John Wesley Powell; Horace Tabor; Tombstone; George Wheeler.
  Jan 22: Movement and Messages: Communications Revolution
    REAW: Adams Express Co.; Atchison, Topeka & Santa Fe Railroad; Brigham Young Express & Carrying Co.; Burlington Northern Railroad; John Butterfield; Central Overland California and Pike Peak's Express; *Central Pacific Railroad; Chicago & Northwestern RR; *Credit Mobilier; Charles Crocker; Denver & Rio Grande RR; Grenville Dodge; William Fargo; John Murray Forbes; Gadsden Purchase:

Jay Gould; E. H. Harriman; James J. Hill; Ben Holladay;
Holladay's Stagecoach Lines; Mark Hopkins; Collis P. Huntington;
Theodore Judah; Alexander Majors; Overland Mail Co.; Pacific
Mail Steamship Co.; Pony Express; George Pullman; *railroad
land grants; **railroads; Russell, Majors & Waddell; *Southern
Pacific Railroad; stagecoach; Leland Stanford; *telegraph;
*transcontinental railroad surveys; transportation overland;
*Union Pacific Railroad; U. S. Mail Steamship Co.; Henry Villard;
William B. Waddell; Wells Fargo & Co.

Week 3: Wasting the Indians
  Jan 25: Civil War and Indian War
    REAW: Apache; *army on the frontier; Henry Carrington; Cheyenne-Arapaho
    War; John M. Chivington; Cochise; Fetterman Massacre; forts
    (Civil War and after); Grattan Massacre; guns; Hancock Campaign;
    William S. Harney; *Indian Wars, 1850-69; Little Crow; *Medicine
    Lodge Treaty; Minnesota Uprising; Powder River Indian Expedition;
    *Sand Creek Massacre.
  Jan 27: The Coming of the Ghost Dance
    REAW: Big Hole, Battle of; Black Elk; *buffalo; Camp Grant Massacre;
    Cheyenne; *Chief Joseph; Crazy Horse; George Crook; *George A.
    Custer; Dull Knife; Eskiminzin; Gall; Geronimo; *Ghost Dance;
    Oliver Howard; *Indian Wars, 1865-91; *U.S. Indian Policy, 1860-90;
    *Little Big Horn, Battle of; Little Wolf; James McLaughlin;
    Modoc War; Nez Perce; *Nez Perce War; Oklahoma; *peace policy;
    Plenty Coups; Red Cloud; Washita, Battle of; Philip H. Sheridan;
    William T. Sherman; Sioux; Sitting Bull; *Wounded Knee Massacre.
  Jan 29: SECTION Andrew Garcia, Tough Trip Through Paradise--skim Part I,
    read Parts II and III closely.

Week 4: World of Enclaves
  Feb 1: Theocracy in a Land of Little Rain: Utah
    REAW: John T. Caine; George Q. Cannon; Deseret; handcart companies;
    William Jennings; *Latter-Day Saints; Mormon Trail; *polygamy;
    Salt Lake City; *Utah; Wilford Woodruff; *Brigham Young;
    Zion's Cooperative Mercantile Association.
  Feb 3: People of Color: Black, Brown, Yellow
    REAW: Pedro Altube; Basques; *Chinatowns; *Chinese, riots against;
    *Chinese-Americans; *Chinese immigration; Gregorio Cortez;
    Juan Cortina; Fung Ching; *Mexican Americans; Joaquin Murieta;
    Negroes in the Far West; *Negroes on the Frontier.
  Feb 5: SECTION Albert Camarillo, Chicanos in a Changing Society, pp 1-141.

NOTE: Before turning in the first paper assignment, everyone is expected to
have read William Strunk and E. B. White's The Elements of Style. Past
experience indicates that everyone could use some work on their writing,
and this book is a relatively painless and pleasant way to begin thinking
about the problem. Week 4 is the appropriate time to read this book.

Week 5: Tall Grass and Pine Trees
FIRST FILM: SIRINGO
Feb 8: Ranches and Ranges
 REAW: Andy Adams; Clay Allison; *barbed wire; Frank Canton; *cattle
   associations; cattle brands; *cattle industry; *cattle towns;
   Cattle Kate; Jesse Chisholm; John S. Chisum; John Clay; John
   King Fisher; Hugh Glenn; John W. Iliffe; JA Ranch; *Johnson
   County War; Richard King; King Ranch; *Lincoln County War;
   John T. Lytle; Joseph G. McCoy; Maxwell Land Grant Co.;
   Shanghai Pierce; saddles; sheep ranching; *Charles Siringo;
   Granville Stuart; Alexander Swan; *Texas fever; XIT Ranch.
Feb 10: Taking the Forest
 REAW: *Paul Bunyan; fisheries-the West; *lumber industry; *lumberjack.
Feb 12: SECTION Charles Siringo, A Texas Cowboy.
   N.B.: One half of the class will be writing its first paper
   on this book, and will be expected to turn it in today.

Week 6: The Grain Connection
Feb 15: Busting the Sod
 REAW: colleges and universities; English language (agrarian American
   English); Hamlin Garland: *Homestead Act; immigration; Kansas;
   *land policy, 1789-1896; *public domain; *sod house; Timber &
   Stone Act; Timber Culture Act.
Feb 17: Bonanza Farms and Boards of Trade
 REAW: *bonanza farming; corn production; *dry farming; Imperial Valley;
   Irvine Ranch; Minnesota; *wheat production.
Feb 19: SECTION John Ise, Sod and Stubble
   Maisie & Richard Conrat, The American Farm, pp 62-93
   N.B.: The other half of the class will be writing its first
   paper on this book, and will be expected to turn it in today.

Week 7: Corporations and Conflicts
Feb 22: The Farmers' Alliance
 REAW: *agrarian movements; William Jennings Bryan; Annie Diggs;
   Ignatius Donnelly; *elections of 1892, 1896; *Granger laws;
   Greenback Party; Industrial Army Movement; Oliver H. Kelley;
   Mary E. Lease; William A. Peffer; People's Party, Kansas;
   *Populism; *silver issue; Jerry Simpson; James B. Weaver.
Feb 24: Miners and Wobblies
 REAW: Harry Bridges; Cripple Creek; *Cripple Creek Strikes; *William
   Haywood; *Industrial Workers of the World; *labor movement;
   Pinkerton Detective Agency; Charles Siringo; Western Federation
   of Miners.
Feb 26: SECTION Bill Haywood, Autobiography, pp 1-173.
   George Tindall, Populist Reader, pp 11-41, 60-73, 90-103.

Week 8: Assault on Tribalism
March 1: Reform and the Indians, 1869-1928
 REAW: Adolph Bandelier; Carlisle Indian School; Edward S. Curtis;
   *Henry L. Dawes; *Indian Affairs Bureau; *Indian Rights Association;
   *U.S. Indian Policy, 1860-1920; Helen Hunt Jackson; *peace policy;
   Robert Welsh.

March 3: MID-TERM EXAMINATION
March 5: NO SECTION

SPRING BREAK: You're encouraged to take along the two books on which
you'll be doing your final paper--since they're novels or memoirs,
they may not even feel so much like schoolwork.... Steinbeck's Grapes
of Wrath would also be good to take along, since you'll be seeing the film.

Week 9: Saving the Land, Reforming the People
    March 22: Western Progressivism
        REAW: Kate Barnard; William E. Borah; California; Hiram Johnson;
        George Norris; Lincoln Steffens; woman suffrage.
    March 24: Conservation or Preservation: The Battle for Hetch Hetchy
        REAW: Boone & Crocket Club; *Carey Act; *conservation movement;
        Interior Dept.; Aldo Leopold; *Elwood Mead; *John Muir;
        national parks and monuments (scan this); National Park Service;
        *Francis Newlands; *Newlands Reclamation Act; *Gifford Pinchot;
        **reclamation and irrigation; *Theodore Roosevelt; Carl Schurz;
        Sierra Club; William E. Smythe; wilderness; Yellowstone National
        Park; Yosemite National Park.
    March 26: SECTION Samuel Hays, Conservation and the Gospel of Efficiency,
        pp 1-174, 261-76.

Week 10: Dust Bowl and New Deal
    SECOND FILMS: PLOW THAT BROKE THE PLAINS, GRAPES OF WRATH
    March 29: The Crisis of American Agriculture
        REAW: *agricultural expansion; corn production; cotton production;
        *dust bowl; Woody Guthrie; *Okies; *John Steinbeck; Henry
        Wallace; wheat production.

Week 11: Imagining the West
    THIRD FILMS: GREAT TRAIN ROBBERY, BATTLE OF ELDERBUSH GULCH, STAGE COACH
    April 5: Landscape and Myth, Frontiers and Heroes
        REAW: Don't be intimidated by this list--it contains all the images
        and image-makers relevant to this week, and it's mainly here
        for your wandering delight. Keep track of the asterisks and
        you won't go crazy. artists of western surveys; H. H. Bancroft;
        P.T. Barnum, Sam Bass; Roy Bean; Ambrose Bierce; Albert
        Bierstadt; Billy the Kid; Black Bart; Herbert Eugene Bolton;
        Bonnie & Clyde; S. H. Borglum; Kit Carson; Butch Cassidy;
        Willa Cather; Badger Clark; Calamity Jane; Walter Van Tilburg
        Clark; *Cody, Buffalo Bill; E. I. Coves; *cowboy; cowboy
        clothing; Edward S. Curtis; Dalton gang; *dime novels;
        Earp brothers; Edna Ferber; Mary Hallock Foote; gambling;
        Pat Garrett; T. Gilcrease; Graham-Tewksbury Feud; Zane Grey;
        A. B. Guthrie; John Wesley Hardin; Bret Harte; Wild Bill Hickok;
        Doc Holliday; Tom Horn; Emerson Hough; humor; Indian captivity
        narratives; William H. Jackson; Jesse James; Will James;
        law and order; Jake McClure; Larry McMurtry; federal marshall;
        Bat Masterson; Karl May; Michael & John Meagher; Joaquin Miller;
        Thomas Moran; *music, western; *music about the West; National
        Cowboy Hall of Fame; John G. Neihardt; Frank Norris; *novel, western;

Annie Oakley; *photography; Henry Plummer; *prints; Frederic
Remington; Eugene M. Rhodes; John Ringo; *rodeo; Will Rogers;
O. E. Rölvaag; Rough Riders; Charles M. Russell; O. C. Seltzer;
Belle Starr; Wallace Stegner; *Wild West Show; Owen Wister;
Younger Brothers.
    Recommended: If you're at all interested in the problem of
imagery and ideology in the popular culture of the West,
Henry Nash Smith's Virgin Land is superb and highly recommended.
You may find it of help in writing your final paper.
April 7: Hollywood's West
    REAW: Walt Disney; *films, western; *motion picture industry;
*radio and television, westerns on.
    Recommended: Jack Nachbar's Focus on the Western has a number
of essays, of varying quality, on this film genre. Robert
Warshow's "Movie Chronicle: The Westerner" is a real
classic (pp 45-56) which you should try to read if possible.
April 9: SECTION: You are expected to have read the pair of books you
have chosen for your final paper by this time, and four
people will give reports on these books so that everyone
will have an idea of what is in them when we discuss them
next week. (See list of titles in the section on readings above.)

Week 12: Transformations of War
FOURTH FILMS: LONE RANGER (radio), SETTLERS VALLEY (B Western), HIGH NOON
April 12: Airplanes and Internments.
    REAW: *aerospace industry; airlines; Boeing Airplane Co.;
Howard Hughes; *Japanese-Americans; *Japanese immigration;
Henry Kaiser; Nevada Proving Ground.
April 14: Power Shift: Metropolis West
    REAW: California; *cities, growth of; Dallas; Denver; Disneyland;
Fort Worth; gambling-Nevada; Amadeo P. Giannini; Ford Ferguson
Harvey; William Randolph Hearst; Houston; Las Vegas;
*Los Angeles; Phoenix; *roads and highways; *San Francisco;
Seattle; *tourist travel.

Week 13: Today's West
FIFTH FILM: GIANT
April 19: Energy from Texas to Alaska
    REAW: Alaska; Alaska purchase; John G. Brady; Albert Fall;
fisheries-Alaska; Ernest Gruening; Hawaii; H. L. Hunt;
W. W. Keeler; King Ranch; Cap Lathrop; *oil industry;
*uranium mining.
April 21: Colonialism, Ecology, and the Sage Brush Rebellion
    REAW: Cesar Chavez; *Chicano Liberation Movement; *conservation
movement; Vine Deloria; Charles Edwardson; Hector P. Garcia;
Corky Gonzales; *Indian Power Movement; Ken Kesey; Larry
McMurtry; Reiss Tijerina; Wyoming.

ERRORS, ADDENDA, AND CORRECTIONS TO SYLLABUS

Please make the following changes on your course syllabus:

David Potter, <u>The Impending Crisis</u>, is no longer required reading.
It is, however, strongly recommended for the first week of class.
Spend the bulk of your reading time wandering through REAW.

Rodman Paul, <u>Mining Frontiers of the Far West</u>, is the required
reading for the second week of classes even though there are no
sections. Read it quickly but in its entirety.

For SECTION on April 16, we will be discussing the final papers;
there is no other reading assignment aside from REAW.

For SECTION on April 23, the reading is John McPhee, <u>Coming into
the Country</u>.

Week 10 of the syllabus is incomplete. It should read as follows:

Week 10: Dust Bowl and New Deal
SECOND FILMS: PLOW THAT BROKE THE PLAINS, GRAPES OF WRATH
March 29: The Crisis of American Agriculture
REAW: *<u>agricultural expansion</u>; <u>corn production</u>; <u>cotton production</u>;
*<u>dust bowl</u>; Woody Guthrie; *<u>Okies</u>; <u>John Steinbeck</u>; Henry
Wallace; <u>wheat production</u>.
March 31: Settling With Indians: 20th Century Indian Policy (George Miles)
REAW: *<u>John Collier</u>; Joseph R. Garry; *<u>Indian Affairs Bureau</u>;
*<u>Indian Power Movement</u>; Indian painters; **<u>U.S. Indian Policy,
1920-present</u>; Peyotism.
April 2: SECTION Conrat, pp 124-57, 190-221.
Recommended: John Steinbeck, Grapes of Wrath

<u>Film Schedule</u>:

9 February: SIRINGO

30 March: PLOW THAT BROKE THE PLAINS, GRAPES OF WRATH

6 April: GREAT TRAIN ROBBERY, BATTLE AT ELDERBUSH GULCH, STAGE COACH

13 April: LONE RANGER, SETTLERS VALLEY, HIGH NOON

20 April: GIANT

All showings are on Tuesday nights.

SORRY FOR THE SNAFUS!

University of IOWA

Malcolm Rohrbough

The Frontier in American History

A Reading List

A note on selection. This is a guide to the study of the American Frontier.
Any reading list is a statement of personal preference. This one is even
more so than usual, for the literature in the field is extensive and the
list brief. It does not deal with the frontier in the 20th century--internal
migrations, conservation, political protest movements--and this is a further
expression of my own view of the field. It is possible that the periodical
literature is short changed. There may be other good articles. I couldn't
find them. Some of the works on this list should be read and, in light of
new work or simply the passage of time, re-read. Others should be sampled.
A third group should be faced in a kind of intellectual confrontation. Each
reader may place titles in these categories as he or she wishes. For
myself, I have attempted to find selections from all three, as well as
fiction and a few documents. Suggestions for additions and deletions are
most welcome.

A note on use. I have arbitrarily divided this list under several headings.
Such a selection process is not exact, for some titles belong under more
than one heading--numbers I and XIII are especially difficult in this
aspect--and no work is listed more than once. So the reader should beware
of trying to place any selection within too narrow a framework. Under
each heading, I have tried to move from the general to the more specific,
but I do not see that much is lost by reading out of order. The date is
the year of original publication. Many of the books have gone into later
editions, including paperback. Happy reading.

I. Approaches to the Frontier

Frederick Jackson Turner, The Significance of the Frontier in American History
    (1920).
    _____, The Significance of the Section in American History (1932).
Gene M. Gressley, "The Turner Thesis--A Problem in Historiography,"
    Agricultural History, 32 (1958).
Ray Allen Billington, America's Frontier Heritage (1966).
Merle Curti, The Making of an American Community (1959)
Henry Nash Smith, Virgin Land (1950)
Earl Pomeroy, "Toward a Reorientation of Western History: Continuity and
    Environment," Mississippi Valley Historical Review, 41 (1955).
David M. Potter, People of Plenty (1954), ch. VII.
Richard A. Bartlett, The New Country (1975)
Arthur K. Moore, the Frontier Mind (1957), ch. 3
Daniel J. Boorstin, The Americans: The National Experience (1965),
    parts two and five
W.J. Cash, The Mind of the South (1941), ch. one
Stanley Elkins and Eric McKitrick, "Democracy in the Old Northwest," and
    "The Southwest Frontier and New England," Political Science Quarterly, 69
    (1954)

Robert R. Dykstra, The Cattle Towns (1968)
Frederick Merk, History of the Westward Movement (1978)
Malcolm J. Rohrbough, The Trans-Appalachian Frontier, 1775-1850 (1978)
Robert V. Hine, The American West (1973)
Roderick Nash, Wilderness and the American Mind (1967), ch. 2
Robert F. Berkhoffer, "Space, Time, Culture and the New Frontier,"
    Agricultural History, XXXVIII (1964)
Daniel J. Elazar, "Land Space and Civil Society in America," Western
    Historical Quarterly, V (1974)
Ray Allen Billington, Frederick Jackson Turner (1973)
Louis Hartz, The Founding of New Societies (1969)
Richard C. Wade, The Urban Frontier (1969)
Lawrence H. Larsen, The Urban West at the End of the Frontier (1978)

II. Exploration

John Bartlett Brebner, Explorers of North America, 1492-1806 (1933)
John Bakeless, The Eyes of Discovery (1950)
Francis Parkman, LaSalle and the Discovery of the Great West (1879)
Bernard DeVoto, The Course of Empire (1959), chs. 1-5

III. The Colonial Frontier

Charles Gibson, Spain in America (1966), ch. 9
Cabeza de Vaca, Adventures in the Unknown Interior of America (1961)
Wallace Notestein, The English People on the Eve of Colonization, 1603-1630
    (1954)
Thomas P. Abernathy, Three Virginia Frontiers (1940)
W.J. Eccles, The Canadian Frontier, 1534-1760
Lois K. Mathews, The Expansion of New England (1909)
Charles E. Clark, The Eastern Frontier: The Settlement of Northern New
    England, 1610-1763 (1970)
John Demos, The Little Commonwealth: Family Life in Plymouth Colony (1970)
E. Roy Merrens, "Historical Geography and Early American History,"
    William and Mary Quarterly, 22 (1965)
Carl Bridenbaugh, Myths & Realities (1952), ch. III
Douglas E. Leach, The Northern Colonial Frontier, 1607-1763 (1966)
Jack M. Sosin, The Revolutionary Frontier, 1763-1783 (1967)

IV. Expansion in the New Nation, 1783-1815

Reginald Horsman, The Frontier in the Formative Years, 1783-1815 (1970)
Arthur P. Whiteaker, The Spanish American Frontier, 1783-1815 (1970)
William B. Hamilton, "The Southwestern Frontier, 1795-1817: An Essay in
    Social History," Journal of Southern History, 10 (1944)
Francis S. Philbrick, The Rise of the West, 1754-1830 (1965)
    _____, ed., Laws of the Indiana Territory (1930), introduction
Solon J. and Elizabeth Buck, The Planting of Civilization in Western
    Pennsylvania (1939)

Conrad Richter, The Trees (1940)
William B. Hamilton, Anglo-American Law on the Frontier (1953), introduction
John Filson, The Discovery, Settlement and Present State of Kentucky (1784)

V. The Great Migration, 1815-1850: Northwest and Southwest

Frederick Jackson Turner, The Rise of the New West, 1819-1829 (1906)
____, The United States, 1830-1850 (1935)
R. Carlyle Buley, The Old Northwest (2 v., 1951)
Everett Dick, The Dixie Frontier (1948)
Thomas P. Abernathy, The Formative Period in Alabama, 1815-1828 (1922)
Edward Eggleston, The Hoosier Schoolmaster (1871)
Augustus B. Longstreet, Georgia Scenes (1835)
Joseph G. Baldwin, The Flush Times of Alabama and Mississippi (1853)

VI. The Confrontation with the Native American

Wilcomb E. Washburn, The Indian in America (1975)
Jack D. Forbes, "Frontier in American History," Journal of the West,1 (1962)
William T. Hagen, The Indian in American History (1971)
Carl O. Sauer, Sixteenth Century North America (1971)
Wilcomb E. Washburn, "The Moral and Legal Justification for Depossessing
    the Indians," James Morton Smith, ed., Seventeenth Century America (1959)
Nancy O. Lurie, "Indian Cultural Adjustment to European Civilization," in
    Smith, ibid.
Peter Nabokov, Two Leggings (1967)
N. Scott Momaday, House Made of Dawn (1967)
James L. Thane, "The Montana 'Indian War' of 1867," Arizona and the West
    X (1968)
John G. Neihardt, Black Elk Speaks (1961)
Francis Paul Prucha, American Indian Policy in the Formative Years (1962)
Edward H. Spicer, Cycles of Conquest (1964)
Frank Waters, The Man Who Killed the Deer (1942)
Francis Paul Prucha, "Books on American Indian Policy: A Half-Decade of
    Improtant Work," Journal of American History, LXIII (1976)
William G. McLoughlin and Walter H. Conser, Jr., "The Cherokees in Transition:
    A Statistical Analysis of the Federal Cherokee Census of 1835,"
    Journal of American History, LXIV (1977)
Theodora Kroeber, Ishi (1961)
Robert F. Berhoffer, "The Political Context of a New Indian History,"
    Pacific Historical Review, XL (1971)
Frederick Manfred, Conquering Horse (1959)

VII. Economic Development on the Frontier

Roy M. Robbins, Our Landed Heritage (1942)
Vernon Carstensen, ed., The Public Domain (1963)
____, "A Long Way from the Crow in the Stewpot," The National Observer,
    Oct. 18, 1975.
Malcolm J. Rohrbough, The Land Office Business (1968)

Paul W. Gates, <u>The Illinois Central Railroad and Its Colonization Work</u> (1934)
_____, <u>The Farmer's Age: Agriculture, 1815-1860</u> (1960)
_____, "The Role of the Land Speculator in Western Development,"
    <u>Pennsylvania Magazine of History and Biography</u>, LXVI (1942)
Allan G. Bogue, <u>From Prairie to Corn Belt</u> (1961)
Kenneth W. Porter, "Negro Labor in the Western Cattle INdustry, 1806-1900"
    Labor History, X (1960)

VIII. The Opening of the Far West

David Lavender, <u>Bent's Fort</u> (1954)
Ray Allen Billington, <u>The Far Western Frontier, 1830-1860</u> (1956)
Dale L. Morgan, <u>Jededia Smith and the Opening of the West</u> (1953)
Frederick Merk, ed., <u>Fur Trade and Empire</u> (1932), introduction
William H. Goetzmann, <u>Exploration and Empire</u> (1966)
James L. Clayton, "The Growth and Economic Significance of the Fur Trade,
    1790-1880," <u>Minnesota History</u>, XL (1966)
Dale L. Norgan, "The Fur Trade and Its Historians," <u>Minnesota History</u>, XL (1966)
John S. Galbraith, "British-American Competition in the Border Fur Trade of
    the 1820's," <u>Minnesota History</u>, XXXVI (1959)
Glendwr Williams, "Highlights of the First Two Hundred Years of the Hudson's
    Bay Company," <u>The Beaver</u> (Autumn, 1970)
Frederick Merk, <u>Manifest Destiny and Mission in American History</u> (1963)
_____, <u>The Monroe Doctrine and American Expansion</u> (1966)

IX. The Pacific Northwest

Frederick Merk, <u>Albert Gallatin and the Oregon Problem</u> (1950)
_____, <u>The Oregon Question: Essays in Anglo-American Diplomacy and Politics</u> (1967)
Vernon Carstensen, "The Fisherman's Frontier on the Pacific Coast: The
    Rise of the Salmon-Canning INdustry," in John G. Clark, <u>The Frontier
    Challenge</u> (1971)
Orin J. Oliphant, <u>On the Cattle Ranges of the Oregon Country</u> (1968)
Michael L. Olsen, "Transplantation of Domestic Plants and Animals in the
    Pacific Northwest," <u>Journal of the West</u> 14 (1975)
Donald W. Meinig, <u>The Great Columbia Basin: A Historical Geography 1805-1910</u>
    (1968)

X. The Spanish Borderlands

Eugene C. Barker, <u>Life of Stephen F. Austin</u> (1925)
William C. Binkley, <u>The Texas Revolution</u> (1952)
_____, <u>The Expansionist Movement in Texas, 1836-1850</u> (1935)
Leonard Pitt, <u>The Decline of the Californias</u> (1966)
Paul Horgan, <u>Great River: Rio Grande in North American History</u> (2 vol., 1954)
Carey McWilliams, <u>North from Mexico</u> (1948)
John Francis Bannon, <u>The Spanish Borderlands Frontier, 1513-1821</u> (1970)
Daniel J. Garr, "A Rare and Desolate Land: Population and Race in
    Hispanic California," <u>Western Historical Quarterly</u>, VI (1975)

Jane Dysart, "Mexican Women in San Antonio, 1830-1860: The Assimilation
     Process," Western Historical Quarterly, VII (1976)
Herbert Eugene Bolton, "The Mission as a Frontier Institution in the
     Spanish American Colonies," American Historical Review, XXIII (1917)

XI. The Great Basin

Leonard Arrington, Great Basin Kingdom (1959)
Thomas F. O'Dea, The Mormons (1957)
Fawn M. Brodie, No Man Knows My History: The Life Story of Joseph Smith (1945)
Robert Flanders, Nauvoo: Kingdom on the Mississippi (1955)
Rodman W. Paul, "The Mormons as a Theme in Western Historical Writing-"
     Journal of American History, LIV (1967
Merle W. Wells, "The Idaho Anti-Mormon Test Oath, 1884-1892,"
     Pacific Historical Review,24 (1955)

XII. Mining

Rodman W. Paul, Mining Frontiers of the Far West, 1848-1880 (1963)
     , California Gold: The Beginning of Mining in the Far West (1947)
Harwood Hinton, "Frontier Speculation: A Study of the Walker Mining Districts,"
     Pacific Historical Review, XXIX (1960)
W. Turrentine Jackson, Treasure Hill: Portrait of a Silver Mining Camp (1963)
Duane Smith, Rocky Mountain Mining Camps (1967)
Mark Wyman, "Industrial Revolution in the West," Western Historical Quarterly,
     V (1971)
Charles H. Shinn, Mining Camps: A Study in American Frontier Government (1884)

XIII. The Great Plains

Walter Prescott Webb, The Great Plains (1931)
James C. Malin, The Grassland of North America (1956) chs. 11, 15, 22, 3,
     4, 12, 18, 19, 10, 24-26.
Fred A. Shannon, The Farmer's Last Frontier (1945)
Gilbert C. Fite, The Farmer's Frontier, 1865-1900 (1966)
Robert G. Bell, "James C. Malin and the Grassland of North America,"
     Agricultural History, XLVI (1972)
Wallace Stegner, Wolf Willow (1962)
     , Beyond the Hundreth Meridian (1954)
Mari Sandoz, Old Jules (1935)
Ole E. Ralvaag, Giants in the Earth (1927)
     Hamlin Garland, Boy Life on the Prairie (1899)
     , A Son of the Middle Border (1917)
Howard R. Lamar, Dakota Territory, 1861-1889 (1956)
James C. Malin, Winter Wheat in the Golden Belt of Kansas (1944)
Willa Cather, My Antonia and O Pioneers

UNIVERSITY OF VIRGINIA

Dorothy Ross

HIUS 315

The Gilded Age

Fall Term   Professor Ross

Class:
   The class will meet on Tuesdays and Thursdays at 12:30 p.m.
   Approximately every third meeting of the class will be set
   aside to discuss the assigned readings. Be prepared to discuss the readings at that time. One-third of your final grade
   will be based on the class discussion.

Readings:
   The readings listed below are required. All books have been
   placed on reserve in the Reserve Book Room of Alderman Library.
   Those books marked with an asterisk are available in paperback
   editions at the Newcomb Hall Bookstore.

Examinations:
   There will be a mid-term examination during the class period,
   and there will be a final examination. Each will count for
   one-third of the final grade.

The Problem

1. Introduction to the course.

2. Agrarian community and industrial nation.

3. Discussion.

   * Horatio Alger, Ragged Dick

The Capitalists

4. The search for profit.

5. The search for order.

6. Discussion.

   Joseph Wall, Andrew Carnegie, chapters 11, 15, 16.

The Workers

7. Standards of living and quality of life.

8. Working class organization: why was there so little?

9. Discussion.

> * Herbert Gutman, <u>Work, Culture, and Society in Industrializing America</u>, p. 1-118.
> * Melvyn Dubofsky, <u>Industrialism and the American Worker, 1865-1920</u>, ch. 1, 2.

The Farmers

10. Who were the Populists and what did they want?

11. Black farmers in the South: the vise of poverty and race.

12. Discussion.

> * Lawrence Goodwyn, <u>The Populist Moment</u>, Introduction and ch. 1-6.
> * Richard Hofstadter, <u>The Age of Reform</u>, p. 23-59.

* * * * * * * * * *

13. Mid-term examination.

* * * * * * * * * *

The Middle Class

14. Aspiration, anxiety and guilt

15. Discussion

> * William Graham Sumner, <u>What Social Classes Owe to Each Other</u>

16. The crisis of the Republic.

17. Discussion.

> * Edward Bellamy, <u>Looking Backward</u>

The Political System

18. Party politics.

19. National government and judicial government.

20. Discussion.

     * Morton Keller, <u>Affairs of State</u>, ch. 7, 14
     * William L. Riordon, <u>Plunkitt of Tammany Hall</u>

Crisis in the 1890's

21. National and judicial government continued: the ICC.

22. 1896: year of decision?

23. Discussion.

     Keller, <u>Affairs of State</u>, ch. 15.
     Goodwyn, <u>The Populist Moment</u>, ch. 7 to the end of the book.
     Hofstadter, <u>The Age of Reform</u>, p. 94-130.

The New Middle Class

24. Science, specialization and reform.

25. Social science, critical and contained.

26. Discussion.

     * Charlotte Perkins Gilman, <u>Women and Economics</u>

Conclusion

27. <u>Gemeinschaft</u> and <u>Gesellschaft</u>

     * Robert Wiebe, <u>The Search for Order</u>, Preface, p. 1-163.

10.371
Fall, 1982   Professor Higham

ETHNIC PATTERNS IN AMERICAN HISTORY

The aims of this course are: (1) to develop and
sharpen the ability to think comparatively about different
kinds of people; (2) to understand the dynamics of American
society by studying one of its most distinctive and important
dimensions; (3) to gain a deeper understanding of one's own
particular heritage.

The assigned readings are all available in paperback
at the Book Store (I hope). They include three histories,
three novels, and one personal memoir:

Wilcomb Washburn, The Indian in America
Glenn Altschuler, Race, Ethnicity and Class in American
   Social Thought
Carl Degler, Neither Black Nor White

Vilhelm Moberg, The Emigrants
Harriet Arnow, The Dollmaker
Abraham Cahan, The Rise of David Levinsky

Jerre Mangione, Mount Allegro

In addition to the weekly assignments from the
above books, each student is responsible for an eight to
ten page paper, due around the end of the term. Unless
special arrangements for a different topic are made with
the instructor, the paper should deal with the life of one
or more of your grandparents in historical context.

Week of

Date	Topic	Reading
Sept. 9	Englishmen and Indians	Begin Washburn
Sept. 16	U.S. Indian Policy	Finish Washburn
Sept. 23	Slavery: Origins and Character	Degler, complete
Sept. 30	Early European Immigration	Moberg, complete
Oct. 7	The Chinese	No assignment
Oct. 14	Free Blacks in the 19th Century	Begin Cahan
Oct. 21	The "New Immigration"	Finish Cahan
Oct. 28	Work, Family, and Radicalism	Altschuler, complete
Nov. 4	Ethnic Leadership and Mobilization	Begin Mangione

Week of

Nov. 11	Repression and Resistance	Finish Mangione
Nov. 18	The Flight from Ethnicity	Begin Arnow
Dec. 2	The Ethnic Revival	Finish Arnow
Dec. 9	Contemporary Dilemmas	No assignment

BIBLIOGRAPHY

I. International Comparative Studies

Foner, Laura, and Genovese, Eugene, eds., Slavery in the New World: A Reader in Comparative History (1969).

Fredrickson, George M., White Supremacy: A Comparative Study in American and South African History (1981).

Hartz, Louis, The Founding of New Societies (1964).

Mason, Philip, Patterns of Dominance (1970).

Isaacs, Harold R., Idols of the Tribe: Group Identity and Political Change (1975).

Van den Berghe, Pierre L., Race and Racism: A Comparative Perspective (1967).

II. Ethnic Contrasts in American Society

Mann, Arthur, The One and the Many: Reflections on the American Identity (1979).

O'Dea, Thomas F., The Mormons (1957).

Eaton, Clement, The Growth of Southern Civilization, 1790-1860 (1961).

Glazer, Nathan, and Moynihan, Daniel P., Beyond the Melting Pot: The Negroes, Puerto Ricans, Jews, Italians, and Irish of New York City (rev. ed., 1970).

Gordon, Milton M., Assimilation in American Life. The Role of Race, Religion, and National Origins (1964).

Hollinger, David A., "Ethnic Diversity, Cosmopolitanism and the Emergence of the American Liberal Intelligentsia," American Quarterly, 27:133-151 (May, 1975).

Bodnar, John and others, Blacks, Poles and Italians in Pittsburgh, 1900-1950 (1981).

Polenberg, Richard, One Nation Divisible: Class, Race and Ethnicity in the United States since 1938 (1980).

Steinberg, Stephen, The Ethnic Myth: Race, Ethnicity and Class in America (1981).

Kelley, Robert, The Cultural Pattern in American Politics (1979).

Hareven, Tamara K., ed., Anonymous Americans. Explorations in Nineteenth-Century Social History (1971). See essays by Stephan Thernstrom, Lawrence Levine, and Timothy Smith.

Higham, John, ed., Ethnic Leadership in America (1978).

Smith, Timothy L., "Native Blacks and Foreign Whites. Varying Responses to Educational Opportunity," Perspectives in American History, 6:309-339 (1972).

Sowell, Thomas, Ethnic America: A History (1981).

McLoughlin, William G., "Red Indians, Black Slavery and White Racism: America's Slaveholding Indians," American Quarterly, 26:367-385 (October, 1974).

Fox, Dixon Ryan, Yankees and Yorkers (1940).

Jensen, Richard, The Winning of the Midwest: A Social History of Midwestern Elections, 1888-1896 (1971).

Holli, Melvin G. and Jones, Peter d'A., The Ethnic Frontier: Essays in the History of Group Survival in Chicago and the Midwest (1977).

III. Indians

Nichols, Roger L. and Adams, George R., eds., The American Indian: Past and Present (1971).

Sheehan, Bernard W., Seeds of Extinction. Jeffersonian Philanthropy and the American Indian (1973).

Slotkin, Richard, Regeneration Through Violence. The Mythology of the American Frontier, 1600-1860 (1973).

Spicer, Edward H., Cycles of Conquest: The Impact of Spain, Mexico and the U.S. on Indians of the Southwest (1962).

Axtell, James, The European and the Indian (1981).

Washburn, Wilcomb, The Indian in America (1975).

Ellis, Richard N., ed., The Western American Indian: Case Studies in Tribal History (1972).

Wallace, Anthony F. C., The Death and Rebirth of the Seneca (1969).

IV. Blacks

Davis, David B., The Problem of Slavery in Western Culture (1966).

Drake, St. Clair, and Cayton, Horace D., Black Metropolis.

Williamson, Joel, New People: Miscegenation and Mulattoes in the United States (1980).

Wilson, William J., The Declining Significance of Race (1978).

Fogel, Robert W. and Engerman, Stanley, Time on the Cross. The Economics of Negro Slavery, 2 vols. (1974).

Fredrickson, George, The Black Image in the White Mind (1971).

Gutman, Herbert G., The Black Family in Slavery and Freedom (1976).

Genovese, Eugene, Roll, Jordan, Roll: The World the Slaves Made (1974).

Harlan, Louis R., Booker T. Washington, Vol. 1 (1973).

Huggins, Nathan I., Harlem Renaissance (1971).

Jordan, Winthrop, White Over Black (1968).

Levine, Lawrence, Black Culture and Black Consciousness (1977).

Meier, August, Negro Thought in America, 1880-1915 (1963).

Meier, August, and Rudwick, Elliott, From Plantation to Ghetto (3rd ed., 1976). The best brief survey of Afro-American history.

Mullin, Gerald, Flight and Rebellion: Slave Resistance in Eighteenth-Century Virginia (1972).

Osofsky, Gilbert, Harlem, 1890-1930 (1966).

Wood, Peter H., Black Majority: Negroes in Colonial South Carolina (1974).

V. European Immigrants: General

Abbott, Edith, ed., Historical Aspects of the Immigration Problem: Select Documents (1926).

"Dislocation and Emigration. The Social Background of American Immigration," Perspectives in American History, vol. 7 (1973).

Thomas, Brinley, Migration and Economic Growth (2nd ed., 1973).

Holt, Michael F., "The Politics of Impatience: The Origins of Know-Nothingism," Journal of American History, 60:309-331 (Sept., 1973).

Cole, Donald B., Immigrant City: Lawrence, Massachusetts, 1845-1921 (1963).

Higgs, Robert, "Race, Skills and Earnings: American Immigrants in 1909," Journal of Economic History, 31:420-428 (June, 1971).

Handlin, Oscar, The Uprooted (2nd ed., 1973).

Jones, Maldwyn, Destination America (1976).

Taylor, Philip, The Distant Magnet: European Emigration to the U.S.A. (1971).

Park, Robert E., and Miller, Herbert A., Old World Traits Transplanted (1921).

Gleason, Philip, ed., Catholicism in America (1970).

Lemon, James, The Best Poor Man's Country: A Geographical Study of Early Southeastern Pennsylvania (1972).

Davis, Allen F. and Haller, Mark H., The Peoples of Philadelphia: A History of Ethnic Groups and Lower-Class Life, 1790-1940 (1973).

Higham, John, Send These to Me: Jews and Other Immigrants in Urban America (1975).

_____, Strangers in the Land: Patterns of American Nativism, 1860-1925 (1955).

145

Ehrlich, Richard L., ed., Immigrants in Industrial America: 1850-1920 (1977).

VI. European Immigrants: Specific Nationalities

Thomas, William J. and Znaniecki, Florian, The Polish Peasant in Europe and America, 2 vols. (1918).

Golab, Caroline, Immigrant Destinations (1977).

Handlin, Oscar, Boston's Immigrants (1959). The Irish.

Fishman, Joshua, Language Loyalty in the United States (1966). Germans, Ukranians, French Canadians, Mexicans.

Howe, Irving, The World of Our Fathers (1976). Eastern European Jews.

Hvidt, Kristian, Flight to America (1975). Danes

Sklare, Marshall, America's Jews (1972).

Saloutos, Theodore, The Greeks in the United States (1964).

Erikson, Charlotte, Invisible Immigrants: The Adaptation of English and Scottish Immigrants in Nineteenth-Century America (1972).

Hosteter, John A., Amish Society (3rd ed., 1980).

Walker, Mack, Germany and Emigration, 1816-1885 (1964).

Leyburn, James G., The Scotch-Irish: A Social History (1962).

Barton, Josef, Peasants and Strangers (1975). Italians, Slovaks, Rumanians.

Novak, Michael, Rise of the Unmeltable Ethnics (1971). Slavs.

Yans-McLaughlin, Virginia., Family and Community: Italian Immigrants in Buffalo, 1880-1930 (1977).

Prpic, George J., The Croatian Immigrants in America (1971).

VII. Other Groups

Barth, Cunther, Bitter Strength: The Chinese in the U.S., 1850-1870 (1964).

146

Daniels, Roger, The Politics of Prejudice (1962). Japanese.

Fuchs, Lawrence, Hawaii Pono: A Social History (1961).

Pitt, Leonard, The Decline of the Californios (1966).

Lee, Rose Hum, The Chinese in the United States (1960).

Gonzales, Nancie, The Spanish-Americans of New Mexico (1969).

Meier, Matthew S., and Rivera, Feliciano, The Chicanos: A History of Mexican-Americans (1972).

VIII.   General Reference

Thernstrom, Stephan, ed., Harvard Encyclopedia of American Ethnic Groups (1980).

HARVARD UNIVERSITY
DEPARTMENT OF HISTORY

Stephan Thernstrom

History 90p

Immigration and Ethnicity
Fall, 1981

Required Reading (All assigned articles are to be found in Thernstrom,
Harvard Encyclopedia of American Ethnic Groups or on reserve in
the History Department Library.)

Sept. 29   "Concepts of Ethnicity"; "American Identity and Americanization";
            "Immigration: History of U.S. Policy"; "Naturalization and
            Citizenship"; "Prejudice and Discrimination, History of"; "Survey
            Research"; Gleason, "The Melting Pot: Fusion or Confusion?" [reserve]

Oct. 6   Ward, Cities and Immigrants; "Immigration: Economic and Social
            Characteristics"; "Immigration: Settlement Patterns and Spatial
            Distribution"; "Family Patterns".

Oct. 13   "Germans"; "Irish"; "Danes"; "Mormons"; "Loyalties: Dual and
            Divided"; "Leadership"; "Labor"

Oct. 20   Rischin, The Promised City; "Armenians"; "Romanians"; "Education"

Oct. 27   Glazer and Moynihan, Beyond the Melting Pot; Thernstrom, The Other
            Bostonians, chs. 6 and 7 (reserve)

Nov. 3   Petersen, Japanese Americans

Nov. 10   Novak, The Rise of the Unmeltable Ethnics; "Pluralism: A Political
            Perspective"; Patterson, "The Revival of Ethnicity: With Special
            Reference to the U.S." (reserve)

Nov. 17   "Afro-Americans"; "West Indians"; "Prejudice and Discrimination,
            Policy Against"; "Intermarriage"; The Other Bostonians, ch. 8;
            Sowell, "Ethnicity in a Changing America" (reserve)

Nov. 24   Camarillo, Chicanos; "Spanish"; "Cubans"; "Central and South
            Americans"; Thernstrom, "E Pluribus Plura--Congress and Bilingual
            Education" (reserve)

Paper   Each student will be expected to prepare a 20-25 page research
            paper based upon research in primary sources. The class meetings
            on Dec. 1, 8, and 15 will be given over to oral reports on your
            findings. Papers are due Jan. 5.

148

UNIVERSITY OF MICHIGAN

HISTORY 396

Section 005

Colloquium: The Immigrant Experience In America

Syllabus   3633 Haven Hall

Fall Term 1982   764-6353/971-8562

Gerald F. Linderman   Office Hours: Tuesdays
                                                         4:15 – 5:45 and by
                                                         appointment

    The course is designed to explore the personal and collective experience
of immigrants arriving in the United States during the nineteenth and twentieth
centuries. Categories of special interest will include immigrant expectation
and adaptation; the tension between ethnic exclusiveness and assimilation; the
fit of the immigrant within the new city and its politics; native-born reactions;
and the condition of ethnicity in contemporary America. One or more meetings
may call on members of local ethnic communities to convey particular ethnic
patterns.

    Tentative marking requirements include vigorous class discussion and
several short analytical essays. The course does not form part of a Departmental
sequence, nor do special background or prerequisite courses bear on its
successful completion.

Required Texts

    Michael Arlen, Passage to Ararat (Farrar, Straus, Giroux)
    Abraham Cahan, The Rise of David Levinsky (Harper Colophon)
    L. Dinnerstein and D. Reimers, Ethnic Americans (Dodd Mead)
    Richard Gambino, Blood of My Blood (Doubleday Anchor)
    Akemi Kikumura, Through Harsh Winters (Chandler and Sharp)
    Helen Lopata, Polish Americans (Prentice-Hall)
    Barbara Myerhoff, Number Our Days (Touchstone: Simon & Schuster)
    Y.G. and B.D.B. Nee, Longtime Californ' (Pantheon)
    Edwin O'Connor, The Last Hurrah (Bantam)
    Piri Thomas, Down These Mean Streets (Vintage)

    Course-Pack (Available at Dollar Bill Copying, 611 Church Street; 665-9200)

Class Schedule and Reading Assignments

    September 9   Introduction

    September 16   The Immigrant Experience:
                         Dinnerstein and Reimers, Ethnic Americans

    September 23   The Irish Experience:
                         O'Connor, The Last Hurrah; Course-Pack Article on the
                         Irish (22 pages)

149

September 30	The Jewish Experience: Cahan, _The Rise of David Levinsky_; Course-Pack Article on the Jews (28 pages)
October 7	The Jewish Experience: Myerhoff, _Number Our Days_
October 14	The Polish Experience: Lopata, _Polish Americans_; Course-Pack Article on the Poles (17 pages)
October 21	Film Showing: Me and The Colonel (Danny Kaye and Curt Jurgens) First Critical Essay Due No Reading Assignment
October 28	The Italian Experience: Gambino, _Blood of My Blood_: Course-Pack Article on the Italians (16 pages)
November 4	The Japanese Experience: Kikumura, _Through Harsh Winters_; Course-Pack Article on the Japanese (11 pages)
November 11	The Chinese Experience: Nee and Nee, _Longtime Californ'_; Course-Pack Article on the Chinese (18 pages)
November 18	The Armenian Experience: Arlen, _Passage to Ararat_; Course-Pack Article on the Armenians (14 pages)
November 25	Thanksgiving
December 2	Visit with Ms. Patricia Yeghissian Second Critical Essay Due No Reading Assignment
December 9	The Puerto Rican Experience: Thomas, _Down These Mean Streets_; Course-Pack Article on the Puerto Ricans (10 pages)

History Colloquium:

The Immigrant Experience in America

Reading Questions

Questions Pertinent to Dinnerstein-Reimers' Ethnic Americans

1. What exactly are those Puritan-Pilgrim values which early established themselves as the "American" values?

2. The authors stress colonial-period tensions between the English majority and German and Scotch-Irish minorities. How is the problem ultimately resolved? And how do you judge the desirability of that solution as a general prescription for ethnic conflict?

3. Why do nineteenth-century immigrants come to America? Are they generally more pushed than pulled or the reverse?

4. What are the principal problems that immigrants encounter upon their arrival in this country?

5. If there is so much animosity against immigrants, why does it not quickly reflect itself in the political process as a legal prohibition against the acceptance of additional immigrants? And why do not the immigrants defend themselves by establishing a united front?

6. It is no wonder that native Americans were more hostile to the New Immigrants than to the Old, for the former make no commitment to this country and wish only to take their wages and return to their homelands at the first opportunity. Please evaluate this position.

7. The unwillingness of the United States to accept large numbers of European Jews in the late 1930s reveals the power of American anti-Semitism. Please comment on this assertion.

8. What factors account for the diminution of ethnic animosity in recent years?

9. Mexican-Americans tolerate longer than other ethnic groups the absence of improvement in the basic conditions of their lives. Why do they endure what others have protested?

10. Why do the Germans achieve greater social mobility than the Irish? Why do the Jews rise faster than other New Immigrant groups?

11. On page 140, the authors contend that "...we are on the threshold of the disappearance of the European ethnic minorities." Do you agree? And if so, how do you account for the 1960s resurgence of interest in ethnic affiliation?

12. On the basis of your reading to date, what national immigration policy would you advocate that the United States adopt today?

Questions Pertinent to Edwin O'Connor's The Last Hurrah

1. What accounts for Irish preoccupation with the political process?

2. Frank Skeffington does not lack enemies. What is the basis of Amos Force's hostility? Of Nathaniel Gardiner's opposition? Of Roger Sugrue's? Of the Cardinal's?

3. If it is reasonable to view the mayor as a complex amalgam of "Irish" and "American" attitudes and traits, where in the behavior of Frank Skeffington does one find the explicitly Irish?

4. What is a wake?

5. How is the Skeffington political machine supported?

6. Is Frank Skeffington corrupt?

7. In what ways do those men whose story we follow think about and interact with women?

8. Weinberg, Gorman and Mangan each offer an explanation of what in the end goes wrong. Why does Frank Skeffington suffer defeat?

Questions Pertinent to Abraham Cahan's The Rise of David Levinsky

1. What are the proximate and secondary considerations prompting David
    Levinsky to emigrate? Is he more pushed than pulled, or the reverse?

2. What are the principal points at which David Levinsky's preconseptions
    of the United States clash with American social reality?

3. What are the principal points at which American popular professions
    clash with American social and political reality?

4. What is "education" and how can David Levinsky at once so value it and
    so disparage its results in those around him?

5. Why, given the hardships that he endures, is David Levinsky not more
    receptive to labor organization? to socialism?

6. When Andrew Carnegie first read Herbert Spencer, "light came in a flood
    and all was clear." Why should David Levinsky--so different, so distant
    from Andrew Carnegie--respond in the same way?

7. What in the end does David Levinsky decide it means to be an "American"?

8. Is David Levinsky victor or victim? And if the latter, who or what is
    the source of his oppression?

Questions Pertinent to Barbara Myerhoff's <u>Number Our Days</u>

1. How would you characterize the relationship between parents—
    i.e. those with whom Barbara Myerhoff speaks at the Aliyah
    Senior Citizens Center — and their children? To what degree
    is immigrant-ethnicity a contributor to the problem? Or is
    the problem satisfactorily explained by differences in age,
    in experience, etc?

2. Why do Center members recall with fondness their lives in
    Eastern European <u>shtetls</u>? And what does Shmuel the Filosofe
    mean when, in reply to such a question, he answers, "Because
    it (the <u>shtetl)</u> was ours"?

3. What is Survivor's Guilt and how does it enter the lives of
    people at the Center?

4. If Yiddish culture insists on the subordination of women — they
    are, after all, denied opportunities for education and religious
    participation and thought to be nothing in their own right — how
    is one to account for what appear to be elements of extraordinary
    strength and assertiveness in those women to whom the book intro-
    duces us?

5. How do Center members think about the Gentile world? In images
    favorable or threatening to their own interests?

6. Do you think Shmuel right in his assertion that Judaism is quite
    capable of working well without God or Zionism?

7. The Evil Eye and magic, demons and curses — how can one take
    seriously the interactions of people who believe in such
    phenomena? And who are constantly so angry and so disputatious?

8. Why, if Sadie had named Anna, would the breach have become
    irreparable?

9. What do Center people believe it is to be a Jew?

Questions Pertinent to Lopata's <u>Polish Americans</u>

1. What is the distinction which Milton Gordon draws between cultural pluralism and structural pluralism? Which characterizes American society?

2. How valuable do you think the notion of the Triple Melting Pot?

3. What does the author intend by the term "ethclass"? And why is it more germane to the Polish experience than to that of other immigrant groups?

4. Hopes for an independent Poland and for a Jewish homeland in Palestine might have been expected to establish affinity between Polish and Jewish immigrant groups, but the patterns of American society hindered such co-operation. Please comment.

5. What are the qualities which Poles believe constitute their national character? Would not one expect such values to make of Poles the most materially successful of the immigrant groups? And how valid do you believe the conception of national character? Is there, for example, an American national character?

6. What, according to the author, is status competition and what is its import to the Polish community?

7. Polish Americans both bring with them and encounter here problems unique to themselves. Please comment.

8. Polish Americans are anti-Semitic and anti-Black, are they not?

9. In what ways are Polish immigrants aided by their ethnic backgrounds? In what ways obstructed?

Questions Pertinent to Richard Gambino's <u>Blood of My Blood</u>

1. Why is there so much more Italian emphasis on the family than among native-born Americans?

2. How can one possibly believe that "the law works against the people"?

3. What are the differences between the immigrant, second and third generations in their orientation towards Italian culture? In their conceptions of marriage?

4. Is it, do you think, easier to be a second or third generation Italian-American?

5. The author believes that aspects of <u>uomo segreto</u> are no less admirable than American honesty, trust, fair-dealing, etc., because the latter, while preached, are not practiced. Do you agree?

6. Why do Italian-Americans not strive in pursuit of the traditional American aspiration of buying bigger and buying better?

7. What are the bases of Italian-Black animosity?

8. What, according to the author, is the Italian-American's problem and what the solution?

Please master the meanings of the following terms:

contadino   comparragio
famiglia   Mezzogiorno
rispetto   l'uomo de Pazienza
pieta   la serietà
la via vecchia

Questions Pertinent to Akemi Kikumura's _Through Harsh Winters_

1. Why should the author's mother feel shame vis-a-vis relatives who remained in Japan? And why should she desire their forgiveness?

2. In what ways does the mother appear representative of Japanese women who emigrate to the United States? In what ways untypical?

3. How would you characterize the relationship between husband and wife as prescribed by the mores of the Japanese-American community? And which of its prescriptions depart from those governing Anglo-American marriages?

4. What are the extent and nature of the author's parents' contacts with the larger white American society?

5. Is Mama's estimate of Papa higher or lower than you own?

6. Why do Mama's children not behave or treat her as she believes proper?

7. Does Mama regard herself as a success or as a failure? By American cultural definitions of what constitutes a good life, is she a success or a failure?

8. What are the strengths of Japanese-American child-rearing practices? The weaknesses? Do such practices generally advance or retard the pace of the children's Americanization?

9. In what ways did the internment-camp experience of World War Two affect Japanese Americans?

10. What aspects of Japanese culture appear most persistently in contemporary Japanese Americans? And which have proven most vulnerable to disintegrative forces?

Questions Pertinent to the Nees' Longtime Californ'

Please read the Introduction; from mid-page 9 through page 10 of the Prologue;
Chapters 1-15, omitting pages 30-59, 73-80, 83-90, 96-mid-105, 117-135, 141-147,
177-181, 213-227, 266-271, 280-288, 324-328, 360-362.

1. Contrasts between Chinese Americans and Japanese Americans:

    (a) Why do Chinese return to the homeland more frequently than the Japanese?

    (b) Why do Chinese social organizations rival one another, while Japanese
        organizations do not seek to dominate one another?

    (c) Why do Chinese Americans take up criminal activity?

    (d) One must conclude that while the Japanese immigrant experience has been
        remarkably successful, that of the Chinese should be adjudged a failure.
        Please evaluate this contention.

2. The control of Chinatown by the Six Companies is both despotic and anachronis-
   tic and should be overthrown, do you not agree?

3. What are the tongs? What functions did they serve originally? And which do
   they continue to fulfill today?

4. Why is it that many of Chinatown's young seem unaffected by the anti-Chinese
   animosity of white American society?

5. Why should we worry about the situation of the new Chinese immigrants? That
   process which incorporated earlier arrivals will work again, and recent
   arrivals will in the end be no worse off than their predecessors. Please
   gauge the validity of this position.

6. Which propositions do you favor?

    (a) I would rather grow up as the child of Japanese American parents/I would
        rather grow up as the child of Chinese American parents.

    (b) Chinatown's garment shops are a disgrace to proper employer-employee rela-
        tionships and should be closed down/The intimate, personal atmosphere
        and the flexibility of Chinatown's garment shops more than offset their
        below-average wage scales and justify their continuation.

7. Ethnic institutions have in other cases prepared and strengthened those within
   for their entry into the larger society. Chinatown, however, has ill served
   this function, and Chinese Americans would today be better off had that
   enclave long ago disappeared. Please comment on this contention.

8. How are Chinatown's problems to be addressed? By the recognition that Chinese
   Americans are, with Blacks and Chicanos, members of an exploited class? By
   development of pride in the Chinese heritage? By accelerating movement into
   middle-class America and professional status? What exactly is your
   prescription?

Questions Pertinent to Michael Arlen's _Passage to Ararat_

1. In what ways does the author become aware of his own Armenianism?

2. Where is Armenia?

3. What is it about Michael Arlen's initial contacts with New York City Armenians that so disconcerts him?

4. What does William Saroyan mean when he says, "An Armenian can never not be an Armenian"?

5. "To be an Armenian," says Sarkis, "is to have this intolerable weight of sadness on one's soul," but Armenians appear to add masochistically to their burden by recalling endlessly that long-ago experience of the Massacres. Please evaluate this contention.

6. Michael Arlen's story, despite the author's protestations to the contrary, is simply one of a son troubled by an unsatisfactory relationship with a father now dead. Ethnicity _per se_ is of little importance. Do you agree with this argument?

7. Is the remembrance of the Massacres, as Michael Arlen several times suggests, a "poison"? And do you agree with him that "the Jews handled their nightmare better"?

8. Why _do_ the Turks kill Armenians? And why, if Armenians did nothing to merit Turkish enmity, should Armenians come to blame themselves almost as they blame the Turks?

9. Are you convinced by the profundity of the effects that the author describes as taking place within himself as a result of his journey to Armenia?

Questions Pertinent to Piri Thomas' Down These Mean Streets

1. Harry H.L. Kitano contends in Japanese Americans (pages 6-7) that of four
   groups in the United States--Blacks, Jews, Catholics and Puerto Ricans--
   "only the Puerto Rican has not been culturally assimilated ... that is,
   has not taken on the values, skills, and behaviors of the host, middle-
   class American society." Does the evidence of Piri Thomas' book support
   or challenge this notion?

2. Puerto Rican youths lack any sense of community and thus such concomitants
   as respect for public property. Witness the graffiti with which they
   cover New York City subway cars.

   Please comment on this contention.

3. What are Piri Thomas' feelings for his father? For his mother? Do they
   derive principally from Hispanic cultural values or from the city's
   immediate social environment?

4. What are Piri Thomas' attitudes towards himself? Do they derive principally
   from Hispanic cultural values or from the city's immediate social environment? And what for him constitutes success?

5. How would you characterize Piri Thomas' feelings about Italians, Jews, Irish?

   He remarks at one point that X is a good White, Y a bad White, but his
   friend Brew denies the distinction; no, he says, white is white.

   Which position does the evidence of the book itself seem to support?

6. Blacks and Puerto Ricans seem to suffer the same animosities and the same
   obstructions. Why, then, do they not unite against their oppressors?

7. How does Piri Thomas find it possible to justify to himself the encounter
   with the homosexuals, an episode that he admits fills him with disgust?
   His theft of money from a Puerto Rican woman? The child he fathers in a
   loveless relationship? And what is it that ultimately convinces him that
   his basic values are destructive of himself and others?

History 571, Seminar 1   Thomas Archdeacon

Immigration and Ethnicity in Recent American History

Meeting 1   January 21

An Overview of Immigration to the U.S.A.

Recommended Reading: Maldwyn Jones, American Immigration.

Meeting 2   January 28

Recent Immigration Issues

    Thomas L. Bernard, "United States Immigration Laws and the
        Brain Drain," International Migration, VIII (1970), 31-38.
    William S. Bernard, "America's Immigration Plicy: Its Evolution
        and Sociology," International Migration, IV (1965-66),
        pp. 234-45.
    _____, "Immigrants and Refugees: Their Similarities,
        Differences, and Needs," International Migration, XIV (1976),
        pp. 267-81.
    Monica Boyd, "The Changing Nature of Central and Southeast Asian
        Immigration to the United States, 1961-1972," International
        Migration Review, VIII (1974), pp. 507-20.
    Charles B. Keely, "Temporary Workers in the United States,"
        International Migration, XIII (1975), pp. 106-11.

Meeting 3   February 4

Mexican and Caribbean Immigrants

    Jose H. Alvarez, "The Movement and Settlement of Puerto Rican
        Migrants within the United States," International Migration
        Review, II (1967-68)
    Roy Simon Bryce-Laporte, "New York City and the New Caribbean
        Immigration: A Contextual Statement," International Migration
        Review, XIII (1979)
    Jorge A. Bustamante, "Undocumented Immigration from Mexico:
        Research Report," International Migration Review, XI (1977),
        pp. 147-77.
    Alejandro Porter, "Toward a Structural Analysis of Illegal
        (Undocumented) Immigration," International Migration Review,
        XII (1978), pp. 469-84.
    Josh Reichert & Douglas S. Massey, "Patterns of US Immigration
        from a Mexican Sending Community: A Comparison of Legal and
        Illegal Migrants," International Migration Review, XIII (1979),
        pp. 599-623.

Meeting 4   February 11

Concepts of Acculturation and Assimilation

        Milton M. Gordon, Assimilation in American Life.

Meeting 5   February 18

The Melting Pot and Beyond

> Eugene I. Bender & George Kagiwado, "Hansen's Law of 'Third
>   Generation Return' and the Study of American Religious
>   Ethnic Groups," _Phylon_, XXIX (1968), pp. 360-70.
> Bernard Lazerwitz, "Religious Identification and Its Ethnic
>   Correlates," _Social Forces_, LII (1973), pp. 204-20.
> R.A. Schermerhorn, "Ethnicity in the Perspective of the
>   Sociology of Knowledge," _Ethnicity_, I (1974), pp. 1-14.
> Harry S. Stout, "Ethnicity: The Vital Center of Religion in
>   America," _Ethnicity_, II (1975), pp. 204-24.

Recommended: Will Herberg, _Protestant-Catholic-Jew_.

Meeting 6   February 25

The Lenski Thesis

> Gary D. Bouma, "Beyond Lenski: A Critical Review of Recent
>   'Protestant Ethic' Research," _Journal for the Scientific Study
>   of Religion_, 12 (1973), pp. 141-55.
> David L. Featherman, "The Socioeconomic Achievement of White
>   Religion-Ethnic Subgroups: Social and Psychological Explanations,"
>   _American Sociological Review_, 36 (1971), pp. 207-22.
> Norval D. Glenn and Ruth Hyland, "Religious Preference and
>   Worldly Success: Some Evidence from National Surveys,"
>   _American Sociological Review_, 32 (1967), pp. 73-85.
> Joseph Veroff, Sheila Field, and Gerald Burin, "Achievement
>   Motivation and Religious Background," _American Sociological
>   Review_, 27 (1962), pp. 205-17.

Recommended: Gerhard Lenski, _The Religious Factor_.

Meeting 7   March 4

Ethnic Groups and Economic Achievement

> Andrew M. Greeley, _Ethnicity, Denomination, and Inequality_.

Recommended: Thomas Sowell, ed., _American Ethnic Groups_.

Meeting 8   March 11

Residential Segregation

> Wendell Bell, "A Probability Model for the Measurement of
>   Ecological Segregation," _Social Forces_, 33 (1954), pp. 357-64.
> Avery M. Guest and James A. Weed, "Ethnic Residential
>   Segregation: Patterns of Change," _American Journal Sociology_,
>   81 (1976), pp. 1088-1111.
> Nathan Kantrowitz, "Ethnic and Racial Segregation in the New
>   York Metropolis," _American Journal of Sociology_, 74 (1969),
>   pp. 685-95.

Stanley Lieberson, "The Impact of Residential Segregation
on Ethnic Assimilation," Social Forces, 40 (1961), pp. 52-57.
_____, "Suburbs and Ethnic Residential Patterns,"
American Journal of Sociology, 67 (1962), pp. 673-81.

Meeting 9   March 18

Spring Break

Meeting 10   March 25

Social Contacts Amoung Ethnic Groups

Jon P. Alston, William A. McIntosh, and Louise M. Wright, "Extent
of Inter-marriage among White Americans," Sociological Analysis,
37 (1976), pp. 261-64.
Bartolomeo J. Palisi, "Ethnic Patterns of Friendship," Phylon, 27
(1966), pp. 217-25.
Peter C. Pineo, "The Social Standing of Ethnic and Racial
Groupings," Canadian Review of Sociology and Anthropology, 14
(1977), pp. 147-55.
C. Price and J. Zubrzycki, "The Use of Inter-Marriage Statistics as
an Index of Assimilation," Population Studies, 16 (1962),
pp. 58-69.
John Finley Scott, "The American College Sorority: Its Role in
Class and Ethnic Endogamy," American Sociological Review,
30 (1965), pp. 514-27.

Meeting 11   April 1

Ethnic Politics

Walter O. Borowiec, "Perceptions of Ethnic Voters by Ethnic
Politicians," Ethnicity, I (1974), pp. 267-78.
Andrew M. Greeley, "Political Participation among Ethnic Groups
in the United States," in Greeley, ed., Ethnicity in the United
States: A Preliminary Reconnaissance, pp. 121-55.
Michael Parenti, "Ethnic Politics and the Persistence of Ethnic
Identification," American Political Science Review, LXI (1967),
pp. 717-26.
Gerald Pomper, "Ethnic and Group Voting in Nonpartisan Municipal
Elections," Public Opinion Quarterly, XXX (1966), pp. 79-97.

Meeting 12   April 8

Ethno-Religious Voting Behavior

Andrew R. Baggaley, "Religious Influence on Wisconsin Voting,
1928-1960," American Political Science Review, LVI (1962),
pp. 66-70.
Jerome M. Clebb and Howard W. Allen, "The Cities and the Election
of 1928: A Partisan Realignment?" American Historical Review,
74 (1969), pp. 1205-20.
Philip B. Converse et. al., "Stability and Change in 1960: Reinstating
Election," American Political Science Review, LV (1961),
pp. 269-80.

Vincent P. DeSantis, "American Catholics and McCarthyism,"
   Catholic Historical Review, LI (1965), pp. 1-30.
Mark R. Levy and Michael S. Kramer, The Ethnic Factor, pp. 225-52
   ("Epilogue: The 1972 Election").

Meeting 13   April 15

Ethnics and Contemporary Social Issues

   Andrew M. Greeley, "Response to Urban Unrest: The Case of
      Jews and the Poles," in Greeley, ed., Ethnicity in the United
      States, pp. 217-51.
   Norman H. Nie et al., "Political Attitudes among American
      Ethnics: A Study of Perceptual Distortion," in Greeley, ed.,
      Ethnicity, pp. 186-216.
   Larry R. Peterson and Armand L. Mauss, "Religion and the 'Right
      to Life': Correlates of Opposition to Abortion," Sociological
      Analysis, XXXVII (1976), pp. 243-54.
   John F. Stack, Jr., "Ethnicity, Racism, and Busing in Boston:
      The Boston Irish and School Desegregation," Ethnicity, VI
      (1979), pp. 21-28.

Meeting 14   April 22

American Ethnic Cultures in Comparison

   Andrew M. Greeley & William C. McCready, "Ethnic Problem
      Drinking," unpublished NORC pager, 1978.
   William C. McCready, "The Persistence of Ethnic Variation in
      American Families," in Greeley, ed., Ethnicity, pp. 156-76.
   Nicholas Robak & Sylvia Clavan, "Perception of Masculinity
      among Males in Two Traditional Family Groups," Sociological
      Analysis, 36 (1975), pp. 335-46.
   Edward A. Suchman, "Sociomedical Variations among Ethnic Groups,"
      American Journal of Sociology, 70 (1964), pp. 319-32.
   Berthold B. Wolff & Sarah Langley, "Cultural Factors in Response
      to Pain: A Review," American Anthropologist, 70 (1968),
      pp. 494-501.

Meeting 15   April 29

Ethnicity and Race

   William J. Wilson, The Declining Significance of Race.

Recommended: Nathan Glazer and Daniel P. Moynihan, Beyond the Melting
                Pot, revised edition, Introduction.

Meeting 16   May 6

Concluding Discussion

History 165S.1
Fall, 1982
MWF 9-9:50
West Duke 101

Peter H. Wood
205 East Duke
Office hours: Wed. 2-4
or by appointment

RACE AND SOCIETY IN AMERICA: HISTORICAL AND CULTURAL PERSPECTIVES

This class is the core course for the Race and Society Program. It is open to members of that program and to a limited number of other students by permission of the instructor.

Emphasis in the first two thirds of the course will fall on the inter-relations of Native Americans, Afro-Americans and Euro-Americans in the 17th through the 19th centuries, including a comparison of U.S. race relations with those of South Africa. In the third part of the course, attention will be given to the Hawaiian, Puerto Rican, Japanese and Chinese experiences. The purpose is not only to learn about divergent American groups but to trace the sources, continuities and shifts of ethnic and racial attitudes and understanding. (The course is not a substitute for more extensive Duke courses dealing with the history of Blacks, Indians, or Asian-Americans, but it may serve as a stimulus toward taking such courses.)

Reading will be in both primary and secondary sources and will include "literary" as well as "historical" material. Books are on closed reserve in Perkins and East Campus Library (single copies) and all may be purchased at the Regulator Bookshop at 720 Ninth Street near East Campus. Paperbacks recommended for individual or joint purchase are:

William Shakespeare, The Tempest (Signet)
Richard Drinnon, Facing West (Meridian)
George Fredrickson, White Supremacy (Oxford)
John Neihardt, Black Elk Speaks (Pocket)
Frederick Douglass, Narrative of the Life of Frederick Douglass (Signet)
Paul Jacobs, To Serve the Devil (Vol. II) (Vintage)

Since class discussion is central to the course, it is important to do the reading in advance and bring the assigned book to class. There will be written assignments during weeks two and ten, and there will be a final exam. But since this is a seminar, much of what you get out of the course (including a final grade) will depend upon regular attendance and participation in the class.

PART ONE: NATIVES AND NEWCOMERS (1600-1900)

WEEK ONE:

Sept. 1   Introductory Session (no reading).
     3   Andre Lopez, Pagans in Our Midst, read pp. v-xvii and browse in the
           main part of the book.

WEEK TWO: PROSPERO, CALIBAN AND US

Sept. 6   Lopez, Pagans: browse further. Then choose a specific item, image or
           theme and WRITE A BRIEF 2 OR 3 PAGE PAPER TO BE TURNED IN AT THE START
           OF CLASS. Identify your topic clearly (list page or pages), and
           state your personal reactions and ideas in an organized and compelling
           way. If not typed, the paper should be neatly handwritten with wide
           margins and numbered pages; it should have a title.

Sept. 8   Shakespeare, <u>The Tempest</u>, Acts I-II and the section of historical
            source documents in Signet edition.
       10   Finish <u>The Tempest</u>.

WEEK THREE:

Sept. 13   No Reading: but plan to attend a viewing of <u>The Tempest</u> Sunday night,
            Sept. 12 at 7 p.m., in the Video Room of Perkins Library (Perkins 211).
            Friends are welcome.

Sept. 15   Richard Drinnon, <u>Facing West</u>, introduction and chs. 1-3, pp. xi-xx,
            3-34.
       17   Drinnon, <u>Facing West</u>, chs. 4-5, pp. 35-61 AND ALSO John Mason, <u>A
            Brief History of The Pequot War</u> (on reserve for this course and
            History 112)

WEEK FOUR:

Sept. 20   Drinnon, <u>Facing West</u>, Part II, chs. 6-10, pp. 65-116.
       22   Drinnon, <u>Facing West</u>, Part III, chs. 11-13, pp. 119-164.
       24   Drinnon, <u>Facing West</u>, Part III, chs. 14-15, pp. 165-215.

WEEK FIVE: IMAGES OF RACE IN NINETEENTH CENTURY AMERICA

            Assignments for these two days will be
Sept. 27   built on responses to Drinnon's essays. Individuals will be asked to
            test out his methods and
       29   hypotheses by examining works of art and literature which focus on
            non-Europeans.
Oct.   1   Films: <u>The Lakota</u> and/or <u>The Clash of Cultures</u>

WEEK SIX: BLACK ELK: HOLY MAN OF THE OGLALA SIOUX

Sept. 4   John G. Neihardt, <u>Black Elk Speaks</u>, preface and chs. 1-7, pp. 1-76.
       6   <u>Black Elk</u>, chs. 8-16, pp. 77-163.
       8   <u>Black Elk</u>, chs. 17-25 and postscripts, pp. 164-238.

PART TWO: AFRICA AND AMERICA

WEEK SEVEN: THE ORIGINS OF RACIAL SLAVERY

Oct. 11   Fredrickson, <u>White Supremacy</u>, ch. 1 (Settlement and Subjugation)
      13   Fredrickson, <u>White Supremacy</u>, ch. 2 (The Rise of Racial Slavery)

FALL BREAK

WEEK EIGHT: EVOLVING RACE RELATIONS IN TWO SOUTHS

   NOTE: During weeks 8-11, there will be an art exhibit concerning "The Image
            of the Black in Western Art" in the Hanks Lobby of the Bryan Center,
            and there will also be a series of four Thursday Lectures sponsored
            by the Race and Society Program relating to the exhibit. Time and
            place will be announced. You are cordially invited to attend and
            bring friends.
Oct. 18   FALL BREAK
      20   Fredrickson, <u>White Supremacy</u>, ch. 3 (Race Mixture and the Color Line)
      22   Fredrickson, <u>White Supremacy</u>, ch. 4 (Liberty, Union and White Supremacy)
            (Film in Class - <u>Last Grave at Dimbaza</u>)

WEEK NINE: EXPERIENCING THE COLOR LINE

Oct. 25 <u>Narrative of the Life of Frederick Douglass</u>, pp. v-64.
  27 <u>Narrative</u>, pp. 65-126.
  29 Herman Melville, <u>Benito Cereno</u> (78 pages, copies on reserve. READ THE
        ENTIRE STORY)

WEEK TEN: INDUSTRIALISM AND SEGREGATION

Nov. 1 Fredrickson, <u>White Supremacy</u>, ch. 5 (Industrialism, White Labor, and
        Racial Discrimination)
        Also, look at Judy Seidman, <u>Ba Ye Zwa</u>--one copy on reserve at East
        and West.
  3 Fredrickson, <u>White Supremacy</u>, ch. 6 (Segregation in South Africa
        and the South)
  5 NO CLASS TODAY. BEFORE 5 P.M., TURN IN TO MY BOX IN 102 WEST DUKE
        BUILDING A SIX TO TEN PAGE PAPER ON A TOPIC OF YOUR CHOICE, DEALING
        SPECIFICALLY WITH A SUBJECT WE HAVE ADDRESSED SO FAR IN THE COURSE.
        THE PAPER SHOULD BE TYPED AND PROOFREAD, WITH A TITLE AND CONCLUSION.

PART THREE: RACISM AND IMPERIALISM

WEEK ELEVEN: HAWAII, PUERTO RICO AND U.S. EXPANSION

Nov. 8 Jacobs, <u>To Serve the Devil</u> (Vol. II), Introduction and Part One,
        pp. xv-xxxv, 3-65.
  10 Jacobs, <u>Devil</u>, pp. 271-355
  12 Drinnon, <u>Facing West</u>, chs. 16-19, pp. 219-278

WEEK TWELVE: THE U.S. IN THE ORIENT

Nov. 15 Drinnon, <u>Facing West</u>, chs. 20-22, pp. 279-351 (The Philippines)
  17 Drinnon, <u>Facing West</u>, chs. 23-26, pp. 355-401 (Indochina)
  19 Drinnon, <u>Facing West</u>, chs. 27-30, pp. 402-467 (Vietnam)

WEEK THIRTEEN: CHINES IN AMERICA

Nov. 22 Jacobs, <u>Devil</u>, pp. 66-165

THANKSGIVING HOLIDAY

WEEK FOURTEEN: EAST AND WEST

Nov. 29 Kingston, <u>The Woman Warrior</u>, pp. 1-63
Dec. 1 Kingston, <u>The Woman Warrior</u>, pp. 67-186
  3 Kingston, <u>The Woman Warrior</u>, pp. 189-243

WEEK FIFTEEN: THE JAPANESE

Dec. 6 Jacobs, <u>Devil</u>, pp. 166-222.
  8 Jacobs, <u>Devil</u>, pp. 222-270
  10 Discussion

WEEK SIXTEEN

Dec. 13 REVIEW

DEPARTMENT OF AFRO-AMERICAN STUDIES

THE UNIVERSITY OF WISCONSIN

Course 106-231
Spring 1979-80   Prof. Tom Shick

Introduction to Afro-American History

Afro-American History 231 is being offered this semester as an
introductory course. It is designed primarily for the freshmen and
sophomore level student with little or no previous exposure to the subject.
The approach of the course is topical in nature within a chronological
framework. There will be two formal lectures per week and a fifty
minute discussion period. Scheduling of the discussion sections will be
arranged by the Teaching Assistant, Mr. David Anthony.

One important goal of this course is to give students an orientation
to the nature and scope of Afro-American studies in general. The course
begins chronologically with the African background to the slave trade.
The unique aspects of the Afro-American experience through slavery in
America, the Civil War and the post-Reconstruction period of the nineteenth
century will then become the focus of lectures and reading. The remainder
of the course will highlight the political, economic and cultural struggle
of Afro-Americans in the twentieth century within an explicitly racist
society. Emphasis will be placed on the programs and actions of major
Afro-American leadership such as Frederick Douglass, Booker T. Washington,
W. E. B. DuBois, Martin Luther King, Malcolm X and Marcus Garvey.

There will be three major examinations for this course: two mid-
term exams and a final--all of the specifics about the exams will be
announced at the appropriate time. There will also be periodic quizzes
to help students better prepare for the major examinations.

This course is approved for Human Relations Code points 2 and 3.
Human Relations Code point 2: a study of the values, life-styles, and contributions of racial, cultural, and economic groups in American society.
Human Relations Code point 3: an analysis of the forces of racism, prejudice,
and discrimination in American life and the impact of these forces on the
experience of the majority and minority groups.

The following books are ALL REQUIRED and available in paperback
editions in the campus bookstores:

> John Hope Franklin, From Slavery to Freedom
> John H. Bracey, Jr., August Meier, and Elliott Rudwich, eds.
>   The Afro-Americans: Selected Documents

Course 106-231
Spring, 1979-80

Prof. T. Shick
4214 Humanities

Course Outline

I. Introduction

    Jan. 24: Organizational Matters and Overview

II. The Formation of the African Diaspora

    Jan. 29: The South Atlantic Slave Trade System

           31: Slaves, Sugar, and Plantations

    Reading Assignment: Franklin, pp. 3-53; Bracey, pp. 3-16

III. Servitude: The Road to Slavery in America

    Feb. 5: Origins of Racial Discrimination in Colonial America

       7: Afro-Americans in Colonial South Carolina

    Reading Assignment: Franklin, pp. 54-80

IV. Afro-Americans and the American Revolution

    Feb. 12: Afro-Americans as Patriots and Loyalists

        14: Slavery and "All Men are Created Equal"

    Reading Assitnment: Franklin, pp. 81-131

V. Slavery in Antebellum America

    Feb. 19: The Slave Community

        21: Slavery: Urban and Rural

    Reading Assignment: Franklin, pp. 132-56; Bracey, pp. 17-95

VI. Resistance to Slavery and Its Impact

    Feb. 26: Resistance as a Theme in Afro-American History

        28: Turner, Vesey, Prosser: Strike a Blow and Die

    Reading Assignment: Bracey, pp. 99-156

VII. The Building of Black Institutions in America

    Mar. 4: "Establishing the Base"

       6: Ideology and Institutions: Conflicts over Consensus

    Reading Assignment: Franklin, pp. 157-204; Bracey, pp. 157-214

VIII. National Conflict and Crisis: The Civil War and Reconstruction

    Mar. 11: Lincoln, Slavery, and the Union

       13: Reconstruction

    Reading Assignment: Franklin, pp. 205-250; Bracey, pp. 215-296

IX. The Triumph of Institutionalized Racism

        Mar. 25: Economic Dependency and Exploitation

            27: Disfranchisement and Segregation

    Reading Assignment: Franklin, pp. 251-267; Bracey, 297-362

X. Afro-American Response to Racism

        Apr. 1: Booker T. Washington and Accommodation

           3: DuBois and the Niagara Radicals

    Reading Assignment: Franklin, pp. 268-294; Bracey, pp. 363-393

        Apr. 8: Bound for the Promised Land

          10: Garvey and the Harlem Renaissance

    Reading Assignment: Franklin, pp. 295-382; Bracey, pp. 394-429, 508-578

XI. The Depression and F.D.R.'s "New Deal"

        Apr. 15: Last Hired, First Fired

           17: New Deal or No Deal?

    Reading Assignment: Franklin, pp. 383-421; Bracey, pp. 430-507; 579-618

XII. World War II and Race Consciousness

        Apr. 22: The Domestic Front

          24: March on Washington Movement

    Reading Assignment: Franklin, pp. 422-449; Bracey, pp. 622-649

XIII. The Civil Rights Movement

        Apr. 29: Brown v. Board of Education (1954)

        May 1 : Civil Disobedience

    Reading Assignment: Franklin, pp. 450-505; Bracey, pp. 650-751

XIV. Black Power and Urban Rebellion

        May 6: Ideology and Black Power

          8: Pan-Africanism

    Reading Assignment: Class Handouts

        May 13: Review

UNIVERSITY OF WISCONSIN

DEPARTMENT OF AFRO-AMERICAN STUDIES

A SELECT BIBLIOGRAPHY OF STUDIES IN AFRO-AMERICAN HISTORY

I.   Historiography and Bibliography

Earl E. Thorpe, Black Historians: A Critique 1971
James McPherson, Blacks in America: Bibliographical Essays 1971
Monroe N. Work, A Bibliography of the Negro in Africa and
   America 1928
Leonard Irwin, Black Studies: A Bibliography 1973
Dwight L. Smith, Afro-American History: A Bibliography 1974

II. General Histories

Benjamin Quarles, The Negro in the Making of America 1964
Lerone Bennett, Before the Mayflower 1969
John Hope Franklin, From Slavery to Freedom. Fourth edition 1974
August Meier and Elliott Rudwick, From Plantation to Ghetto.
   Third edition 1976
Langston Hughes and Milton Meltzer, A Pictorial History of the
   Negro in America 1968
James Dorman and Robert Jones, The Afro-American Experience:
   A Cultural History Through Emancipation 1974
Arnold Taylor, Travail and Triumph: Black Life and Culture in
   the South Since the Civil War 1976
Philip Foner, A History of Black Americans 1975
Alex Haley, Roots 1976 (historical fiction)

III. African Background

Basil Davidson, The African Genius 1970
Robert W. July, A History of the African People 1970
Paul Bohannan and Philip Curtin, Africa and Africans 1971
Joseph Harris, Africans and Their History 1972
Harry Gailey, History of Africa from Earliest Times to 1800   1970
Jefferson Murphy, History of African Civilization 1972

IV. Atlantic Slave Trade

Basil Davidson, The African Slave Trade or Black Mother 1961
Philip Curtin, The Atlantic Slave Trade: A Census 1969
Daniel Mannix and Malcolm Cowley, Black Cargoes 1962
Eric Williams, Capitalism and Slavery 1944
W.E.B. DuBois, The Suppression of the African Slave Trade 1896
James Pope-Hennessy, Sins of the Fathers 1968
Ronald Takaki, A Proslavery Crusade 1971
Herbert S. Klein, The Middle Passage: Comparative Studies in the
   Atlantic Slave Trade 1978

V. Blacks in Colonial America

Lorenzo Greene, The Negro in Colonial New England 1942
Gerald Mullin, Flight and Rebellion 1972
Winthrop Jordan, White Over Black 1968
Thad Tate, The Negro in Eighteenth-Century Williamsburg 1965
Edgar J. McManus, Black Bondage in the North 1973
Peter Wood, Black Majority 1974
Lester B. Scherer, Slavery and the Churches in Early America,
    1619-1819 1975
Edmund S. Morgan, American Slavery, American Freedom 1975

VI. Blacks in the Revolutionary Era

Benjamin Quarles, The Negro in the American Revolution 1961
Herbert Aptheker, The Negro in the American Revolution 1940
Arthur Zilversmit, The First Emancipation
Staughton Lynd, Class Conflict, Slavery, and the US Constitution
    1967
Donald Robinson, Slavery in the Structure of American Politics,
    1765-1820 1971
Robert McColley, Slavery and Jeffersonian Virginia 1964
David Brion Davis, The Problem of Slavery in the Age of Revolution,
    1770-1823 1975
Philip S. Foner, Blacks in the American Revolution 1977

VII. Plantation and Urban Slavery

Leslie H. Owens, This Species of Property 1976
Kenneth Stampp, The Peculiar Institution 1956
John Blassingame, The Slave Community 1972
Eugene Genovese, Roll, Jordan, Roll 1974
Stanley Elkins, Slavery 1959
Ulrich B. Phillips, American Negro Slavery 1918 (a racist
    interpretation)
Stanley Engerman and Robert Fogel, Time on the Cross 1974
Richard Wade, Slavery in the Cities 1964
Robert Starobin, Industrial Slavery in the Old South 1970
George Rawick, From Sundown to Sunup 1972
Claudia Goldin, Urban Slavery in the American South 1976
Herbert Gutman, The Black Family in Slavery and Freedom 1976

VIII. Slave Resistance and Rebellion

Herbert Aptheker, American Negro Slave Revolts 1943
Nicholas Halasz, The Rattling Chains 1966
John Lofton, Insurrection in South Carolina 1964
John B. Duff and Peter Mitchell, eds., The Nat Turner Rebellion
    1971
Larry Gara, The Liberty Line: The Legend of the Underground
    Railroad 1961

IX. Black Folklore

Dena J. Epstein, <u>Sinful Tunes and Spirituals: Black Folk
    Music to the Civil War</u> 1977
Newell Niles Puckett, <u>Folk Beliefs of the Southern Negro</u> 1926
Gilbert Osofsky, <u>Puttin' On Ole Massa</u> 1969
Norman Yetman, <u>Life Under the "Peculiar Institution"</u> 1970
Richard Dorson, <u>American Negro Folktales</u> 1967
Zora Neale Hurston, <u>Mules and Men</u> 1935
Harold Courlander, <u>Negro Folk Music, U.S.A.</u> 1963
Leroi Jones, <u>Blues People</u> 1963
Norman Whitten and John Szwed, eds., <u>Afro-American Anthropology</u>
    1970
Lawrence Levine, <u>Black Culture and Black Consciousness</u> 1977

X. Free Black Community

Floyd J. Miller, <u>The Search For a Black Nationality: Black
    Colonization and Emigration, 1787-1863</u> 1975
Leon Litwack, <u>North of Slavery</u> 1961
Howard Bell, <u>A Survey of the Negro Convention Movement</u> 1969
W.H. and J.H. Pease, <u>Black Utopia: Negro Communal Experiments</u>
    1963
Eugene Berwanger, <u>The Frontier Against Slavery</u> 1967
Luther P. Jackson, <u>Free Negro Labor and Property Holding in
    Virginia</u> 1942
John Hope Franklin, <u>The Free Negro in North Carolina</u> 1943
Letitia Brown, <u>Free Negroes in the District of Columbia</u> 1972
E. Franklin Frazier, <u>The Negro Church in America</u> 1964
    _____, <u>The Free Negro Family</u> 1932
Carter G. Woodson, <u>The Education of the Negro Prior to 1861</u> 1915
Carol V.R. George, <u>Segregated Sabbaths</u> 1973
Ira Berlin, <u>Slaves Without Masters</u> 1975

XI. Black Abolitionism

Benjamin Quarles, <u>Black Abolitionists</u> 1969
Herbert Aptheker, <u>The Negro in the Abolitionist Movement</u> 1941
Benjamin Quarles, <u>Frederick Douglass</u> 1948
Arthur H. Fauset, <u>Sojourner Truth: God's Faithful Pilgrim</u> 1938
Earl Conrad, <u>Harriet Tubman</u> 1943
William Farrison, <u>William Wells Brown: Author and Reformer</u> 1969
Herbert Aptheker, ed., <u>One Continual Cry: David Walker's
    Appeal</u> 1965
Jane and William Pease, <u>They Who Would Be Free</u> 1974
Joel Schor, <u>Henry Highland Garnet</u> 1977

XII. Civil War

Dudley T. Cornish, <u>The Sable Arm</u> 1956
James McPherson, ed., <u>The Negro's Civil War</u> 1965
Benjamin Quarles, <u>The Negro in the Civil War</u> 1953

Herbert Aptheker, <u>The Negro in the Civil War</u> 1938
Bell Wiley, <u>Southern Negroes, 1861-1865</u> 1938
John Hope Franklin, <u>The Emancipation Proclamation</u> 1963
James Brewer, <u>The Confederate Negro</u> 1969
V.J. Voegeli, <u>Free But Not Equal</u> 1967
James McPherson, <u>The Struggle for Equality</u> 1964

XIII.   Reconstruction

Robert Cruden, <u>The Negro in Reconstruction</u> 1969
Lerone Bennett, <u>Black Power U.S.A.</u> 1967
W.E.B. DuBois, <u>Black Reconstruction</u> 1935
Joel Williamson, <u>After Slavery</u> 1965
Peter Kolchin, <u>First Freedom</u> 1972
Forrest G. Wood, <u>Black Scare: The Racist Response to Emancipation
    and Reconstruction</u> 1968
Claude F. Oubre, <u>40 Acres and Mule: Freedmen's Bureau and Black
    Land Ownership</u> 1978

XIV.   Post-Reconstruction

C. Vann Woodward, <u>Reunion and Reaction</u> 1951
                 , <u>Origins of the New South, 1877-1913</u> 1951
Rayford Logan, <u>The Betrayal of the Negro</u> 1954
Philip Durham and E.L. Jones, <u>Negro Cowboys</u> 1965
Stanley Hirshon, <u>Farewell to the Bloody Shirt</u> 1962
Willard Gatewood, <u>Black Americans and the White Man's Burden,
    1898-1903</u> 1975

XV.   Era of Washington and Dubois

August Meier, <u>Negro Thought in America, 1880-1915</u> 1963
Louis R. Harlan, <u>Booker T. Washington</u> 1972
Francis Broderick, <u>W.E.B. DuBois: Negro Leader in a Time of
    Crisis</u> 1959
Elliott Rudwick, <u>W.E.B. DuBois: A Study in Minority Group
    Leadership</u> 1961
Emma Lou Thornbrough, <u>T.Thomas Fortune</u> 1972
Stephen Fox, <u>The Guardian of Boston: William Monroe Trotter</u> 1970
Charles F. Kellogg, <u>A History of the NAACP</u> 1967
John D. Weaver, <u>The Brownsville Raid</u> 1970

XVI.   Migration, Urbanization, And Emigration

James Weldon Johnson, <u>Black Manhattan</u> 1930
Claude McKay, <u>Harlem: Negro Metropolis</u> 1940
St. Clair Drake and H. Cayton, <u>Black Metropolis</u> 1945
Gilbert Osofsky, <u>Harlem: The Making of a Ghetto</u> 1966
Seth Scheiner, <u>Negro Mecca</u> 1965
Clyde Vernon Kiser, <u>Sea Island to City</u> 1969
Florette Henri, <u>Black Migration: 1900-1920</u> 1975
Allan Spear, <u>Black Chicago</u> 1967
Edwin Redkey, <u>Black Exodus</u> 1969

Elliott Rudwick, Race Riot at East St. Louis   1964
William Tuttle, Race Riot: Chicago in the Red Summer of
     1919   1970
David Gordon Nelson, Black Ethos: Northern Urban Negro
     Life and Thought, 1890-1930   1976

XVII.   Black Labor

Sterling Spero and A. Harris, The Black Worker   1931
Charles Wesley, Negro Labor in the U.S., 1850-1925   1927
Herbert Northrup, Organized Labor and the Negro   1944
F. Ray Marshall, The Negro and Organized Labor   1965
Herbert Hill, Black Labor and the American Legal System   1976

XVIII.   Garveyism

John Henrik Clarke, ed., Marcus Garvey and the Vision of
     Africa   1974
E. David Cronon, Black Moses   1955
Amy Jacques Garvey, Garvey and Garveyism   1963
_____, Philosophy and Opinions of Marcus Garvey
     1923
Tony Martin, Race First   1976

XIX.   Harlem Renaissance

Harold Cruse, The Crisis of the Negro Intellectual   1967
Nathan Huggins, Harlem Renaissance   1971
Langston Hughes, The Big Sea   1940
Alain Locke, ed, The New Negro   1925
Nathan Huggins, ed., Voices From the Harlem Renaissance   1976

XX.   Depression And War

Ralph Bunche, The Political Status of the Negro in the
     Age of FDR   1975
Raymond Wolters, Negroes and the Great Depression   1970
T. Arnold Hill, The Negro and Economic Reconstruction   1937
Gunnar Myrdal, An American Dilemma   1944
Richard Sterner, The Negro's Share 1943
Roi Ottley, New World A-Coming   1943
Richard Dalfiume, Fighting on Two Fronts   1969
Charles S. Johnson, Shadow of the Plantation   1934
Herbert Garfinkel, When Negroes March 1959
Dan T. Carter, Scottsboro   1969
Ulysses Lee, The Employment of Negro Troops   1966
Charles H. Martin, The Angelo Herndon Case and
     Southern Justice   1976

XXI.   Civil Rights Movement

August Meier and Elliott Rudwick, CORE   1973
William Berman, Politics of Civil Rights in the Truman
     Administration   1970
Donald McCoy and R.T. Ruetten, Quest and Response   1973
Anthony Lewis, Portrait of a Decade
Benjamin Muse, The American Negro Revolution   1968
Lerone Bennett, Confrontation: Black and White   1965
David L. Lewis, King: A Critical Biography   1970
John P. Roche, The Quest for the Dream   1964
Louis Lomax, The Negro Revolt   1962
Howard Zinn, SNCC: The New Abolitionists   1964
Steven Lawson, Black Ballotts: Voting Rights in the South,
     1944-1969

XXII.   Black Power And Black Nationalism

E.U. Essien Udom, Black Nationalism: A Search for Identify in
     America   1962
Theodore Draper, The Rediscovery of Black Nationalism   1970
Harold Isaacs, New World of Negro Americans   1963
C. Eric Lincoln, The Black Muslims in America   1961
Stokely Carmichael and C.V. Hamilton, Black Power   1967
Eldridge Cleaver, Soul on Ice   1968
Bobby Seale, Seize the Time   1970
Peter Goldman, Death and Life of Malcom X   1974
Malcolm X, Autobiography of Malcolm X   1965
H. Rap Brown, Die, Nigger, Die   1969
Louis Lomax, When the Word is Given   1964
George Jackson, Soledad Brother   1970
Robert L. Allen, Black Awakening in Capitalist America   1969
James H. Cone, Black Theology and Black Power   1969
Rodney Carlisle, The Roots of Black Nationalism   1975
Alphonso Pinkney, Red, Black and Green: Black Nationalism
     in the United States   1976

1/31/77

1980-81 SUPPLEMENT

II.   Jeanne Noble, <u>Beautiful, Also, Are the Souls of My</u>
       <u>Black Sisters: A History of Black Women in America</u>   1978

V.   A. Leon Higginbotham, Jr., <u>In the Matter of Color: Race and</u>
       <u>the American Legal Process</u>   1978

VII.   Albert J. Raboteau, <u>Slave Religion</u>   1978
       Thomas L. Webber, <u>Deep Like the Rivers: Education in the Slave</u>
          <u>Quarter Community</u>   1978
       William L. VanDeburg, <u>The Slave Drivers</u>   1979
       Nathan I. Huggins, <u>Black Odyssey</u>   1977

IX.   Daryl C. Dance, <u>Shuckin' and Jivin': Folklore from Contemporary</u>
       <u>Black Americans</u>   1978

XIII.   Thomas Holt, <u>Black Over White</u>   1977
       Leon F. Litwack, <u>Been in the Storm So Long: The Aftermath of</u>
          <u>Slavery</u>   1979
       Roger Ransom and Richard Sutch, <u>One Kind of Freedom: Economic</u>
          <u>Consequences of Emancipation</u>   1977

XIV.   Nell I. Painter, <u>Exodusters</u>   1977
       Gerald Gaither, <u>Blacks and the Populist Revolt</u>   1977
       Joseph H. Cartwright, <u>The Triumph of Jim Crow: Tennessee Race</u>
          <u>Relations in the 1880s</u>   1979

XV.   William Toll, <u>Resurgence of Race: Black Social Theory from</u>
          <u>Reconstruction to the Pan-African Conferences</u>   1979
       Robert L. Zangrando, <u>The NAACP Crusade Against Lynching, 1909-</u>
          <u>1950</u>   1980

XVI.   Tom W. Shick, <u>Behold the Promised Land: A History of Afro-</u>
       <u>American Settlers in the 19th-Century Liberia</u>   1980
       Kenneth L. Kusmer, <u>A Ghetto Takes Shape: Black Cleveland,</u>
          <u>1870-1930</u>   1976

XVII.   August Meier and Elliott Rudwick, <u>Black Detroit and the Rise</u>
          <u>of the UAW</u>   1979
       Jervis Anderson, <u>A. Philip Randolph</u>   1972
       William H. Harris, <u>Keeping the Faith</u> [Randolph]   1977

XX.   John B. Kirby, <u>Black Americans in the Roosevelt Era</u>   1980
       Harvard Sitkoff, <u>A New Deal for Blacks</u>   1978

XXI.   Howell Raines, <u>My Soul is Rested</u>   1977
       David J. Garrow, <u>Protest at Selma</u>   1978
       William H. Chafe, <u>Civilities and Civil Rights: Greensboro, N.C.</u>
       <u>and the Black Struggle for Freedom</u>   1980

XXII.   Bobby Seale, <u>A Lonely Rage</u>   1978
       Sterling Stuckey, <u>Ideological Origins of Black Nationalism</u>   1972

BROWN UNIVERSITY

COMPARATIVE AMERICAN SLAVERY

R.S. Jones

History 197C

Fall Term 1983

This course attempts to understand why slaves were treated more harshly in some parts of the Americas than in others.

Nature of the Course

The course will meet, as a seminar, once a week on Tuesdays. Each student is to come to seminar with three written questions based on the assigned readings for the week. These questions should stimulate discussion and demonstrate the student has both read the assigned material and reflected on it. Simple questions such as, "What did Hoetink mean on page 287," are not acceptable. Students may bring more than three questions in for discussion by the seminar. Students may also submit a _bonus_ question which ties the week's assigned readings to previous seminar discussion and readings. The written questions _must_ be turned in at the _beginning_ of the seminar, but students should retain a copy for their own records, and for the purpose of discussion.

In addition to submitting weekly questions each student must:

(a) Complete a short (eight pages, typewritten, double-spaced, _plus_ notes) paper in which a first effort is made to sort out the forces which determined the treatment of slaves in the New World. Footnotes are particularly important as the student must demonstrate not only what sources he/she has used but how he/she has used them. In constructing this paper, the student should take into consideration that he/she will be asked to critique it in the second paper. The first paper is due on FRIDAY, OCTOBER 7 at 4 PM.

(b) Complete a substantial paper (thirty pages, typewritten, double-spaced, _plus_ notes) in which the student manifests a more sophisticated, knowledgeable perspective on the forces which determined the treatment of slaves than was possible in the first paper. He/she is expected to correct, buttress, critique, defend, and expand on arguments presented in the first paper, and to build upon the readings, discussion, and questions presented by other students in the seminar in constructing the paper. Full credit must not only be given to written sources, but to the questions and ideas presented by students in seminar. The second paper is due on MONDAY, DECEMBER 12 at 4 PM.

Grades

Grades are based on the two papers, the quality of the required questions submitted over the course of the term, and attendance. As the course meets but once a week, failure to regularly attend will make it impossible for a student to earn a grade higher than "C." In borderline cases, regular submission of _bonus_ questions and the quality of participation in seminar will be taken into consideration. A "C" is awarded for satisfactory completion of work, while grades above "C" are reserved for outstanding, creative effort. Students may elect the course for SAT, NC.

Textbooks

The following books are required reading and may be purchased at the Brown University Bookstore:

G. M. Fredrickson, _White Supremacy_

(Textbooks continued)

M. Harris, Patterns of Race in the Americas

R. Hart, Slaves Who Abolished Slavery (Volume I)

A. L. Higginbotham, In the Matter of Color

S. W. Mintz and R. Price, An Anthropological Approach to the Afro-American Past: A Caribbean Perspective

E. Williams, Capitalism and Slavery

The bulk of the books and articles assigned for this course have been placed on reserve in the Rockefeller Library. The calendar below indicates when works are to be read. The student is expected to complete his/her readings prior to the weekly class meeting.

Calendar
Week of:

9/13   COMPARATIVE SLAVERY IN THE CONTEXT OF HEMISPHERIC RACE RELATIONS
        Higginbotham, Part One.
        R. S. Jones, "Race Relations in the Colonial Americas: An Overview."
            Humboldt Journal of Social Relations, Spring/Summer (1974): 73-82.
        F. Tannenbaum, Slave and Citizen, all.
        Williams, Chapters 4 and 9-13.

9/20   EUROPEANS VIEW AFRICANITY
        Fredrickson, Chpt. 1.
        Higginbotham, Part Three.
        W. Jordan, White Over Black, Chpt. 1.
        J. Kovel, White Racism: A Psychohistory, Chpt. 4.
        L. Rout, The African Experience in Spanish America, Chpt. 1.

9/27   CHRISTIAN THOUGHTS AND DEEDS
        E. Goveia, "Comment on Anglicanism, Catholicism, and the Negro Slave."
            Comparative Studies in Society and History (1966): 328-330.
        Hart, Chpt. 6.
        H. S. Klein, Slavery in the Americas, Part III.
        M. Morner, Race Mixture in the History of Latin America, Chpt. 4.

10/4   ECONOMICS, IMPERIALISM, AND RACE
        D. B. Davis, The Problem of Slavery in Western Culture, Chpt. 8.
        E. D. Genovese, The World the Slaveholders Made, Chpt. 1.
        Hart, Chpts. 1, 3, 4.
        H. S. Klein, Slavery in the Americas, Part IV.
        H. Shapiro, "Eugene Genovese, Marxism, and the Study of Slavery."
            Journal of Ethnic Studies (1982): 87-100.

10/7   FIRST PAPER DUE

10/11   NUMBERS AND CONSEQUENCES
        R. Bastide, African Civilizations in the New World, Chpts. I, II, VIII, IX.
        Harris, all.
        A. Kulikoff, "The Origins of Afro-American Society in Tidewater
            Maryland and Virginia." William and Mary Quarterly (1978): 226-259.
        E. J. McManus, Black Bondage in the North, Chpt. 12.

10/18   PATTERNS OF SETTLEMENT
         G. N. Bolland, The Formation of a Colonial Society, Chpts. 4-6.
         F. W. Knight, The Caribbean, Chpt. 3.
         M. Onwood, "Impulse and Honor: The Place of Slave and Master in
             the Ideology of Planterdom." Plantation Society in the Americas
             (1979): 31-56.
         J. S. Otto, "Slaveholding General Farmers in a Cotton County."
             Agricultural History (1981): 167-178.

10/25   LEGAL STRUCTURES
         Higginbotham, any two chapters from PART TWO.
         E. J. McManus, Black Bondage in the North, Chpts. 4, 5.
         R. Mellafe, Negro Slavery in Latin America, Chpt. 5.
         L. Rout, The African Experience in Spanish America, Chpt. 13.
         A. A. Sio, "Interpretations of Slavery: The Slave Status in
             the Americas." Comparative Studies in Society and History
             (1965): 289-308.

11/1   MIXED ATTITUDES ABOUT MIXED BLOODS
         C. N. Degler, Neither Black nor White, Chpt. V.
         Fredrickson, Chpt. III
         H. Hoetink, The Two Variants in Caribbean Race Relations, Part Three.
         W. Jordan, "American Chiaroscuro: The Status and Definition of
             Mulattoes in the British Colonies." William and Mary Quarterly
             (1962): 183-200.
         M. Morner, Race Mixture in the History of Latin America, Chpt. V.

11/8   IDEOLOGY AND ACTION
         M. Craton, Searching for the Invisible Man, Part Two.
         Fredrickson, Chpts. II, IV.
         Hart, Chpt. 5
         Higginbotham, Part Four.

11/15   THE EVOLUTION OF RACIST THOUGHT
         J. Gratus, The Great White Lie, Chpts. 20-23.
         F. W. Knight, Slave Society in Cuba During the Nineteenth Century,
             Introduction and Chpts. 1 and 3.
         P. Mauro, "Tensions and the Transmission of Tensions in the European
             Expansion to America." Plantation Society in the Americas (1979):
             149-159.
         E. S. Morgan, American Slavery American Freedom, Chpts. 11, 13-16, 18.
         G. B. Nash, Red, White, and Black, Chpt. 9.

11/22   INFORMAL DISCUSSIONS OF COURSE PAPERS

11/23-27 THANKSGIVING RECESS

11/29   BLACK RESISTANCE
         Hart, Chpt. 8.
         R. S. Jones, "Transformation of Maroon Identity in Jamaica." Blacks
             On Paper (1975): 94-100.
         R. S. Jones, "Identity, Self-Concept and Shifting Political Allegiances
             of Blacks in the Colonial Americas." Western Journal of Black
             Studies (1981): 61-74.
         L. Rout, The African Experience in Spanish America, Chpt. 4.
         P. H. Wood, Black Majority, Chpt. XII.

12/6   BLACK IDENTITY
         H. Hoetink, The Cultural Links," pp. 20-40 in M. E. Crahan and F. W.
             Knight, Africa and the Caribbean.
         R. S. Jones, "Slavery in the Colonial Americas." Black World (1975):
             28-39.
         R. S. Jones, "Structural Isolation and the Genesis of Black Nationalism
             in Colonial North America." Colby Library Quarterly (1979): 252-266.
         B. K. Kopytoff, "The Early Political Development of Jamaica Maroon
             Societies." William and Mary Quarterly (1978): 287-307.
         Mintz and Price, all.

12/12   SECOND PAPER DUE

                              R. S. Jones
                              History and Afro-American Studies

R.S. Jones

Afro-American Studies 106

Fall Term, 1983

The course aims not only at making students familiar with life within the slave community in the United States, but at making them familiar with the many recent studies of slavery. Afro-American Studies 106 is therefore both a course in history and historiography. At the end of the semester each student will be expected to prepare a substantial paper on the slave community.

Nature of the Course

The course will meet, as a seminar, once a week on Thursday. Each student is to come to seminar with three written questions based on the assigned readings for the week. These questions are intended to stimulate discussion and to demonstrate the student has both read the assigned materials and reflected on them. Simple questions such as, "What did Genovese mean on page 369?" are not acceptable. Students may bring more than three questions in for discussion by the seminar. Students may also submit a bonus question which ties the week's assigned readings to previous seminar discussion and readings. The written questions must be turned in at the beginning of the seminar, but students should retain a copy for their own records, and for the purpose of discussion.

In addition to submitting weekly questions each student must:

(1) Complete a short (eight pages, typewritten, double-spaced, plus notes) paper in which a first effort is made to understand the nature of the slave community. Footnotes are extremely important in this paper as the student must demonstrate not only what sources he/she has drawn upon, but just how these sources have been used. In constructing this paper the student should take into consideration that he/she will be asked to critique and build upon in the second paper. The first paper is due on FRIDAY, OCTOBER 7 at 4 PM.

(2) Complete a substantial paper (thirty pages, typewritten, double-spaced, plus notes) in which he/she manifests a more sophisticated, knowledgeable perspective on the slave community than was possible in the first paper. The student is expected to defend, correct, critique, buttress, and expand upon arguments presented in the first paper, and to build upon the readings, ideas, and questions presented by other students in the seminar. Full credit must therefore not only be given to published sources, but to other students in seminar. The second paper is due on MONDAY, DECEMBER 12 at 4 PM.

Grades

Grades will be based on the two papers, the quality of the required questions submitted over the course of the semester, and attendance. As the course meets only once a week, failure to regularly attend will make it impossible for a student to earn a grade higher than "C." In borderline cases, regular submission of bonus questions and the quality of participation in seminar will be taken into consideration. A "C" is awarded for satisfactory completion of work, while grades above "C" are reserved for outstanding achievement. Students may elect the course for SAT/NC.

Textbooks

The following books are required reading and may be purchased at the Brown University Bookstore:

J. W. Blassingame, The Slave Community (revised, enlarged edition)

(Textbooks continued)

E. D. Genovese, _Roll, Jordan, Roll_

L. H. Owens, _This Species of Property_

G. P. Rawick, _From Sundown to Sunup_

W. L. Rose, _Slavery and Freedom_

Portions of other books are also required reading for this course. These have been placed on three hour reserve in the Rockefeller Library. The calendar below indicates when they are to be read. The student is expected to complete his/her readings _prior to_ the weekly meeting of the seminar.

CALENDAR
Date:

9/8   INTRODUCTION No required readings.

9/15   HISTORIANS VIEW THE SLAVE COMMUNITY
           D. B. Davis, "Slavery and the Post-World War II Historians," in
           S. W. Mintz, _Slavery, Colonialism and Racism_.
           S. M. Elkins, _Slavery_, Chpt. I.
           Rawick, Chpt. 1.
           Rose, Chpt. 12.

9/22   AFRICAN VALUES IN THE SLAVE COMMUNITY
           M. F. Berry and J. W. Blassingame, _Long Memory_, Chpt. 1.
           Blassingame, Chpts. 1, 2.
           Rawick, Chpt. 2
           P. H. Wood, _Black Majority_, Chpts. 4, 6.

10/6   CONTROLLING SLAVES
           Blassingame, Chpt. 7.
           Genovese, Book ONE, Part 1.
           Rawick, Chpt. 4.
           Rose, Chpt. 2
           K. M. Stampp, _The Peculiar Institution_, Chpt. IV.

1C/7   FIRST PAPER DUE

10/13   THE SLAVE COMMUNITY IN ENVIRONMENTAL CONTEXT
           Genovese, Book THREE, Part 2.
           Owens, Chpts. 2, 3.
           R. Sutch, Chpt. Six in P. A. David, _et. al._, _Reckoning with Slavery_.

10/20   HIERARCHY IN THE SLAVE COMMUNITY
           Genovese, Book THREE, Part 1.
           R. M. Miller, _Dear Master_, Part II.
           Owens, Chpts. 5, 6, 7.
           R. S. Starobin, _Letters of American Slaves_, Part One.
           W. L. Van DeBurg, _The Slave Drivers_, Chpts. 1, 2, and Conclusion.

10/27   THE ECONOMIC ASSIMILATION OF SLAVES
           P. A. David and Peter Temin, Chpt. One in P. A. David, _et. al._,
           Reckoning with Slavery.
           R. W. Fogel and S. L. Engerman, _Time on the Cross_, Chpt. Six and
           Epilogue.
           Genovese, Book TWO, Part 2.

H. G. Gutman and R. Sutch, Chpt. Two in P. A. David, _et. al._, _Reckoning with Slavery_.
K. M. Stampp, INtroduction to P. A. David, _et. al._, _Reckoning with Slavery_.

11/3   RELIGION IN THE SLAVE COMMUNITY
Genovese, Book TWO, Part 1.
A. J. Raboteau, _Slave Religion_, Chpts. 5, 6.
Rawick, Chpt. 3.
G. S. Wilmore, _Black Religion and Black Radicalism_, Chpt. I.

11/10   FAMILY LIFE IN THE SLAVE COMMUNITY
Blassingame, Chpt. 4.
Genovese, Book ONE, Part 2.
H. G. Gutman, _The Black Family in Slavery and Freedom_, Chpts. 1, 8.
Owens, Chpt. 9.
Rawick, Chpt. 5

TUESDAY, 12/12 INFORMAL DISCUSSION OF PAPERS.

11/23-27   THANKSGIVING RECESS.

12/1   SLAVE PERSONALITIES
Blassingame, Chpt. 8.
E. Fox-Genovese and E. D. Genovese, _Fruits of Merchant Capital_, Chpt. 5.
K. M. Stampp, _The Peculiar Institution_, Chpt. III.
Ownes, Chpt. 10.

12/8   RACISM, SLAVERY, AND THE SLAVE COMMUNITY
Blassingame, Chpt. 6
G. M. Fredrickson, _White Supremacy_, Chpt. II.
E. S. Morgan, _American Slavery American Freedom_, Chpts. 15, 16.
Rawick, Chpt. 4.
P. H. Wood, _Black Majority_, Chpt. VIII.

MONDAY, 12/12 FINAL PAPER DUE.

                            R. S. Jones, Afro-American
                            Studies Program and
                            History Department

BROWN UNIVERSITY

Problems in Afro-American History

Brown University   Fall Term, 1980
History 166   Graduate Level
Rhett Jones

This course is an overview of some of the issues important in Afro-American history.
It makes use of social scientific concepts and the student is expected to come to grips
with sociological and anthropological perspectives on the black past.

Nature of the Course

The course will meet twice a week with the Tuesday and Thursday sessions devoted to
lectures for the first five or six weeks of the class. Beginning about the sixth week
of class the Thursday sessions will be devoted to student led discussions on course related topics.

In addition to leading a discussion, each student must meet the following requirements:

(a) He must turn in a short outline of his proposed term paper on or before
Tuesday, 10/14 at 4 P.M. He must consult with the instructor concerning the
paper prior to that date.

(b) He must take and pass a take-home examination distributed on Tuesday,
10/21 and due on Tuedsay, 10/28 at 4 P.M.

(c) He must successfully complete a brief--15-20 pages typewritten, double-spaced--
paper on or before Monday, 12/23 at 4 P.M.

(d) He must take and pass a take-home final examination distributed on Monday,
1/12 and due on Monday, 1/19 at 4 P.M.

Grades

Grades are calculated on the basis of the two take-home examinations and the paper,
with each counting a third. In border-line cases consideration will be given to attendance, performance in leading discussion, class participation, and improvement over the
course of the term. A "C" is given for satisfactory completion of all work; grades
above this level are reserved for outstanding, creative work. Students may elect the
course for SAT/NC.

Textbooks

The following books are required reading and may be purchased at the Brown Bookstore:

    J.W. Blassingame, The Slave Community
    R.D. Brown and S.G. Rabe (eds.), Slavery in American Society.
    L.W. Levine, Black Culture and Black Consciousness.
    J. Maquet, Africanity: The Cultural Unity of Black Africa.
    W. Rodney, How Europe Underdeveloped Africa.
    F. Tannenbaum, Slave and Citizen: The Negro in the Americas.

Other publications have been placed on reserve in the Rockefeller Library. The
calendar below indicates when particular works are to be read. The student is expected
to complete his readings prior to the Thursday of the week in which they are assigned.

-2-

Calendar

Week of
9/16   THE NATURE OF SOCIOLOGICAL HISTORY
        H. Cruse, "Black and White: Outlines of the Next Stage: Part I," in
          Black World, January, 1971.
        A.M. Pescatello, Power and Pawn: The Female in Iberian Families, Societies,
          Cultures, Chpt. 6, Epilogue.
        Rodney, Chpt. 1.

9/23   THE CULTURAL UNITY OF WEST AFRICA
        Maquet, pp. 4-101.
        Rodney, Chpts. 2-4.

9/30   AFRICANISMS IN THE NEW WORLD
        Blassingame, Chpts. 1,2.
        R. Bastide, African Civilizations in the New World, Chpts. II, VIII, IX.
        C. Palmer, Slaves of the White God, Chpts. 5-7.

10/7   RACE IN THE COLONIAL AMERICAS, I
        Brown and Rabe, Chpt. I
        Tannenbaum, all.
        F.N. Okoye, "Chattel Slavery as the Nightmare of the American Revolutionaries,
          William and Mary Quarterly, January, 1980.
        A.J.R. Russell-Wood, "Iberian Expansion and the Issue of Black Slavery,"
          American Historical Review, February, 1978.
        L. Rout, The African Experience in Spanish America, Chpt. 4.
        C. Degler, "Plantation Society," Plantation Society in the Americas,
          February, 1979.

10/14   RACE IN THE COLONIAL AMERICAS, II
                Term Paper Outlines Due.
        Brown and Rabe, Chpt. III.
        R.S. Jones, Race Relations in the Colonial Americas: An Overview," Humboldt
          Journal of Social Relations, Spring/Summer, 1974.
        R.S. Jones and A. Dzidzienyo, "Africanity, Structural Isolation and Black
          Politics in the Americas," Studia Africana, Spring, 1977.
        E. Genovese, From Rebellion to Revolution, Chpt. 1.

10/21   STRUCTURAL ISOLATION AND THE GENESIS OF BLACK NATIONALISM
                First Examination Distributed.
        A. Kulikoff, "The Origins of Afro-American Society in Tidewater Maryland and
          Virginia," William and Mary Quarterly, April, 1978.
        H. Hoetink, Slavery and Race Relations in the Americas, Chpt. 1.
        R. Price, Maroon Societies, Introduction.
        Blassingame, Chpt. 3.

10/28   NATIVE AMERICANS AND AFRO-AMERICANS IN HEMISPHERIC PERSPECTIVE
                First Examination Due. M.W. Helms, "Negro or Indian," pp. 157-172 in
          A. Pescatello, Old Roots in New Lands
        D.F. Littlefield, Africans and Seminoles, Chpt. 10.
        R.S. Jones, "Black and Native American Relations before 1800," Western Journal
          of Black Studies, September, 1977.
        W.G. McLoughlin, "Red Indians, Black Slavery and White Racism: America's
          Slaveholding Indians," American Quarterly, October, 1974.

T. Perdue, <u>Slavery and the Evolution of Cherokee Society</u>, Chpts. 3, 4.

11/4   THE STRUCTURE OF SLAVERY
Brown and Rabe, Chpts. II, IV.
Blassingame, Chpts. 5, 6.
Levine, Chpts. 1, 2.

11/11   COMMUNITIES OF SLAVES
Blassingame, Chpts. 7, 8.
Levine, Chpt. 3.
H.G. Gutman, <u>The Black Family in Slavery and Freedom</u>, Chpts. 3, 5, 8.

11/18   SOCIAL ROOTS OF BLACK THOUGHT, I
W.G. Marston and T.L. Van Valey, "Role of Residential Segregation in the
    Assimilation Process," <u>ANNALS</u>, January, 1979.
H.C. Triandis (ed.), <u>Variations in Black and White Perceptions of the Social
    Environment</u>, Chpts. 3,6.

11/25   SOCIAL ROOTS OF BLACK THOUGHT, II
Levine, Chpts. 5-6.
E.J. Slawski and J. Scherer, "The Rhetoric of Concern: An Urban Desegregated
    School," <u>Anthropology and Education Quarterly</u>, Winter, 1978.
J.E. Blackwell, <u>The Black Community</u>, Chpt. 10.

11/26 - 11/30   THANKSGIVING RECESS.

12/2   THE BLACK FAMILY: IMAGES AND REALITIES
Blassingame, Chpt. 4.
H.G. Gutman, <u>The Black Family in Slavery and Freedom</u>, Chpt. 10, and Afterword.
L. Rainwater and W.L. Yancey, <u>The Moynihan Report and the Politics of Contro-
    versy</u>, Chpts. 1-4.
E. Spraights, "Some Dynamics of the Black Family," <u>Negro Educational Review</u>,
    July-October, 1973.

12/9   RACE AND CLASS IN HEMISPHERIC PERSPECTIVE
B. Bernstein, "Social Class, Language, and Socialization in P. Giglioli (ed.),
    <u>Language and Social Context</u>.
W. Labov, "The Logic of Nonstandard English," in Giglioli.
M.Z. Black, "Characteristics of the Culturally Deprived Child," in J.L. Frost,
    and G.R. Hawkes (eds.), <u>The Disadvantaged Child</u>.
D. Henderson, "The Assault on Black Culture Through the Labeling Process,"
    <u>Journal of Afro-American Issues</u>, Winter, 1975.
D.C. Thompson, <u>Sociology of the Black Experience</u>, Chpts. 3, 4.

12/16   CONTINGENCY DAY.

12/18 - 1/4   CHRISTMAS RECESS.

12/23   TERM PAPER DUE.

1/12   FINAL EXAMINATION DISTRIBUTED.

1/19   FINAL EXAMINATION DUE.

R.S. Jones, Afro-American Studies
and History

AFRO-AMERICAN STUDIES DEPARTMENT

Course 106-261
Spring 1981
Tuesday and Thursday: 11:00 - 12:30   Professor Herbert Hill

UNIVERSITY OF WISCONSIN
HISTORY OF BLACK LABOR: FROM COLONIAL TIMES
TO THE PRESENT

This course will be a history of black labor from the colonial period to
the present. Beginning with an examination of the first slave laws based on
race, the development of a dual racial labor system in America will be studied
in each major period of the black experience. Black labor force characteristics,
before and after emancipation will be analyzed within changing economic
contexts. A major theme will be the relationship between white and black
workers in a racist society. The role of organized labor and its effect on the
struggles of black workers will be analyzed in successive periods with
emphasis on the black response to white labor working class behavior. Major attention
will be given to the history of black labor organizations in the past and in
the present. A comprehensive analysis will be made of the effects of government
policy, and employer and labor union practices on the status of black workers.
The consequences of automation and technological change for black labor in
the contemporary period will be studied as will such issues as the changing
judicial preception of employment discrimination, the role of federal contract
compliance and the effects of anti-poverty programs among the urban black
population. The social characteristics of the stable black working class
that has been central to black protest and to community institutions for many
generations will be studied. The history of the black worker will be examined
within the changing context of racial conflict in American society.

Organization

Each session will consist of a lecture followed by discussion. A
separate discussion section will meet with the T.A. at a time to be assigned.

Requirements

1. Participation in discussion sections
2. Two-hour examinations
3. Short term paper, reading report, or project (1 of 3 choices)

Required Reading

Herbert Hill, Black Labor and the American Legal System
Georgakas, Dan, Detroit: I Do Mind Dying
John Blassingame, The Slave Community
Robert Starobin, Industrial Slavery in the Old South
Sterling Spero and Abram Harris, The Black Worker
Richard C. Wade, Slavery in the Cities

Session I.   Introduction

Session II-III.   The Colonial Period

              Development of slave laws based on race. Unique
              character of the slave labor system on the North
              American continent. Action by white workingmen
              against free black labor. The importance of slave
              labor in capital accumulation. Slavery as a system
              of labor exploitation and racial control.

              Assigned Readings

              Required: Winthrop D. Jordan. White Over Black
                           Chapter II.
              Recommended: Edmund S. Morgan. American Slavery,
                           American Freedom.
                           Lorenzo J. Greene. The Negro in Colonial
                           New England, Ch. 4
                           Peter Wood. Black Majority, Ch.
                           Gerald Mullin. Flight and Rebellion.

189

Session IV-V.   The Southern Plantation System at the Beginning of the
Nineteenth Century.

Demographic and economic conditions in three areas;
the Chesapeake region, the Carolina region and the
Back Country. Social consequences of the plantation
as an economic unit. The black worker as the basic
labor force.

Assigned Readings

Required: John Blassingame, The Slave Community.
Richard Wade. Slavery in the Cities,
pp. 110-189.
Recommended: Harvey Wish. Slavery in the South,
Section on Nat Turner.

Session VI-VII.   Industrial Slavery.

Required: Robert Starobin, Industrial Slavery in
the Old South, pp. 3-189.
Recommended: Wade, Slavery in the Cities, pp.

Session VIII-IX.   Reconstruction and Post-Reconstruction.

The process of racial occupational eviction, North
and South. The Black Codes, labor contracts and the
perpetuation of the master-servant relationship. The
rise and fall of the National Labor Union and the
Colored National Labor Union. The emergence of
Booker T. Washington.

Assigned Readings

Required: W. E. B. DuBois. Back to Slavery: excerpts
from Black Reconstruction in America.
Booker T. Washington, "The Negro and the
Labor Problems of the South," in Howard
Brotz, ed., Negro Social and Political
Thought, pp. 401-405.
Recommended: Roger Shugg, The Origins of Class Struggle
in Louisiana, Ch. 8.

Session X-XI.   The Anti-Oriental Agitation and the Rise of Working
Class Racism.

Organized labor's crusade against Asians legitimizing
racist ideology within the working class, reinforced
discriminatory patterns and provided a new model and
justification for racial exclusion policies by unions
against black workers. A central stage in the development of racial caste system and in the formation of
working class racism after the Civil War.

Assigned Readings

Required: Alexander Saxton, The Indispensable Enemy,
Ch. 2.
Herbert Hill, "Anti-Oriental Agitation
and Working-Class Racism," Transaction/
Society (February, 1973), pp. 43-54.
Recommended: James Bryce. The American Commonwealth,
Vol. II, Ch. 89.

Session XIII-XIV.   The Racial Policies and Practices of the American
Federation of Labor and its Predecessors.

The American Federation of Labor as representing the
primary American labor tradition. The Industrial
Workers of the World representing the secondary tradition
of radical unionism. The triumph of craft unionism and
racial exclusion. Consequences of the A.F. of L's
refusal to organize the unskilled and mass-production
workers. New patterns of racial segregation.

Assigned Readings

Required: Herbert Hill, "The Racial Practices of
                 Organized Labor in the Age of Gompers,"
                 in Ross and Hill, Employment, Race and
                 Poverty.
                 Sterling Spero and Abram Harris, The
                 Black Worker, Ch. 2, 4, 5, 7.
Recommended: Philip S. Foner, History of the Labor
                 Movement in the United States, Vol. 3,
                 Ch. 8 and 9.

Session XV-XVI.   European Immigration and Black Labor.

Conflicts between European immigrant workers and black
labor in northern industry. The function of institutions
of social preparedness and the Americanization process.
Violence against the black community from the Civil War
draft riots to the East St. Louis massacre in 1917 and
the Chicago race riot in 1919.

Assigned Readings

Required: William Tuttle, Labor Conflict and Racial
                 Violence: the Black Worker in Chicago,
                 1894-1919. (Bobs-Merrill reprint).
                 Spero and Harris, The Black Worker, Ch. 8,
                 11, 12, 18.
Recommended: Elliott M. Rudwick, Race Riot at East St.
                 Louis. Ch. 11.
                 Allen Grimshaw, Racial Violence in the
                 United States, pp. 38-42.
                 Gary Nash and Richard Weiss, The Great Fear,
                 pp. 45-70.

Session XVII-XVIII.
Ideologies of Protest and Black Labor.

Three ideological tendencies:

1. The Garvey Movement
2. The Communist Party
3. The N.A.A.C.P.

<u>Assigned Readings</u>

Required: E. David Cronon. <u>Marcus Garvey</u>, pp. 1-58
Ralph Bunche. "The Programs, Ideologies,
Tactics and Achievements of Negro Better-
ment and Interracial Organizations," in
Broom and Selznick, <u>Sociology</u>.
Wilson Record. <u>The Negro and the Commu-
nist Party</u>, Ch. 3

Recommended: E. David Cronon. <u>Black Moses</u>.
Theodore Vincent. <u>Black Power and the Garvey
Movement</u>.
Tony Martin. <u>Race First</u>.
Angelo Herndon, "A Negro Communist Tells What
the Party Meant to Him," in Broderick and
Meier, <u>Negro Protest Thought in the
Twentieth Century</u>.

SESSION XIX-XX..
The Great Depression and

The resurgence of the industrial unionism and the organization of black labor in mass-production industries; steel,
auto, packinghouse, etc. The role of the United Mine
Workers of America and black labor problems. Attitudes
of black leaders and community organizations toward
labor unions.

<u>Assigned Readings</u>

Required: Raymond Wolters. <u>Negroes and the Great
Depression</u>, pp. 98-148, 169-187.
Herbert Hill, <u>Black Labor and the African
Legal System</u>, Ch. 3-4.

Session XXI-XXII.
The Rise of the C. I. O.

<u>Assigned Readings</u>

Required: Sylvia Woods, "You Have to Fight for Freedom"
(xerox reserve)

Matthew Ward, <u>The Indignant Heart</u>
(xerox reserve).
Julius Jacobson, ed., <u>The Negro and the
American Labor Movement</u>, Ch. 5

Exam

192

Session XXIII-XXIV.

      The Black Railroad Worker, The Brotherhood of Sleeping
Car Porters and the March on Washington Movement.

      The role of A. Philip Randolph, Chandler Owen and other
black radicals in labor organizations during the 1920's,
1930's and early 1940's. Influence of "The Messenger,"
edited by Randolph. History of black job eviction on
the nation's railroads and response of workers through
direct action and litigation. The March on Washington
Movement and the struggles for FEPC. President Franklin
D. Roosevelt issues Executive Order 8802 in 1941. Consequences of first Federal Fair Employment Practice
Committee.

Session XXV-XXVI.

      Investigations and findings of World War II FEPC in
selected industries.

      Philadelphia transit strike of 1944 and racially motivated
labor conflict in Detroit and other cities.

      <u>Assigned Readings</u>

      Required: Herbert Hill, <u>Black Labor and the American
                      Legal System,</u> Ch. 5-12.

Session XXVIII-XXIX.

      The Economics of Race and Class in Urban Society.

      The dual racial labor system and its social consequences.

      <u>Assigned Readings</u>

      Required: Doeringer and Piore, <u>Internal Labor Mar-
                      kets and Manpower Analysis,</u> Ch. 2, 3, 7.
                      Kenneth Clark, Dark Ghetto, Ch. 3.
                      <u>Report of the National Advisory Commission
                      On Civil Disorders,</u> pp. 124-136
      Recommended: Julius Jacobson, ed., <u>The Negro and the
                      American Labor Movement,</u> Ch. 7.

      Prospects for the Future.

Session XXX-XXXI.

Black Labor Today.

Implications of Census data regarding economic and
social conditions of black wage earners. Patterns of
discrimination in basic sectors of the economy. The
emergence of civil rights law and employment discrimination.
Implications of the case law under Title VII of the
Civil Rights Act of 1964. Conflict and seniority issues
over preferential hiring. Failure of federal contract
compliance. Sources of resistance to change.

<u>Assigned Readings</u>

Required: Herbert Hill, <u>Black Labor and the American
Legal System</u>, Introduction and Ch. 1.

Recommended: Herbert Hill, "Whose Law--Whose Order:
The Failure of Federal Contract Compliance,"
in Charles V. Hamilton, ed., <u>The Black
Experience in American Politics</u>.

Session XXXII.

Prospects for the Future.

Required: Dan Georgakas, <u>Detroit: I Do Mind Dying</u>
St. Martin's Press.

INTRODUCTION TO CHICANO HISTORY
History 2/Chicano Studies 2
University of California, Riverside

Fall, 1982   Carlos E. Cortés
TuTh 2-3:30   Office: LibS. 4153
Watkins 1101   Office Hours: TuTh 3:40-4:30

Scope: Chicano Studies 2/History 2 (Introduction to Chicano History) focuses
on the historical heritage of the Mexican American from Spanish and Indian
origins to the Chicano Movement, with an emphasis on the Chicano experience
since 1846. Throughout the course we will (1) examine the myths currently
clouding Chicano history and (2) attempt to establish the realities of the
Chicano historical experience.

Course Requirements: There will be one ten-page term paper, an optional midterm
examination on Tuesday, November 9, and a required final examination covering
the entire course. For students who take the optional midterm--the term paper
and midterm will each be worth thirty percent of the course grade and the
final examination will be worth forty percent. For students who do not take
the midterm examination--the term paper and final examination will each be
worth fifty percent of the course grade.

     In the term paper students will write either (1) a brief history of a
Mexican-American family, (2) a brief history of a Mexican-American community,
(3) a comparative critical analysis of two books which deal in some way with
the Chicano historical experience (books required for this course and anthologies
are unacceptable), or (4) a short research paper on some aspect of Chicano
history, as approved by the instructor. Unless you request otherwise, I will .
keep and use all family history papers as part of a long-range research project
on the historical origins of UCR Chicano students. Therefore, family history
papers will not be returned. Should you wish your family history paper returned
with comments, please submit two copies of the paper.

     Term paper deadlines are November 23(+), December 2(o), and December 9(-).
Students who turn in their papers by Tuesday, November 2, will receive their
grades by Thursday, November 4, to help in their decision whether or not to
take the optional midterm examination on November 9. Papers submitted after
December 9 will receive reduced grades. Papers submitted after Friday, December
16, will receive severely reduced grades. As some papers will be kept on
file, students should be sure to make copies of their papers before submitting
them.

     The UCR Learning and Study Skills Center hopes to offer an Adjunct Study
Skills course in conjunction with Introduction to Chicano History. It will be
taught by Pat Moran, who will describe the course at our first class meeting.
Student interest will determine the fate of the adjunct course, so students
should seriously consider this option, which has proven of significant value
to students during the past six years.

Required Reading

Rodolfo Acuna. OCCUPIED AMERICA. A HISTORY OF CHICANOS.

Robert Miller (ed.). LA CRONICA.

David J. Weber (ed.). FOREIGNERS IN THEIR NATIVE LAND. HISTORICAL ROOTS OF THE MEXICAN AMERICANS.

Recommended Reading

James D. Bennett and Lowell H. Harrison. WRITING HISTORY PAPERS.

David Kyvig and Myron Marty. YOUR FAMILY HISTORY. A HANDBOOK FOR RESEARCH AND WRITING.

Course Schedule

I. The Roots of Mexican America.

October 5   (Tues.) -- Introduction.

October 7   (Thur.) -- What Are the Spanish and Indian Roots of Chicanos?

October 12   (Tues.) -- What Societal Similarities and Differences Developed in the Various Regions of Northern Mexico?
--FOREIGNERS, pp. 1-50
--LA CRONICA, Issue 1, 1835

October 14   (Thur.) -- What Has Been the Legacy of These Regional Experiences?
             Films: The Dream of Don Guadalupe
                     Tierra Amarilla: The People of Chama Valley

October 19   (Tues.) -- In What Ways Did Anglo-Americans Penetrate into Northern Mexico?
--OCCUPIED, pp. 1-11
--FOREIGNERS, pp. 51-93, 101-116

October 21   (Thur.) -- In What Respects Did the U.S.-Mexican War Affect the Lives of Mexican Northerners?
--OCCUPIED, pp. 11-17
--FOREIGNERS, pp. 93-99, 117-138, 161-162
--LA CRONICA, Issue 2, 1848

October 26   (Tues.) -- What Rights, Protections, and Dilemmas Did the Treaty of Guadalupe Hidalgo and the Gadsden Purchase Establish for Mexican Americans?
--OCCUPIED, pp. 17-23
--FOREIGNERS, pp. 99-100, 162-168

II. The Nineteenth Century after the U.S. Conquest

October 28 (Thur.) -- What Challenges and Problems Did the Coming of Anglo-
American Society Create for Chicanos?
--FOREIGNERS, pp. 139-160, 169-202
--LA CRONICA, Issue 3, 1859

November 2 (Tues.) -- In What Ways Did Chicanos Respond to the Anglo-
American Challenge?
--OCCUPIED, pp. 24-120
--FOREIGNERS, pp. 203-225

November 4 (Thur.) -- How did the Chicano Experience Vary from Region to
Region?
--FOREIGNERS, pp. 226-254
--LA CRONICA, Issue 4, 1877

November 9 (Tues.) -- Optional Midterm Examination (covering lectures and
reading assignments through November 2)

November 11 (Thur.) -- Why Did Some Chicanos Resort to Violence to Meet the
Anglo-American Challenge?
Multi-Media Presentation: The Chicano Social Bandit

November 16 (Tues.) -- Who Were the Leading Figures of Chicanos Resistance?
--LA CRONICA, Issue 5, 1980

III. The Twentieth Century

November 18 (Thur.) -- How Did the Dramatic Increase in Mexican Immigration
Affect Chicano Society?
--OCCUPIED, pp. 121-136, 190-213, 299-315
--FOREIGNERS, pp. 225-260
--LA CRONICA, Issue 6, 1915

November 23 (Tues.) -- What Special Dilemmas Did the Great Depression
Create for Chicanos?
--OCCUPIED, pp. 136-143, 213-255, 316-323
--LA CRONICA, Issue 7, 1933

November 30 (Tues.) -- What Did World War II and Its Aftermath Mean for
Mexican Americans?
--OCCUPIED, pp. 144-162, 256-268, 323-349
--LA CRONICA, Issue 8, 1954

December 2 (Thur.) -- What Historical Factors Contributed to the Emergence
of the Chicano Movement?
Film: Yo Soy Chicano
--OCCUPIED, pp. 162-189, 268-298

December 7   (Tues.) -- What Is the Chicano Movement and What Significance
             Does It Have for Contemporary and Future U.S. Society?
             --OCCUPIED, pp. 350-427
             --LA CRONICA, Issue 9, 1969

December 9   (Thur.) -- How Does the Chicano Experience Look in Retrospect?
             Film: Mexican Americans: Viva la Raza

December 13 (Mon., 11:30 a.m - 2:30 p.m.) -- Final Examination

AMERICAN—JEWISH HISTORY TO 1914

This course will survey the history of the American-Jewish community from the Colonial period until World War I. Special emphasis will be placed on the religious reforms that evolved in America; on the interaction between the German and Eastern European immigrants; the agents of Americanization that developed to facilitate the accomodation of the immigrant to the American scene and to the emergence of a uniquely American brand of Zionism.

REQUIRED TEXTS:

Higham, J.	Strangers in the Land
Karp, A.	
Feingold, Henry	Zion in America or Glazer, N. American Judaism
Goren, Arthur	New York Jews and the Quest for Community
Jones M.	American Immigration
Korn B.	American Jewry and the Civil War
Howe, I	World of Our Fathers
Metzger, I.	A Bintel Brief

I. European Background

Katz, Jacob	Tradition and Crisis	pp. 11-41 (on reserve)
Feingold	pp. 1-19	

II. Colonial Period

Glazer	Chapter 1
Feingold	pp. 20-51
Jones	pp. 39-63
Karp	pp. 21-34

III. The German—Jewish Migration

Feingold	pp. 52-67
Jones	Chapters III, IV.
Karp	pp. 35-64

IV. The Economic Adjustment of the German Jew

Jones	Chapter V
Feingold	pp. 68-95

V. The Civil War

Korn	American Jewry and the Civil War

VI. Nativism and American Antisemitism

Jones	Chapters VI, VII.
Karp	pp. 90-116
Higham, J.	Strangers in the Land

WINTER QUARTER 1981
Professor Lipstadt   AMERICAN JEWISH HISTORY TO 1914

VII. <u>Reform Judaism</u>

Feingold   pp. 96-112
Glazer   Chapter III

Additional readings to be announced

VIII. <u>The Eastern European Migration: First Wave</u>
Howe   pp. 5-118, 225-255
IX. <u>The "uptown/Downtown Split</u>

Goren, A.   <u>New York Jews and the Quest for Community</u>
Feingold   pp. 142-157
Howe   pp. 119-147
Metzger, I.   <u>A Bintel Brief</u>
IX. <u>Jewish Labor Movement</u>

Karp   pp. 148-178
Howe   pp. 287-324, 148-169

XI. <u>Conservative Judaism</u>

Additional readings to be announced
Feingold   pp. 179-193
Glazer   Chapter IV

XII. <u>American Zionism</u>
Urofsky, M.   <u>American Zionism: From Herzl to the Holocaust</u>
Cohen, Naomi   <u>American Jews and the Zionist Idea</u>
Feingold   pp. 194-207
Halpern, Ben   "The Americanization of Zionism, 1880-1930,"
                            <u>American Jewish History</u>, September 1979
                            (On reserve)

XIII. <u>American Politics and American Responses</u>

Howe   pp. 360-413

200

THE BERNARD M. BARUCH COLLEGE
COURSE OUTLINE - THE HISTORY OF THE JEWS IN
AMERICA

History 3560 FH24, T, Th, 9:40-10:55, Room 1420   Prof. H.L. Feingold
                                                  Fall, 1983

Required Text: H.L. Feingold, Zion in America. The Jewish Experience
                 From Colonial Times to the Present (soft cover-
                 Hippocrene, hard cover-Twayne)
                 H.L. Feingold, A Midrash On American Jewish History -
                 State Univ. of N.Y. Press

CALENDAR OF DISCUSSION TOPICS AND ASSIGNED READINGS:

9/13,15   Orientation to course. Overview of American Jewish History
          Read: Feingold, Revised preface and Introduction
                 Midrash, preface IX-XV.

9/20   Old World Background-Colonial beginnings
          Read: Feingold, Chpt. I

9/22   The development of religious toleration, the Puritan
          connection, the Sephardic character.
          Read: Feingold, Chpt. 2

9/27,29   Jews in the Colonial economy; the Jewish bridge, the
          Caribbean Nexus.
          Read: Feingold, Chpt. 3

10/4,6   German Jews in America
          Read: Feingold, Chpt. 5
                 Midrash, Chpt. II
10/11   Jews in the ante bellum economy, the peddlers journey
          Read: Feingold, Chpt. 4

10/13   Jews in ante-bellum politics: slavery and the Civil War
          Read: Feingold, Chpt. 6

10/18,20 The Reform Movement in America
          Read: Feingold, Chpt. 7

10/25   The immigration of Eastern Jewry, pushes and pulls
          Read: Feingold, Chpt. 8
10/27,31 The Lower East Side: Shtetl in microcosm
          Read: Feingold, Chpt. 9
                 Midrash, Chpt. IV, V

11/1   "Uptown V. Downtown," Conflict and Philanthropy
          Read: Feingold, Chpt. 10

11/3 -   <u>EXAMINATION AND FIRST BOOK REVIEW DUE</u>

11/8 -   ELECTION DAY - NO CLASSES

11/15,17 The Jewish labor movement and Yiddish culture in
          America
          <u>Read:</u> <u>Feingold,</u> Chpt.11; <u>Midrash</u>, Chpt. VI

11/22   The Conservative movement, a new religious synthesis
          <u>Read:</u> <u>Feingold</u>, Chpt. 12; <u>Midrash,</u> Chpt. VIII, Chpt. X
          (Orthodoxy)

11/24-26 THANKSGIVING DAY RECESS - NO CLASSES

11/29,12/1 The genesis of American Zionism
          <u>Read:</u> <u>Feingold</u>, Chpt. 13

11/6   Jewish organizational life, AJ Comm, A J Cong. Kehillah
          <u>Read:</u> <u>Feingold</u>, Chpt. 14
                  <u>Midrash</u>, Chpt. VII

11/8   American Jewish political culture
          <u>Read:</u> <u>Feingold</u>, Chpt. XV

11/13   Jews and American foreign relations
          <u>Read:</u> <u>Feingold</u>, Chpt. XIV
                  <u>Midrash</u>, Chpt. XII

11/15   Accommodation, exclusion and crisis, life in the <u>twenties</u>
          <u>and thirties</u>
          <u>Read:</u> Feingold, Chpt. XVII
                  Midrash - chpt. XI

11/20   The Roosevelt administration and the Holocaust
          <u>Read:</u> Feingold, Chpt. XVII
                  Midrash, chpt. XIII
          The American Jewish condition today: problems and prospects
          <u>Read:</u> <u>Feingold</u>, chpt. XIX, Epilogue-"Towards Jewish Survival
                      (Midrash -chpt.XIV) Intermarriage and
                  group survival American Jewry and Israel, where now?
                  Leadership in American Jewry
                  How much power does American Jewry have?
                  How effective is Jewish education?
                  New developments in the Jewish family,
                  synagogue, secular organizations, etc..
                  The vitality of Orthodoxy in America
                  Why so many Jewish radicals?
                  How serious a problem is American anti Semitism?
                  Should there be women in the rabbinate?
                  Jews in the economy, sports, theatre,
                  journalism, science, medicine, law, universities, etc.

<u>FINAL EXAM. - 2nd BOOK REVIEW DUE</u>

This agenda is a flexible guide for our class discussions.
Primarily it enables you to plan your work, especially
the reading, so that you have a sense of security.
You not only know what will happen every day this semester
but having prepared beforehand you will find that your
comprehension of what is happening in class improves and
you are able to participate with ease and intelligence.
The reading furnishes you with the needed background for
class discussion. There are two noncummulative examinations
scheduled based on class lectures and reading. You will be
specially prepared for them beforehand. In addition, all
students must submit at least **two** <u>book-reviews</u> for which
you will be instructed on how to prepare in class. Students
who consider themselves candidates for the grade of <u>A</u> or <u>B</u>
should plan to do at least one additional book review and
preferable two. Attendance is always taken and you are
cautioned not to allow yourself more than three cuts.
Please see me of you find yourself exceeding that limit.
Each class discussion is accompanied by a board outline
designed to facilitate your note taking. For those
students who encounter special problems I am available in
my office Room 1509 on Tuesday from 100-2:00 PM

"For Those Who Gladly Teach"

THE EDITORS

WARREN SUSMAN, professor of history at Rutgers
University, is a former vice-president of the American
Historical Association. While chair of the AHA's Teaching
Division, he visited history classes in colleges and high
schools in more than thirty states. In 1981, he served as
chair of the program committee for the annual convention of
the Organization of American Historians. Holder of a Ph.D.
in history from the University of Wisconsin, he is the
author of Culture and Commitment (N.Y.: Braziller, 1972), a
collection of essays on American cultural history to be
published in the spring of 1984 by Pantheon, and a number of
articles and reviews. During 1983-84, he was a fellow at the
Woodrow Wilson International Center for Scholarship at the
Smithsonian Institution in Washington, D.C.

JOHN W. CHAMBERS, assistant professor of history at
Rutgers University, was the first recipient of the Emily L.
Gregory Award for Outstanding Teaching at Barnard College,
Columbia University. After receiving his Ph.D. in history
from Columbia University in 1973, he taught at Barnard until
1980. Awarded Fulbright and Rockefeller Fellowships, he is
the author of The Tyranny of Change: America in the
Progressive Era, 1900-1917 (N.Y.: St. Martin's Press, 1980)
and the forthcoming To Arm a Nation: The Origin of the
Modern Military Draft and State-Building in the United
States as well as editor of Draftees or Volunteers: A
Documentary History of the Debate over Military Conscription
in the United States, 1787-1973 (N.Y.: Garland Pub. Co.,
1975) and The Eagle and the Dove: The American Peace
Movement and United States Foreign Policy, 1900-1922 (N.Y.:
Garland Pub. Co., 1976).

TABLE OF CONTENTS

VOLUME II

VOLUME III

Documents have been reproduced from the originals as submitted.

WOMEN'S HISTORY

D. WOMEN AND RELIGION

E. WOMEN AND EDUCATION

F. SOCIAL HISTORY, WOMEN AND WORK

G. THEORY AND METHODOLOGY

Documents have been reproduced from the originals as submitted.